BALLOU LI
BUENA VISTA CO
STORM LAKE, IOWA 50588

D0934235

PR 1933 .K6 K57 1991
Kiser, Lisa J., 1949-
Truth and textuality in
 Chaucer's poetry

DEMCO

Truth and Textuality in Chaucer's Poetry

LISA J. KISER ಶ್

ಶ್ Truth and Textuality in Chaucer's Poetry

UNIVERSITY PRESS OF NEW ENGLAND

Hanover and London

© 1991 by University Press of New England, Hanover, N.H. 03755
All rights reserved
Printed in the United States of America   5   4   3   2   1
CIP data appear at the end of the book

FOR JIM

Contents

Acknowledgments

It is a pleasure to thank those individuals and institutions who have supported, in one way or another, the preparation of this book. Grateful acknowledgment is made to the Houghton Mifflin Company for permission to reprint material from *The Riverside Chaucer*, edited by Larry D. Benson, Third Edition, © 1987 by the Houghton Mifflin Company. I would also like to acknowledge *Papers on Language and Literature* and the Board of Trustees of Southern Illinois University for permission to reprint portions of chapter one, which originally appeared in "Sleep, Dreams, and Poetry in Chaucer's *Book of the Duchess*," *Papers on Language and Literature* 19 (1983): 3–12. Chapter two originally appeared as "Eschatological Poetics in Chaucer's *House of Fame*," *Modern Language Quarterly* 49 (1988): 99–119, and parts of chapter five appeared as "*The Legend of Good Women*: Chaucer's *Purgatorio*," *English Literary History* 54 (1987): 741–60. I would like to thank the editors of these journals for allowing me to reprint these sections of my argument.

For help in the early stages of writing, I am grateful to my colleagues Christian Zacher, Alan Brown, and the late Stanley Kahrl. At various stages of research and production, I relied on the good will and hard work of Martha Kallstrom, Beth MacDaniel, John Hofmeister, Michael Szczepanik, and Natalie Tyler. Special gratitude is owing to Amy Goodwin and Susan Oakes for the high quality of their intellectual and technical contributions toward the finished product. To G. Micheal Riley, Dean of the College of Humanities, and to the Board of Trustees of The Ohio State University I extend my gratitude for providing me with a Special Research Assignment in 1986 and a Faculty Professional Leave in

1987–88 to undertake this study. The readers and staff of the University Press of New England have been generous with their comments and suggestions for revision, all of which have made this a better book. Finally, my greatest indebtedness is to James Battersby, for he has substantially enriched both text and life.

January 1991   L.J.K.

Truth and Textuality in Chaucer's Poetry

Chaucer's "Art Poetical"

ᴖᴄ It is no novel idea that Chaucer's narrative poetry consistently exposes the limitations of human knowledge and calls into question the accessibility of "truth." The insecurity and bewilderment his dream-vision narrators project, the slow but continual erosion of certainty in the voice that narrates *Troilus and Criseyde,* and the radical perspectivism that serves as the structural basis for *The Canterbury Tales*—these are all aspects of Chaucer's art with which readers are familiar, and which might be considered characteristic features of his distinctive poetic style. Even within the action represented by Chaucer's poems, characters often find themselves in situations that highlight the incompleteness of their knowledge: Troilus and Criseyde act in ignorance of the menacing future; the figures in *The Knight's Tale* make choices in the stark absence of Christianity's guidance; the Reeve's miller and students grope in the dark of a fabliau bedroom; and the Canon's Yeoman, who is represented as having a rich personal experience with alchemy, still does not understand its deepest secrets—to name a few.

But there are, of course, more subtle ways in which Chaucer expresses his convictions about the inconclusiveness of the human search for "truth." Poets themselves are shown to be untrustworthy sources of knowledge and truth, through Chaucer's typical narrator, a poet figure who is always portrayed as having discernible biases, individualized rhetorical purposes, idiosyncratic views, and deeply subjective responses to the material he sets forth—even when he confidently claims to be objective in his narration. Moreover, the narrators—for example, the Canterbury pilgrims—who are embedded within the boundaries of the typical Chaucerian frame usually also betray another set of specific delusions, thus compounding the interpretive difficulties that face the readers of Chaucerian texts. Taken as a whole, these narrative strategies combine to produce the picture of an author who is extremely reluctant to make authoritative claims, one who systematically refuses to acknowledge the existence of any mind-independent "reality" to which the reader may appeal in the search for new knowledge through his poetry.

Chaucer's skepticism, however, and his interest in subverting traditional medieval notions of written authority, run deeper than the position commonly attributed to him—that he wrote to show that respected authorities conflict in their ethical and philosophical interests or claims, and that the problems created by these competing systems are not easily resolvable.[1] To be sure, authorities do conflict in Chaucer's works, and his narrators are portrayed as having sponsoring biases that undermine their reliability; indeed, these characteristic components of Chaucer's verse alone would constitute sufficient evidence to support the position that writers do not convey to us any authoritative truths, but merely what they think (or want) these truths to be. But Chaucer's poetry tests monistic and objectivist claims even further by persistently questioning how much we can trust even the sturdiest sources of medieval authority, the phenomenal realms of history and experience. Lying behind most of the action described or reported in Chaucer's works is the implication that in the recent or distant past something "really happened" that his narrators are trying to recover. And as they attempt to record and transmit the event, we become privy to a series of remarkable failures, each project beset with a different array of perplexing and unsolvable problems.

Chaucerians may not be accustomed to seeing all the poet's works as essentially historical projects, yet each one undeniably presents us with some kind of attempt to record the facts about past persons and events. The main project of The Book of the Duchess is to recover and record the virtues of an actual woman, deceased at the time of writing; Troilus and Criseyde and The Legend of Good Women make actual claims or strong suggestions about their real-life origins in classical history; The Canterbury Tales sets up a fictional historical event (the pilgrimage), which its narrator-witness tries to recapture; and The House of Fame and The Parliament of Fowls are both identified as records of factual dreams in which the narrator seeks either true stories about lovers or the revelatory nature of love itself. Each of Chaucer's poems, in other words, creates slightly different conditions designed to test the same hypothesis—that writing conveys historical or experiential truth. And taken as a whole, Chaucer's corpus systematically and comprehensively tries to disprove that view.

Chaucer's interest in foregrounding the problematics of recovering history and experience was surely stimulated by the popularity of his-

torical narratives and eye-witness records among the members of his
fourteenth-century audience. Ranulf Higden's *Polychronicon, Brut,* and
the putatively historical French romances were "best-sellers" in late medieval England, reaching a wide and various audience, and Froissart's
Chronicle was presented to Chaucer's own king. We know that aristocratic demand for didactic histories about both distant and recent times
was generally high during Chaucer's lifetime; library catalogues and
other documents testify to the active accumulation of a large number of
chronicles, universal histories, and exempla collections that could furnish courtly and bourgeois readers with both practical and philosophical
lessons to be learned from the past.[2] And although most medieval authors would have recognized that the writing and interpretation of history was rhetorically defined and ideologically motivated, in that one
selected, arranged, and read historical material with certain previously
formed moral and political precepts in mind, they were nonetheless reluctant to abandon the old idea that history and fiction were two distinctly different kinds of narrative, history being "the true" and fiction
the "not true," possibly because God's creation (that is, history) was
invested with an authority that human creations simply could not have.
As Richard Firth Green suggests about the works which provided (or
claimed to provide) their audiences with knowledge of the past, "there
is little doubt that the numerous 'histories' of Troy, Thebes, and Alexander, or even of Arthur, Charlemagne, and Godfrey of Bouillon, were
read largely as sober, factual accounts."[3]

The fourteenth century was indeed an age in which the ancient distinction between poetry and historiography was still honored by many
audiences. After all, authorities as respected as Aristotle, Plato, Cicero,
Isidore of Seville, and Macrobius had, in various ways, articulated or
preserved the distinction, even when they doubted that the two-term
model was adequate to all texts. Isidore, for example, in the following
passage, though he implies that some "historical" reports may not be
entirely truthful, still believes in the truth/fiction dichotomy and the idea
that eye-witness historical reporting is true: "Among the ancients no-
body wrote history except those who had been involved in it, and had
seen the things they were going to write about. It is better that we observe with our eyes that which has happened than that we infer things
about it through hearsay, for what is seen is revealed without lies."[4] Macrobius, working with a Ciceronian model, elaborates on the basic two-
term scheme by subdividing *fabula* (fiction) into narratives that are
wholly fictitious and those that have elements of truth "treated in a fictitious style."[5] And Boccaccio, whose defense of poetry pointedly argues

against an uncomplicated two-term scheme, was very clearly addressing readers who still relied on the "fact/fiction" dichotomy as a standard by which to judge the writing of poets.[6] The whole issue of truth and fictionality in medieval literary theory is, of course, enormously complex—but there can be no doubt that Chaucer was writing at a time when the distinction between fact and fiction was honored by many readers, some of whom seem to be represented by the implied and fictional audiences of his poetry.

Each of Chaucer's works responds to the reductive truth/fiction model by actually adopting it at first; each poem states (or strongly implies) that there is some kind of historical reality authorizing the work, some real-life event that is to be recreated for the reader. But then each work, after embracing the scheme, systematically critiques it from within, showing time after time that even eye-witness participants in historical events cannot, even if they desperately want to, report truthfully about them. Chaucer's narrator-historians, then, end up demonstrating that historiographical narrative and fiction show more resemblances than differences and that the old distinction between history and poetry obscures the essential ways in which these two kinds of writing are alike. Through his narrator-historians, Chaucer very nearly advances the radical thesis that there is no such thing as history or experience prior to its textualization in some rhetorically organized and socially determined fictional form.

One of the primary ways in which Chaucer undermines the authoritative status of narrative truth is by calling attention to the profoundly textual nature of his own historical projects. Chaucer's narratives, though their speakers usually make large claims for their truth, depend more often on other poems for their referential base than on any consistent mimetic or realistic principle of composition. Even when Chaucer's narrators are not recording dreams and are thus claiming to represent some mind-independent reality, Chaucer quickly makes it clear that these narrators are deluded, that there are no facts independent of one's construction of them. That is, Chaucer's works always represent heavily mediated versions of "reality" that self-consciously call attention to the distortions and fictionalizations of life that literature always provides, because this strategy serves to confirm his argument about the basically illusory relationship between texts and life. Often alluding specifically to the work of his literary forebears, and sometimes actually structuring his works in imitation of other medieval poems, Chaucer routinely reminds his readers that they should seek the referents of his poems (and *all* poems) chiefly in other works of literature—not in the raw materials of life. And, although Chaucer's poetry has much to teach us about life and the human condition, it does not do so by means of conventional realism. Rather, Chaucer textualizes his vision of the world mainly by showing that his poems are based on other people's possible (and other poets' actual) constructions of it. To circumscribe the referential claims of his poetry even further, he often takes as the primary subject of his poems, not life, but the nature and function of writing itself.

Chaucer also calls attention to his poetry's de-authorized stance by addressing the complex personal, social, and institutional forces that shape the activities of poets and readers alike. More than any other medieval poet (except perhaps Boccaccio), Chaucer is fond of dramatically representing the wide range of interpretive strategies that readers bring to literary works. Although this is true mainly of the works traditionally assigned to his later career (the *Troilus, The Legend of Good Women,* and *The Canterbury Tales*), where he creates fictional audience figures who respond—often idiosyncratically—to the work at hand, his interest in what individual readers get from books is also visible in the readers who are the narrators of *The Book of the Duchess, The House of Fame,* and *The Parliament of Fowls.* That readers derive from books only what they want or expect from them is, I think, a major Chaucerian assumption, and it is worked out together with Chaucer's larger argument that texts corrupt rather than preserve the historical information they offer. For *even if* historical or revelatory truth were available in some trustworthy text (which it is not), in the very process of interpreting that text readers would inevitably distort it.

Furthermore, when those readers then become writers, they transmit this already distorted material by tailoring it further to suit the specific interests, tastes, and expectations of a new audience. Indeed, Chaucer's narrator-historians are almost always represented as performing their reporting tasks in the presence of socially characterized readers who end up profoundly affecting the way in which these reports are transmitted. The specific social and political forces that Chaucer includes in his representations of oral delivery show him to be very much an investigator into how the production of texts is socially determined and politically motivated. In the verbal transmission of "truth" from age to age or text to text, it becomes clear that it is always sacrificed so that the fit between poem and audience can be closer. As I will argue, this sociopoetic view of transmission is crucial to the dynamics of Chaucer's texts, especially in their deployment of the poet-narrator's stance toward his material in the presence of implied or fictional audiences.

In this study, then, I explore the ways in which Chaucer addresses the issue of literary authority and narrative truth in each of his major works. In *The Book of the Duchess,* which shows sophisticated experimentation with the management of narrative voice, Chaucer has his narrator's dream aid him in addressing the difficult problem of how a poet can be expected to evoke the "real," that is, to describe and eulogize a real person without inevitable falsification of the truth he is trying to capture. As an extended meditation on the discontinuity between art and life, this poem—which might also discharge an actual poetic commission and thus raise important questions about the political entanglements that control artistic production—forcefully confronts many of the issues that Chaucer's later poems will continue to address.

The House of Fame, The Parliament of Fowls, and *The Legend of Good Women* also raise fundamental poetic issues relating to representation in general. But these poems focus more explicitly on how the narrator's reading material (drawn mainly from the visionary tradition) shapes and controls both his fictional dreams and the poems that recount them. Structured by means of analogies that relate writing to love, these revelatory dream-visions find the source of their authority in the sponsoring biases of their dreaming narrators, thus mocking the typical authorial claims one finds in the medieval visionary tradition. *The House of Fame* and *The Legend of Good Women* are especially indebted to the poetry of Dante for their structure; indeed, these poems mock the *Commedia*'s truth-claims and Dante's realist poetics by imitating certain Dantean concepts only to undermine them.

Troilus and Criseyde, too, manifests Chaucer's interest in the basically intertextual nature of literary art. As a work that is purportedly (and, to some extent, actually) a translation of another work, one that makes historical claims, the *Troilus* raises issues involving literary reception and the social and institutional bases of hermeneutic behavior, demonstrating both thematically and through its narrative structure that the self-interests and social interests of those who perceive inevitably govern their interpretations and define for them the nature of historical and textual truth. Moreover, erotic betrayal in the *Troilus*'s action is analogous to authorial betrayal, for the progress of the love affair is reflected in the narrator's betrayal of his source text. Dante again is important to Chaucer here, for the *Troilus* toys with the *Commedia*'s innovative literary synthesis of earthly and heavenly love before finally rejecting its certainties in favor of a much more troubled view of literature's potential to reflect amatory truth, especially in a culture with a divided or contradictory view of earthly love.

Finally, in *The Canterbury Tales,* Chaucer experiments with literature that purportedly refers to life, for in this work his narrator is portrayed as a recorder of a true event—not a dream or another work of literary art. Yet even in this seemingly radical departure from the literariness of his earlier poems, Chaucer takes great pains to signal to his readers that any writer's attempt at capturing the "truth" of an experience, or even the consistent illusion of truth, is deeply problematic, for the many truth-claims advanced by the narrator and the pilgrim speakers within his re-corded frame are repeatedly subverted by the strong competing claims of art and social identity. Time and again in *The Canterbury Tales* we are faced with pilgrim-artists whose assertions about the veracity of what they present in their prologues and tales are shown to be false, sometimes in spite of the pilgrims' own beliefs to the contrary. By ex-amining the claims of a select group of narrators—the Knight, the Miller, the Reeve, the Cook, the Man of Law, the Physician, the Wife of Bath, the Pardoner, and the Canon's Yeoman—this study argues that *The Canterbury Tales* is Chaucer's most complex commentary on the nature of human fictions, for not only does the work offer a variety of representational strategies in the pilgrims' individualized narratives, but it also foregrounds the political and social management of "reality" that motivates human discourse.

Another emphasis of this study that requires introductory comment is its comparative approach, its insistence on the fundamentally intertex-tual nature of Chaucer's poetry. Since Chaucer's poems are more often in dialogue with other works of literature than with any secure extra-textual concept of life, it is worth examining in detail how other texts function in the Chaucerian poems in which they appear. Sometimes, Chaucer's poems reproduce the complex analogies between love and writing that can be found in the self-reflexive texts of the medieval French poets. And his first-person narrative persona owes much to his close reading of *The Romance of the Rose,* in which narratorial authority is often undermined and the impossibility of discerning truth is formally and thematically developed.[7] Like Chaucer, Machaut and Froissart also raise issues in their poems concerning textual truth value, sometimes doing so by means of narrator selves who are clerkly transcribers, much as Chaucer's persona is. Chaucer is clearly joining these poets in a dis-cussion whose terms and concepts had been developed prior to Chau-cer's career as a poet. Indebted as he is to these writers, in his later works he owes most to the Italian poets who came to have a profound influence on him. This study emphasizes that the poetry of Dante and Boccaccio often provides Chaucer's mature work with a convenient starting point for his handling of the textual tradition as a problematic vehicle for "truth." As John Fyler has noted, Chaucer sometimes adopts Ovid's stance toward Vergil's works in his treatment of Dante's poetry.[8] That is, he often brings Dante's poetic achievement to the foreground only to subvert it by comic imitation or to place it in contexts designed to show up its limitations rather than its powers. Dante had raised the ante for all ambitious poets, for he had attempted to "obliterate the boundaries between art and life" and to devise a poetics that would allow him to appropriate "reality" as the raw material of his poetry, in direct imitation of God's own "mimesis."[9] Indeed, by adopting the role of God's scribe, one whose function was to record and interpret the reality that God had "written," Dante granted himself nearly unlimited poetic authority and freedom. In contrast, when Chaucer (taking a cue from Boccaccio before him) adopts the role of "scribe of men," putatively functioning as a mere bookish recorder of what other people—not God—had written, he carves out for himself a poetic identity that pointedly opposes Dante's self-conception, in that it seems to surrender any claim to authority of the kind so central to the Italian poet-theologian's literary (and putatively historical) projects. Yet, as this study will argue, by restricting his attention to the workings of art rather than making claims about the life art purportedly reflects, Chaucer was able to confront—and to some extent call into question—the fundamental theoretical underpinnings of Dante's literary achievement.

Robert M. Jordan, in *Chaucer's Poetics and the Modern Reader*, sketches out some of the ideas that this study will explore, especially the notion that Chaucer's poetry expresses its skepticism through its artifice and evasion of mimetic consistency.[10] Yet Jordan and I differ markedly in the ways in which we approach the poems themselves. Jordan's methodology (loosely based on Todorov's rhetorical poetics) does not encourage historical or social contextualization (such as inquiry into the ways in which audiences implicitly shape Chaucer's texts), nor does it allow him to distinguish among narrators—say, for instance, in *The Canterbury Tales*. Basically rejecting "interpretation" as a useful tool, and restricting his analysis to "verbal surfaces" alone, Jordan also argues against any clear separation between the voice of Chaucer the artificer and the narrative voice that speaks each poem.[11] Although this position is attractive, since it rightly serves to discourage extreme realist or dramatic readings of Chaucer's poems, any position that eliminates the idea of distinctly characterized narrative personae reflecting sharply defined rhetorical purposes will inevitably impoverish study of the skepticism advanced in Chaucer's poetry, for it is often through these distinctive voices (and the rudimentary socialized characters they suggest) that

Chaucer most definitively conveys his distrust of textual claims asserting authoritative truth.

Like Robert Burlin, David Aers, and Judith Ferster, to name three recent critics who have worked closely with the relationships between narrators and the poems they speak, I believe that it is often crucial to identify the nature of each individual narrator's sponsoring concerns, for Chaucer makes many of his most important points about the elusiveness of truth by showing how interpretation is circular. "What one sees depends on who one is," as Ferster writes; "the interpreter sees . . . with and through his prejudices."[12] Moreover, as Robert O. Payne has noted, Chaucer and other medieval rhetoricians were acutely aware of the rhetorical principle of *ethos* (a principle that Jordan avoids), whereby an audience is seen to make judgments about a speaker's character from his words. Indeed, the speaker/language/audience model (a basic communications model) that Payne sees at work in Chaucer's poetry has much explanatory power, since it can begin to account for those aspects of the poetical process that Chaucer's poems most consistently explore.[13]

Indeed, in this study, I will implicitly—and often explicitly—recognize the usefulness of formalist rhetorical models as tools in analyzing Chaucerian narrative. Yet some of the questions traditionally formulated by poststructuralists are also pertinent to any project that attempts to address the operations of language, the dubious authority of all representational activity, and the social texts that shape us. Poststructuralism has indeed provided modern medievalists with a new way to think about Chaucer's distrust of language and his skepticism about any text's ability to represent the "world." The concept of textuality, which I have adopted in a moderated variant, has been useful to me in addressing the social and intertextual qualities of Chaucer's verse because it describes the collapse of texts and sociohistorical contexts into precisely the kind of dizzying hermeneutic tangle that Chaucer himself seems so intent upon weaving. But poststructuralist methodologies, although they are well-equipped to expose the institutional bases of hermeneutic behavior, to carry out structural analyses of social and cultural norms, and to call into question any intrinsic or extrinsic order to which texts refer, are less powerful models if one hopes to examine the cognitive/epistemological concerns of a text, the individual social agency represented in and affected by a text, the representation of cultural conflict due to the variousness present in pluralistic societies, and the very real way in which a single individual is implicated in the production, transmission, and reception of literature.[14] Thus, many extreme forms of poststructuralism threaten to close down the line of inquiry I wish to keep open—the investigation of how Chaucer's texts dramatize, sometimes at the level of the individual interpretive act, the ways in which authors and audiences receive and transmit texts, thereby reconstituting, if not creating, history. In short, I have found the thematics of poststructuralism more useful than its characteristic totalizing operations.

One last point about this study that deserves comment is its assumption throughout that when Chaucer employs concepts such as *truth* and *history*, he is usually employing them loosely, using what philosophers like to call "ordinary language" in the service of "practical reasoning." As much a social creature as every one of his narrators, he very clearly labored to please the widest and most diverse audience possible, probably even ambitiously imagining a future, unknown audience who could derive "sentence" or "solaas" from his works, especially the *Troilus* and *The Canterbury Tales.* We can assume, of course, that some members of his audience would, like Chaucer, have mastered the rigors of Mertonian logic, the subtleties of academic epistemological theory, or the convoluted tradition of historiographical theory. But he often seems to be deploying his arguments about history and hermeneutics in a fashion designed for a relatively untutored audience unfamiliar with academic debate about these and related issues. *Truth* and *history* seem to be crudely and pragmatically defined ("what is out there," "what really happened"), even though Chaucer usually begins with these commonsense definitions in order to assault them from within. This study, then, though at times employing the kind of specialized knowledge that only a few learned members of his audience may have had (close familiarity with Dante's poetics, for example), generally tries to respect the way that Chaucer's texts targeted an audience more diverse than that, one whose concepts were likely to be underexamined (even counterfactual) in terms of their philosophical and theoretical adequacy. In other words, individual hermeneutic acts, in both private and social contexts, are most often represented by Chaucer as components of practical decision making in a complex but communally interactive world.

CHAPTER ONE

True and False "Portrayture" in
The Book of the Duchess

~~⧤~~ **W**hen Chaucer sat down to write *The Book of the Duchess,* he faced many of the same poetic and sociopolitical challenges that generations of court poets before him had encountered. One of these, a dilemma that all hired poets at times must confront, is how one can gracefully, without egregious lying or overt sycophancy, fulfill the duty of a writer of laudatory verse intended primarily to praise those who commissioned it or to respond in specified ways to events involving patrons and their families. Indeed, the special artistic demands of laudatory or occasional verse—principally the demand that it refer directly and unambiguously to court reality—would have presented interesting challenges for fourteenth-century poets such as Machaut and Froissart (Chaucer's most influential models), for these poets, themselves taking cues from *The Romance of the Rose,* had developed an acute sense of the inescapable fictionality of poetry, its predictable distance from authoritative "truth" and its essentially artificial nature. Their experimentation with veracity in dream-frames (dreams being notoriously untrustworthy as vehicles for truth) and with various ways in which to call attention to the textuality of their art showed them to be closely attuned to the complex problems attending any poet's claims to be representing truth or reality accurately. Making no such claims themselves, they often called attention in their poems to the ways in which one's biases, individual experience, or reading material might affect one's perceptions—and thus portrayal—of events or people in the natural world.

Surely much of the hesitation expressed by late medieval court poets also derived from the inherently problematic social situation in which they found themselves. Expected to represent the actual experiences of their patrons and social superiors, they nonetheless needed to avoid the suggestion that they were in any way claiming special knowledge of the courtly codes and privileges restricted to members of the upper class. A court poet needed to attend to matters of literary decorum while completing his assigned task; he could not merely forge ahead with his project of courtly representation without somehow expressing his own unworthiness as a spokesman for his patrons.[1] The strategies poets evolved whereby they could refer to courtly "reality" without making a commitment to the absolute veracity of their references were intricate and aesthetically complex. In addition to developing the literary possibilities inherent in the dream-frame device, they worked out ironic clerkly narratorial personae; they mingled allegorical figures with mimetic or more realistic characters in the same poetic space; they represented their patrons by casting them in fictional guises or in allegorical scenes that only obliquely or by analogy referred to the real-life people involved; and, in general, they playfully exploited, whenever possible, the commerce between "factual" and fictional discourse.[2] By the time Chaucer began his career as a writer, his French poetic predecessors had evolved a variety of artistic devices to help them distinguish their poems from purported utterances of truth, devices which nonetheless could help them fulfill their expected roles as praisers and commemorators of the courtly scene.

Chaucer benefited from the French poets' experimentation with ways in which to call attention to the fictionality of their art, and his debt to them is reflected in all of his poetry—including *The Book of the Duchess,* his first major narrative work. Like the French poets before him, Chaucer needed poetic strategies that could effectively undermine narrative truth at the same time that they allowed a poem to achieve its primary social purpose—in this case to mourn the death and commemorate the virtue of a real woman, Blanche the Duchess, wife of John of Gaunt. *The Book of the Duchess* raises several questions, both literary and social. Is it possible for a poet to capture the truth about another human being? More specifically, can a poet speak with authority about how it is for John of Gaunt, who loved Blanche, to miss her? Even if, by some supernatural transference of direct knowledge, a poet could know such things and therefore be able to claim the authority to speak about them, wouldn't it still be socially presumptuous to claim to be capturing Blanche's reality adequately in a poem's fictional space? Yet wouldn't it appear to be insincere (as well as politically problematic) to praise Blanche in a work that simultaneously called into question its own capacities to tell the truth?

Chaucer's poetic solution to these problems is complex indeed, for not only did it provide him with a strategy to complete the poem's major

work (commemorating Blance "sincerely") but it also allowed him am-
ple room both to question the ability of poetic forms to reflect one's experience of another human being, and to deny his own authority on John
of Gaunt's grief. By creating the fictional situation of the Black Knight
mourning his lady, White, Chaucer escaped the difficulties inherent in
any attempt to represent real people in his poem. As fictional analogues
of his real-life subjects, these two characters needed only to suggest their
real-life counterparts and induce an audience to think of those counterparts and make the connection in their minds as they experienced the
poem. As critics have long realized, the Black Knight is, yet isn't, John
of Gaunt, and White only obliquely refers to Blanche.

This device is interesting in itself, for it freed Chaucer from the obli-
gation of claiming to know the true nature or extent of John of Gaunt's
grief. Moreover, since he was now working with a fictional character, he
was free (as all writers of fiction are) to manipulate his character in any
way he chose. The same is true of the character White—she is only
Blanche by analogy, being primarily a fictional character (and absent except in the Knight's evocation of her). As a result, Chaucer can have his
Knight praise her in any way he chooses—even with stock rhetorical
description—without Chaucer himself having to accept the blame of
misrepresenting, or underrepresenting, the real-life Blanche. Yet because
the Black Knight is indeed a John of Gaunt figure, Blanche's praise seems
to come from the speaker who knew her best—not from the pen of the
distanced and socially inferior poetic "I" who had been commissioned
to write this poem.[3]

The Book of the Duchess would have been intricate enough even if
Chaucer had limited its strategy merely to this one clever device. But in
order to explore the more general issue of the problems inherent in poetic
representation of all kinds, Chaucer uses the Black Knight's own discourse to suggest the impossibility of an adequate fit between life and
the language that aspires to capture it. The Black Knight, because of his
long experience with White, is the only figure in Chaucer's poem with
the authority to speak about her, yet he is portrayed as himself unable
to describe her with any accuracy or self-assurance, even though he
works very hard—and very ingenuously—at the task. Portrayed as a
man whose reminiscing is candid and sincere, the Black Knight allows
his memory to play over the image of White that it has retained, giving
us the impression that he is seeing the deceased woman, the "reality,"
once again: "for be hyt never so derk / Me thynketh I se hir ever moo"
(912–13).

Obsessively announcing that his discourse is true—"trewely" (670,

981, 985, 998, 1075, 1111, 1156, 1240, 1246, 1253, 1281); "y trow trewly" (687); "dredeles" (766, 1272); "soth to seyen" (817, 856, 989, 1090, 1181, 1194, 1221); "For I dar swere, withoute doute" (820); "I trow" (843, 882, 1274); "hyt was soth" (846); "certes y trowe" (853); "I dar swere wel, by the roode" (924); "I durste swere" (929); "I dar swere wel" (972); "And I dar seyn and swere hyt wel" (1002); "be thou siker" (1020); "certes" (1037, 1117); "Nay, leve hyt wel" (1046, 1148); "withoute drede" (1073, 1096); "by my trouthe" (1109); "Before God" (1144); "be ryght siker" (1149); "to seye ryght soth" (1189); "to telle shortly ryght as hyt ys" (1239); "ywis" (1267); "As helpe me God" (1277); "For sothe" (1292); "withoute were" (1296)—the Black Knight is visibly laboring to convey to the listening dreamer his own convictions about the truth of his reportage. Establishing his reliability by strong assurances of veracity, this narrator insists on the legitimacy of his mimetic project—he is trying to tell us that what he is saying about White is true.

Moreover, our trust in his sincerity is bolstered when he shows us that he knows what feigning is and shuns it. Describing Lady Fortune's deceptions, he says she is

"An ydole of fals portrayture . . .
She is the monstres hed ywrien,
As fylthe over-ystrawed with floures.
Hir moste worshippe and hir flour ys
To lyen. . . .
She ys pley of enchauntement,
That semeth oon and ys not soo."   (626–49)

And in describing White, he singles out for special praise her lack of "counterfeit" beauty—" 'Hyt nas no countrefeted thyng; / Hyt was hir owne pure lokyng' " (869–70)—and her absolute refusal to deceive anyone intentionally through her speech:

"Ne lasse flaterynge in hir word,
That purely hir symple record
Was founde as trewe as any bond
Or trouthe of any mannes hond."   (933–36)

"Trouthe hymself over al and al
Had chose hys maner principal
In hir that was his restyng place."   (1003–1005)

"She wolde not fonde
To holde no wyght in balaunce
By half word ne by countenaunce—
But if men wolde upon hir lye—"   (1020–23)

In short, to the Black Knight, one of the highest possible human virtues is that of true "portrayture" and faithful representation. After listening to his personal reminiscences and confessions, it is impossible to take a distrustful view of him; he is enthusiastically (if naively) committed to the view that if he tries hard enough he can make his language accommodate the truth.

Yet in spite of his sincerity and the urgency with which he desires to convey to us the detailed contents of his well-stocked memory, the Knight is still unable to do so adequately. Often slipping into conventional courtly diction (as critics have remarked),[4] he ends up relying on stock hyperbolic poetic language to express intensely personal truths— not necessarily because he wants to do so, but because finding language of one's own (if, indeed, there is such a thing) that can sufficiently capture the high quality of a unique experience is a difficult, if not impossible, task:

> "But which a visage she had thertoo!
> Allas, myn herte ys wonder woo
> That I ne kan discryven hyt!
> Me lakketh both Englyssh and wit
> For to undo hyt at the fulle;
> And eke my spirites be so dulle
> So gret a thyng for to devyse.
> I have no wit that kan suffise
> To comprehende hir beaute." (895–903)

The Knight despairs even of being able to recount satisfactorily the seemingly simple events leading up to his first declaration of love to White: "I not wel how that I began; / Ful evel rehersen hyt I kan" (1203–1204). When he tries to report accurately what White said in return, he ultimately gives up: "I kan not now wel counterfete / Hir wordes" (1241–42), opting for a cursory summary of the gist instead. And to explain their happy life together, he says, would be an impossible task for him: "And thus we lyved ful many a yere / So wel I kan nat telle how" (1296–97). All of his efforts to capture past truth have ended in failure for him; all he can finally say to the dreamer is the baleful exclamation that he has "lost more than thou wenest" (744, 1138, 1306), a phrase that he repeats three times, in spite of the dreamer's polite (but obviously false) assurances that he truly understands the Knight's distress.[5] No one but the Knight himself can know what he is trying to report, because language (not just courtly language, as recent critics have suggested) cannot satisfactorily transmit it.

Chaucer, of course, needing to write his own poem about the real

Blanche, has a task identical to the Knight's in both its scope and its difficulty. For this reason, it is useful to see the Black Knight as the alter-ego of the poem's narrator[6]—not only as a fictionalized John of Gaunt figure, but as a version of the poet himself, whose dream is reflecting back to him his own anxieties about the intimidating poetic task before him. Like the Black Knight (who is portrayed as also a poet), the narrator wants neither to "counterfete" nor to "evel rehersen" the virtues of the lady in question, and he knows quite well that wit and English are not enough to complete the project assigned him. Furthermore, to resort to the conventional language of courtly praise merely in order to get his poem done (as a lying or flattering court poet might do) would be to engage in "fals portrayture," to fictionalize the "truth" by drawing on books rather than on life. But he also knows, like the Black Knight, that finding adequate language of his own is impossible, language itself being an insufficient medium (and a medium always inherited) in which to represent human experience. In his identity as the Black Knight, then, Chaucer tactfully and demurely suggests that any original attempt to eulogize Blanche, however sincerely intended, would in some sense be doomed to failure, since poetry can never be fully answerable to her "truth"; it simply cannot "undo hyt at the fulle" (899). He thus abandons his empirical project of getting at the real, allowing his poem to resist its mimetic program at the same time that it tries to achieve it.

In spite of the central message of *The Book of the Duchess*, that language inevitably fails to capture the "real," Chaucer suggests throughout his text, as any wise beneficiary of patronage would, that poets work very hard at what they do; they are not sluggards who give up in the face of the limitations of their medium. In his role as a poet figure, the Black Knight dramatizes this idea persuasively by engaging in such an energetic struggle to find expression for his thoughts.

Also, by demonstrating that poetry can only result from intense and thoughtful reading (he alludes to Vergil, Ovid, medieval and classical histories, the Bible, contemporary allegorical texts, and epic literature in his attempts to find ways to talk about his life), the Black Knight shows us that the work of a writer begins with the long hours he must spend as a reader, searching his books for the public forms and conventions upon which to work the changes that result in new art. Indeed, the Black Knight deems the virtue of "busynesse" to be next in importance to the virtue of "truth"; what he is most satisfied with in his courtship of White is that he served her "withoute feynynge outher slouthe" (1100). In noting that the hard work of writing poetry kept him from sloth in his youth,

> "for to kep me fro ydelnesse,
> Trewly I dide my besynesse
> To make songes, as I best koude,
> And ofte tyme I song hem loude;
> And made songes thus a gret del,
> Althogh I koude not make so wel
> Songes, ne knewe the art al . . ."   (1155–61)

the Knight implies that idleness and writing poetry are never compatible, even when one's poetic results do not satisfy the rigorous standards of good verse. Poets do not play at their craft; rather, they labor at it.[7]

This idea is pursued not only in the Black Knight's discourse but also in the rest of Chaucer's poem, both in its prologue and in its account of the story of Ceyx and Alcione. The narrator's sleeplessness in the opening lines of the poem's prologue represents his failure to dream. And because dreams in medieval courtly works were often traditionally employed as metaphors for the activities and results of the poetic imagination, the narrator is also noting his inability to write, that is, to engage in the creative and productive work that active poets do.[8] To a poet, whose business is to create often and to create well, sleeplessness is emblematic of a poetically barren state of mind, a period of disturbingly unproductive idleness:

> I have so many an ydel thoght
> Purely for defaute of slep
> That, by my trouthe, I tak no kep
> Of nothing, how hyt cometh or gooth
> Ne me nys nothyng leef nor looth.   (4–8)

That idleness could be demonstrated by the waking state and not by the more obviously inactive state of sleep is an unusual and somewhat nonsensical idea—at least to the nonpoets in Chaucer's audience, who would naturally link sleep with sloth when determining what remuneration a poet deserves for his work. But Chaucer's point here is one that the rest of the poem will attempt to prove—good poets work hard at their "dreams." Observers of a poet at work are not likely to see that closed eyes and idle hands can actually be signs of frenzied poetic activity. Falling asleep, then, is metaphorically the first step toward the fulfillment of a poet's role. It is only "defaute of slep" that constitutes a threat to poetic "busynesse."

The remaining introductory lines of the poem describe the other part of poets' work that might seem to onlookers like idle play—reading. An artist not engaged in active composition might, as the Black Knight has clearly shown, be working equally hard at mastering the poetic tradition by discovering it in books. Turning to Ovid, whose tales will provide the poet with, as he says, "better play" (50) than will chess or any other game, the narrator encounters the tale of Ceyx and Alcione, which makes several very important statements about idleness, poetic labor, and the recovery of the dead, a subject Chaucer finds especially useful for his own commemorative poem involving the loss of a beloved spouse.

In addition to the simple story's thematic appropriateness, the narrator discovers in it an example of the process by which people can be represented in art, a process which he himself is being asked to carry out and which he will narrate so that the reader can compare the Black Knight's (and thus his own) representation of life with that in Ovid's story. Because the narrator so luckily discovers this useful bit of *matere* from his reading, he is now free to sleep and to dream his own poem. Indeed, the narrator's successful search for this useful story is followed by an immediate "lust to sleepe" (273–75).

The Ovidian tale Chaucer retells here (minus the metamorphosis of its original) is significant as a prologue to Chaucer's elegy for Blanche largely because of the character of Morpheus. Like Chaucer, Morpheus is commissioned by a social superior to assuage someone's grief by creating an image of a lost loved one; thus, Morpheus is another of the narrator's doubles. The bereaved mourners, both Alcione and John of Gaunt, are given a chance to "see" their dead mates by means of a visionary experience, Alcione being provided with an actual animation of the dead Ceyx—a re-creation of the real—and John of Gaunt receiving Chaucer's much less ambitious dream-representation of his dead wife. However, the significant difference between the ways in which Morpheus and Chaucer raise the dead by representing them in art must be stressed, for it constitutes the single most important reason for Chaucer's choice of this particular story for use in his poem.

Morpheus, unlike Chaucer's narrator, is an example of true idleness. His sleeping is unproductive and totally unrelated to any subtle process of poetic labor. Of him and his assistant Eclympasteyr Chaucer emphatically writes that they "slep and dide noon other werk" (169). Moreover, the environment in which these deities live is as barren and as unregenerative as their lethargy. They live in a dark valley

> Ther never yet grew corn ne gras,
> Ne tre, ne noght that ought was,
> Beste, ne man, ne noght elles,
> Save ther were a fewe welles
> Came rennynge fro the clyves adoun,
> That made a dedly slepynge soun.   (156–62)

Nothing grows in this infertile valley, and the "welles" that run here are part of the river Lethe (as Ovid makes clear), whose waters signify forgetfulness, not remembrance.[9] As the god of forgetting and the god of sloth, Morpheus sleeps but does nothing else, a point that Chaucer intends us to see as a direct contrast to his own dream-filled and thus highly creative sleeping.

The interlude that follows describes the messenger's comic difficulty in waking up the sleeping deity:

> This messager com fleynge fast
> And cried, "O, how! Awake anon!"
> Hit was for noght; there herde hym non.
> "Awake!" quod he, "whoo ys lyth there?"
> And blew his horn ryght in here eere,
> And cried, "Awaketh!" wonder hyë.
> This god of slep with hys oon yë
> Cast up, and axed, "Who clepeth ther?"   (178–85)

This passage further reinforces Chaucer's desire to paint Morpheus as truly idle. It is next to impossible to arouse the god to action, and even when it is finally done, Morpheus only mechanically fulfills the "artistic" commission that Juno has given him—he retrieves Ceyx's body from the scene of death, gives it voice and animation, and makes it stand before the grieving wife in a vision. Here we have a parodic analogue of Chaucer's own situation: he is writing a commissioned poem to console a grieving spouse, and he will do it through a form of artificial "resurrection." But his act, unlike Morpheus's, is neither a lie nor an effect produced merely to complete the commission. It is more successful than Morpheus's "work of art," even though it fails to achieve the mimetic power of the deity's re-creation of the dead.

Morpheus's work of art, though contrived and mechanical, might at first seem to be an enviously successful accomplishment to a poet who is himself striving to capture the "real" in a work of art, for Morpheus has effortlessly managed to reproduce all the elusive particulars of the dead Ceyx in a startlingly true vision of Ceyx's physical reality. Yet in spite of the mimesis—indeed the true reality—that Morpheus is able to achieve, his work of art is actually an elaborate lie, a counterfeiting of the truth fashioned by an insincere (and slothful) artist. Ceyx only *appears* to be alive and only *seems* to be speaking to Alcione in her vision; in fact, his physical resurrection by the desultory Morpheus is an illusory sham.[10] The re-created Ceyx says it himself when he tells Alcione that she "shul [him] never on lyve yse" (205).

Its effect on Alcione, its primary audience, cannot be said to be successful at all: after "Ceyx" has spoken his few moving words to her, she looks up, presumably expecting to lay eyes on the beloved man who has just spoken to her in her vision, and she sees nothing:

> With that hir eyen up she casteth
> And saw noght. "Allas!" quod she for sorwe,
> And deyede within the thridde morwe.   (212–14)

This false resurrection has obviously failed to console the mourning Alcione in spite of its full re-creation of Ceyx's physical form, for once the lying vision is over, she no longer sees the man that Morpheus had propped before her. One could even argue on the basis of Chaucer's lines that her death from sorrow is actually hastened by Morpheus's cheap trick, for it only strengthens in her mind the realization that her husband is gone. Thus, in their attempts to find an antidote to human grief, the gods have clearly failed.[11]

Human artists must work much harder than Morpheus to evoke the "real" in their art, for they do not have the power to collect scraps of material reality to use as the substance of their craft. Rather, they are limited to the deficient medium of language, whose ability to capture the truth of the things to which it refers is always (as the Black Knight has shown) inadequate to the task. The poet-narrator's dream of the bedroom and the hunt deals further with the difficulties of poetic composition, especially the particular kind that calls for the "real" to be strenuously pursued. The dream opens with the narrator awakening into a May morning, where singing birds, like minor poets, industriously strive to avoid both feigning and sloth:

> For ther was noon of hem that feyned
> To synge, for ech of hem hym peyned
> To fynde out mery crafty notes.
> They ne spared not her throtes.   (317–20)

Yet the poet is indoors, isolated from the natural world and from the events about which his poems are written. His chamber is carefully described: his windows, suffused with light, are glazed with images from classical literature, and his walls are painted with the "text and glose" (334) of *The Romance of the Rose*. This complete environment, from the birds to the chamber decorations, is drawn in such a way as to suggest a particularly artistic atmosphere, for nature's artists (the birds) and former human poets (as represented by their works on the windows and walls) stand here as Chaucer's analogues and models; they are the artists from whom he learns his craft and upon whose works he models his own. The images on the walls and windows are especially interesting, for they imply that poets draw their works less from life than from prior textualizations of it. To use Chaucer's metaphor, the light of the sun may be visible, but only indirectly, as it is mediated by the work of other artists. And the whole environment is part of a bedroom milieu because it is within that room of dreams that he works so diligently at "making." Morpheus's ideal bedroom would be quite different, of course; as the narrator envisions it, it would be designed only for the laziest of artists, for it promotes nothing but deep, inactive, and imageless sleep:

> Of down of pure dowves white
> I wil yive hym a fether-bed,
> Rayed with gold and ryght wel cled
> In fyn blak satyn doutremer,
> And many a pilowe, and every ber
> Of cloth of Reynes, to slepe softe—
> Hym thar not nede to turnen ofte.   (250–56)

The dream-hunt that the poet joins is also an image of his "making." Modeled on the love-hunts of French amatory verse, this episode serves as a structural equivalent to the Black Knight's (and thus Chaucer's) attempt to "capture" Blanche, as critics have noted.[12] But just how cleverly and precisely this episode works as an analogue to the poet's pursuit of his poem has not been fully realized. The metaphor of the hunt had occasionally been used in literary works as a way for artists to suggest their own pursuit of a narrative line or subject matter in the work at hand,[13] and it thus may be functioning in *The Book of the Duchess* merely as an ingenious structural artifice with which Chaucer pairs the literary "hert-hunte" of the Black Knight.

There is another medieval opinion about the hunt, however, that Chaucer is surely acknowledging here, the well-known precept that hunting was a successful antidote for idleness. Hunting manuals routinely addressed this beneficial effect of the sport, usually in words resembling these from *The Master of Game*:

Now shal I preue þe how an huntere ne may by no reson falle yn any of the seuene dedly synnes. ffor whanne a man is ydel and reccheles wiþ oute trauayle and men ben not occupyed to be doyng some þinges and abideþ oþer yn þeire bed oþer in chambres, hit is a þing þe which draweþ men to ymagynacioun of fleshly lust and plaisere. . . . [By hunting] is he lasse ydel . . . for he hath ynowe to do to ymagine, and to þenk on his office.[14]

For Chaucer, the hunt has particular relevance to this poem, for drawing on its common contemporary meaning he can show us that active poets are "pursuing the chase" even though they seem to be sleeping in their "bed oþer in chambres," a feat that the writer of *The Master of Game* might have found unbelievable. In *The Book of the Duchess,* the dream *is* the poetic elegy that Chaucer worked so hard to complete, and the writing (dreaming) of the work is a "game" or sport that is not merely a game alone, like the "better play" of reading that Chaucer showed us before his dream began. Indeed, the poet's seemingly idle life is truly an active one, a point that Chaucer makes through the analogy of the hunt partly so that his patrons will see that they, like poets, have a version of laborious "playing," an activity that can be misread as sloth.

By appropriating this social ritual of his upper-class audience to describe and legitimize his own labor as a poet, Chaucer is also able to defend his underrepresentation of Blanche. As any nobleman in his audience would have realized, energetic pursuit of one's quarry does not necessarily guarantee its capture. The hunters in the dream, who are nothing if not vigorous in their chase, are finally disappointed in their quest for the deer:

> Withynne a while the hert yfounde ys,
> Yhalowed, and rechased faste
> Longe tyme; and so at the laste
> This hert rused and staal away
> Fro alle the houndes a privy way.
> The houndes had overshote hym alle
> And were on a defaute yfalle.
> Therwyth the hunte wonder faste
> Blew a forloyn at the laste.   (378–86)

Like the poet-dreamer and the Black Knight, who never succeed in capturing the image of Blanche, the hunters discover that their pursuit has come to naught. Yet none of these failures in any way suggests that the questers were lax in their duties.

The Book of the Duchess, then, fulfills a difficult poetic assignment without needing to advance any of the questionable claims that normally characterize laudatory and occasional verse. Chaucer does not pretend, for example, that he or his poem can sufficiently describe the lost duchess Blanche; she remains unrepresented at the poem's end. Yet this "failed" elegy actually succeeds in meeting the requirements of its commission because Chaucer's surrogate, the Black Knight, is handled so deftly and well. We are asked to believe what the Knight says about the beauty and virtues of White, not because he ever adequately describes them or escapes the traditional discourse of praise, but because he is absolutely committed to the difficult task of trying. His labored attempt to "catch his quarry" may fail, but we are certainly made to see the "busyness" that informs it.

With this device—as in the rest of the poem—Chaucer also raises the more general philosophical question, Can art ever re-create the "real?" Although Morpheus may come close to answering this perennial aesthetic question, Yes, Chaucer clearly works to undermine the deity's credentials as the super-artist he seems to be. Morpheus's real but desultory resurrection of Ceyx is shown to be an illusory and elaborate lie. His success in literally raising the dead, brought about by magic rather than the laborious crafting of earthly artists, is finally a cheap deception. Moreover, we must not forget that Morpheus himself is only a fiction. Though his miraculous act of raising the dead may be impossible for human artists to repeat, Chaucer makes it clear that were it not for the labor of some earthly artist, Morpheus would have no existence at all. He comes from a book of

> fables
> That clerkes had in olde tyme
> And other poetes, put in rime.   (52–54)

Outside the worlds fashioned by the fiction-makers, there is "god but oon" (237); Morpheus's existence is textual alone.

That art's power to re-create the real is always in question is certainly one of *The Book of the Duchess*'s major philosophical tenets, as it was in the poetry of Chaucer's French predecessors. The origin of art is mainly other art, just as surely as Blanche's elegy comes from books, not life. Even when a poet fancies that he has transcended the confines of literary convention or the frustrating limitations of language's ability to refer to the "real," upon awakening, he is sure to discover some book in his hand—one that has inevitably shaped his dreams and thus his poems:

> Therwyth I awook myselve
> And fond me lyinge in my bed;
> And the book that I hadde red,
> Of Alcione and Seys the kyng,
> And of the goddes of slepyng,
> I fond hyt in myn hond ful even.   (1324–29)

For poems, even those that claim to contain true "portrayture," are no more real than dreams in *The Book of the Duchess*; indeed, as the work's closing lines suggest, they are the same thing:

> Thoghte I, "Thys ys so queynt a sweven
> That I wol, be processe of tyme,
> Fonde to put this sweven in ryme

As I kan best, and that anoon."
This was my sweven; now hyt ys doon.   (1330–34)

By means of the interlocking analogies in *The Book of the Duchess*, then—where play is work, truth is fiction, death is life, and failure is success—the poem nearly takes a deconstructive turn into a total subversion of its own asserted categories. Arguing that writing is always a constitutive activity rather than an imitative one, this poem overtly suggests to its audience that textuality is all writers have, both before mimetic projects are begun and after their completion. There is no significant difference between representing the "real" and imagining the fictional, for each kind of project participates in the same system of textual reclamation. And if there is any notable exchange at all between this poem and its (un)represented world, it is surely just an economic one: John of Gaunt received the poem he had commissioned, and Chaucer got his reward.

CHAPTER TWO

Eschatological Poetics in
The House of Fame

 ⸜ In composing *The Book of the Duchess,* Chaucer
clearly appropriated conventions from French amatory verse, producing
his poem by selecting and manipulating some of the structural devices
and concepts he had found in *The Romance of the Rose* and the works
of Machaut and Froissart. His poem was not only indebted to French
models for its narrative strategy, its structural units, and its diction; it
also attempted to refine and extend the French poets' thematic interest
in the deceptive qualities of literature's representational claims. By foregrounding the discontinuity between art and life, thereby interrogating
his poem's own complicity in the promotion of the dubious informing
assumptions of elegy, *The Book of the Duchess* shows Chaucer's early
involvement in the questions of poetic authority that had been raised in
French verse of the thirteenth and fourteenth centuries.

In *The House of Fame,* Chaucer continues to express his interest in
these issues, but this time he turns to the poetry of Dante for the basic
structure and thematic content of his work. Although he does not abandon what his French models taught him, in *The House of Fame* he ambitiously confronts the forceful claims of the Italian poet-theologian in
a new and differently managed argument about the relationship between
texts and human history, one that comes close to advancing the idea that
the two inhabit separate phenomenal spheres, that there is no such thing
as history prior to some textualization of it. Indeed, Dante's poetry offered Chaucer a strikingly provocative series of poetic claims and disclaimers about history and fiction, for Dante sets himself up as the only
historian of his time able to record the truth about both literal and allegorical "reality."[1]

Much important scholarship on *The House of Fame* has revealed that
the poem imitates texts in the visionary / apocalyptic genre and that it

is some kind of response to the prestigious and respectable tradition of visionary narrative. Dante's influence, which has been well documented, is especially clear in *The House of Fame*'s adaptation of two invocations from the *Commedia,* its use of the device of the golden eagle, and its general interest in reconciling the poetry of secular love with genuine religious vision, an idea that Dante was the first to embody in perfected form.[2] But most critics have rightly seen that Chaucer's response to the writers in the visionary tradition, Dante included, is not without irony— even high comedy—for *The House of Fame* often subverts the common themes and conventions these writers employed in their visions. The comic eagle ride Chaucer shows himself taking on the way to Fame's house and Fame's own grotesque parody of God's judicial role are only two of the scenes that militate against any interpretation of *The House of Fame* as a serious work in the Christian visionary tradition. In tone and in content, there are simply too many massive differences between Chaucer's poem and the works he is imitating for us to see *The House of Fame* as anything but some kind of antivision, a parody of solemn medieval attempts to describe the otherworld to earthbound readers.

Modern critics have done an impressive job of outlining Chaucer's indebtedness to his visionary sources and describing his distinctively subversive tone. For example, Chaucer's proem to Book 1 has been shown to contain elaborate comic statements that undermine the traditional authenticating devices of visionary poets. Sheila Delany notes that the proem provides us with so much "contradictory information about dreams" that it is vain to seek any truth in the dream itself or to hope to learn anything about the validity of dream content in general from it.[3] Others have argued a similar position, some of them even suggesting, as does Robert Burlin, that the proem strongly implies Chaucer's dream should be viewed more as an *insomnium* than a *visio,* that is, as a dream reflecting only the preoccupations and anxieties of the dreamer.[4] But however one may want to categorize Chaucer's dream, it is clear that he himself wishes to make no claims for its truth; he says that he is unsure about either its type or cause. Moreover, the invocation to Morpheus that follows the proem is fraught with irony, since Morpheus's realm, that of fantasy, delusion, and forgetfulness (as we have seen in *The Book of the Duchess*), could hardly be viewed as the source of an authoritative—or even a perfectly remembered—dream.[5]

In addition to these early deauthenticating strategies, *The House of Fame* contains other significant contrasts to poems in the visionary tradition, contrasts that have not yet been described and analyzed. The most important—and the one whose presence and implications this essay will explore—is reflected in Chaucer's calculated avoidance of any claim that he is talking about human lives, either as they may be observed on earth or as they are envisioned in their eternal resting places in the otherworld. Rather, in keeping with his avoidance of any claim to be representing life in *The Book of the Duchess,* he consistently restricts the interests of his text to the nature and destiny of human narratives, both spoken and written, in a comic attempt to avoid the problem of authority that he believed Dante and other visionaries faced. Not wishing to take responsibility for the kind of moral judgment on others' lives that Dante and his predecessors ambitiously shouldered in order to achieve their transcendent literary perspectives, Chaucer takes the safer position of a commentator on the afterlife of words, not souls. In so doing, he clearly avoids the normative theological content of the religious vision, yet he nonetheless depends heavily on the conventions of the genre, casting his poem in the form of sacred visionary texts like Dante's. This strategy allows Chaucer to articulate certain principles central to his poetics and to contrast them implicitly with the views held by his literary forebears, Dante especially.

Chaucer's unique handling of visionary material in *The House of Fame* is made possible largely by the character traits of his narrator, the man who reads and writes about love without ever having experienced it himself. This crucial trait is brought to our attention by the eagle, who says that the narrator "haddest never part" (628) of Love's benefits, being one "of hem that [Love] lyst not avaunce" (640).[6] The narrator is not only ignorant of love and its effect on real people's lives, he is represented as being deficient in general knowledge about other aspects of life around him. Indeed, the self-portrait of "Chaucer" that we receive in Book 2 is worth remembering in detail, for it helps to account for the content of his dream. The eagle remarks to "Geffrey" that

> "thou hast no tydynges
> Of Loves folk yf they be glade,
> Ne of noght elles that God made;
> And noght oonly fro fer contree
> That ther no tydynge cometh to thee,
> But of thy verray neyghebores,
> That duellen almost at thy dores,
> Thou herist neyther that ne this;
> For when thy labour doon al ys,
> And hast mad alle thy rekenynges,
> In stede of reste and newe thynges
> Thou goost hom to thy hous anoon,
> And, also domb as any stoon,

Thou sittest at another book
Tyl fully daswed ys thy look."   (644–58)

The narrator's fondness for books and his absolute withdrawal from life itself are everywhere confirmed by his dream, for instead of describing the otherworld of life (as all visionary poems claim to do), it describes only the otherworld of stories about life, a subject much more suitable to the limited knowledge and personal interests of the reader who lives "thus as an heremyte" (659).

The first major example of Chaucer's textualizing of the visionary genre is found in Book 1, where the narrator begins his journey to the otherworld not with Vergil as his guide (as does Dante in the *Commedia*), but rather with Vergil's story, a guide wholly appropriate to a traveler who habitually relies on books rather than experience for his knowledge. Yet Chaucer does not let us forget that his narrator's encounter with Vergil's story in the Temple of Venus is definitely to be interpreted as part of the poem's visionary machinery, for he repeatedly employs one of the genre's most time-worn conventions, the *I saw* formula, throughout the narration of Book 1.[7] But what he is "seeing" is only a story about events—he witnesses somebody's version of the adventures of Aeneas, not the adventures themselves. In other words, our narrator is a reader during the day, and his vision confirms that he remains one in his dreams.

Exactly whose version of Vergil's story is it that our narrator is seeing in his dream? To ask the narrator's own question about these narrative images, "whoo did hem wirche" (474)? Probably this version of Vergil's story (itself only a version of the truth) is the narrator's own, for in this scene we are faced with just enough self-interested distortion of the basic Vergilian text to suspect that the narrator is seeing what he wants to see: his favorite passages (such as the Dido and Aeneas subplot) come alive in loving detail, but the rest of Vergil's poem is cursorily and dully summarized. Moreover, because the narrator has read Ovid's *Heroides,* too, there are inappropriate Ovidian echoes added to the basic Vergilian story, resulting in a very personalized version of the *Aeneid* based on the imperfect memory and the private concerns of the narrator, who, in a revealing confession of a type unknown to medieval recorders of visions, announces, "Non other auctour alegge I" (314), after he has written down a particularly heart-rending passage of Dido's lament over her lost reputation.

Thus what we have in Chaucer's vision of Venus's temple is not only the carefully maintained illusion that we are dealing with a narrator who has not experienced life for himself, but also an implicit admission that this vision will merely recycle the dreamer's reading material in some novel and personally satisfying shape, providing us with no new or objective knowledge either of the world or of its supernatural dimensions.[8] The result of the first book's undercutting of its own truth and authority, then, is that Chaucer openly admits something that visionary writers (Dante included) would not—their material comes from books and their distant apocalyptic journeys may, in fact, have extended only to the closest library. Moreover, Book 1 suggests that visions and dreams are generally selective versions of those texts upon which they are based, conforming to the visionary's biases and beliefs.

The scene involving Venus's temple presents us with more evidence that Chaucer's vision is designed to report on art instead of life, and that the narrator's interests govern the content of his dream. Venus herself, for example, is not physically present in her temple; rather she is present merely "in portreyture" (131), that is, in an artistic representation on the wall. That the narrator ends up in a building sacred to Venus is itself significant, for his daytime labors as a love-poet will show him to be her devoted servant (615–19), and he later invokes her as the inspiration for his art (516–19). Indeed, Venus's temple—with Venus conspicuously absent—is precisely the place in which we would expect the nonloving writer of amatory verse to tarry in his dreams.

The desert scene that follows Chaucer's visit to the Temple of Venus provides further documentation of this particular dreamer's dependence on texts for his representational activities. Surrounding the temple, the dreamer sees

> but a large feld,
> As fer as that I myghte see,
> Withouten toun, or hous, or tree,
> Or bush, or grass, or eryd lond . . .
> Ne no maner creature
> That ys yformed be Nature
> Ne sawgh I, me to rede or wisse.   (482–90)

That is, once he is outside the temple and thus away from the realm of books, his knowledge of the earth and its creatures abruptly ceases. The real world is clearly a total blank to him, a barren, unpopulated desert that images the unexperienced—and thus unrepresentable—world outside texts.

After Chaucer has established his poem's unique relationship to the visionary tradition in Book 1 and has started to suggest a critique of the claims advanced by its practitioners, he begins to rely—sometimes quite specifically—on Dante's *Commedia* for the structure and subversive significance of his poem. Critics have long noted the resemblance, for example, between Chaucer's eagle and the eagles in Dante's *Purgatorio* 9.19–33 and *Paradiso* 1.62ff.[9] Moreover, the invocation in the Proem to Book 2 is a close adaptation of *Inferno* 2.7–9, with one major alteration in sense: instead of Dante's "O memory that wrote down what I saw," we find Chaucer's invocation of his own "Thought, that wrot al that I mette" (523), a change which carefully reduces Dante's claim that his visionary journey actually occurred to the more modest suggestion that the vision we are about to read had its origin in the dreamer's own head.[10]

There is a further allusion to the *Commedia* in Chaucer's "I neyther am Ennok, ne Elye, / Ne Romulus, ne Ganymede" (588–89), a line that is close in form and meaning to *Inferno* 2.32 and that introduces a passage similar in general content to *Inferno* 2.33–51, where Vergil reassures the frightened Dante about his upcoming journey.[11]

Finally, we must also remember that Dante made the unusual claim that he had taken his journey in the body, not just the spirit; Chaucer's narrator, too, though he follows St. Paul in wondering "wher in body or in gost" (981) he is present, is clearly traveling in all his full-bodied splendor, for the eagle mentions that he is "noyous for to carye" (574).

More important to our understanding of *The House of Fame,* however, is the subtle contrast Chaucer draws between the reasons for his journey and those that Dante lays out in the *Commedia* for his. In Book 2 of the *Inferno,* Vergil explains that he was sent to Dante by Beatrice, who was moved by Dante's love for her to reward him with his journey. Lucy, in reporting to Beatrice on Dante's pitiful state, makes this point clearly: "Beatrice, true praise of God, why do you not succor him who bore you such love that for you he left the vulgar throng? Do you not hear his pitiful lament?" (103–105). Beatrice, responding immediately, sets the wheels in motion for Dante's visit to the otherworlds, a journey that is unmistakably inspired by Dante's long and faithful service as Beatrice's lover.

Chaucer, on the other hand, because he is not a lover but only a writer about love, appropriately describes the inspiration and source for his own extraterrestrial journey as deriving from his literary service alone. The eagle remarks that Jupiter took pity on the industrious and unrewarded poet:

> Certeyn, he hath of the routhe
> That thou so longe trewely
> Hast served so ententyfly
> Hys blynde nevew Cupido,

And faire Venus also,
Withoute guerdon ever yit,
And never-the-lesse hast set thy wit—
Although that in thy hed ful lyte is—
To make bookys, songes, dytees,
In ryme or elles in cadence,
As thou best canst, in reverence
Of Love and of hys servantes eke.   (614–25)

It is fitting, too, that a man who has served Venus and Cupid only through his language should be correspondingly rewarded in his vision by receiving language in return. The eagle announces that Chaucer's writing in service of Love will be repaid with "tydynges," a reward contrasting with that commonly found in love visions, where the dreamer receives an invitation to the God of Love's court, actual physical union with his lady, or, in Dante's transformation of the love vision, a trip into the very presence of Love itself as the mover of the universe. In *The House of Fame,* the narrator's heavenly journey ends, not with a lover, the love-deity, or the origin of Love, but rather with stories about lovers and the origins of those stories, the same step away from love's reality toward textualization that we have come to expect from the poem's "Chaucer," the nonloving reader.

In thinking about the structure and meaning of Chaucer's visit to the palace of Fame, it is instructive to keep in mind the general purpose of Dante's *Commedia.* As described succinctly in the *Letter to Can Grande,* the *Commedia* has two basic interrelated subjects: literally, the poem shows the "state of souls after death"; allegorically, it demonstrates how man, "by good or ill deserts . . . becomes liable to rewarding or punishing justice."[12] In Chaucer's poem, we find a parallel dual purpose, with the expected major substitution of "stories" (or "words") for souls. Cast in Dante's terms, then, Chaucer's poem shows "the state of stories after utterance" and how stories "become liable to rewarding or punishing justice," with Lady Fame as the functional stand-in for Christ the Judge.

That Chaucer was thinking of Dante as he conceived of his comic apocalypse is clearly suggested by the eagle's long pseudo-scientific explanations of how sounds move upward to Fame's house. His doctrine of "kyndely enclynyng" (729–56) adapts to the idea of sound what Dante had written about the soul's natural inclination, through love, toward heaven.[13] Moreover, the eagle's account of how sounds are embodied in Fame's palace,

Whan any speche ycomen ys
Up to the paleys, anon-ryght

> Hyt wexeth lyk the same wight
> Which that the word in erthe spak,
> Be hyt clothed red or blak;
> And hath so verray hys lyknesse
> That spak the word, that thou wilt gesse
> That it the same body be   (1074–81)

implicitly corresponds to Dante's practice in the *Commedia* of lending full human dimension to the souls of the dead. Critics have suggested that *Paradiso* 4.37–48 shows the clearest articulation of this idea,[14] but Statius's words in *Purgatorio* 25.91–108 could qualify at least as well as the inspiration for the Chaucerian passage. In explaining how souls become visible shades, Statius remarks:

As the air, when it is full of moisture, becomes adorned with various colors by another's rays which are reflected in it, so here the neighboring air shapes itself in that form which is virtually imprinted on it by the soul that stopped there; and then, like the flame which follows the fire wheresoever it moves, the spirit is followed by its new form. Inasmuch as therefrom it has its semblance, it is called a shade, and therefrom it forms the organs of every sense, even to the sight. By this we speak and by this we laugh, by this we make tears and sighs. . . . According as the desires and other affections prick us, the shade takes its form; and this is the cause of that at which you marvel. (91–108)

Creatively adapting standard Christian doctrine here to account for the physical substantiality of his characters, Dante is arguing that an individual's appearance and his specific sins and virtues are stamped on the soul, so that after the body's death, the soul still retains an accurate imprint of its possessor's spiritual and physical condition. Therefore, if souls were visible (as they are in the *Commedia*, in a sense), they would each be unique in their appearance, reflecting the distinctive characteristics of the individuals in whom they had previously dwelled.[15] This doctrine and the doctrine behind the eagle's speech on "kyndely enclynyng," are both employed by Chaucer in a Dantean context and for roughly the same Dantean purposes, but Chaucer replaces Dante's "souls" with "words."

The subject matter of Book 3 of *The House of Fame* unambiguously continues Chaucer's interest in the origins and afterlife of language, exploring the inequity, inconsistency, and fickleness of Lady Fame's decisions on the fate of the stories she hears. Chaucer's major point is that human fame (like oblivion) is largely undeserved. We must never lose sight of this primary focus, nor should we unnecessarily allegorize the text, forcing it to serve as an unstable vehicle for Christian doctrine. Yet we cannot ignore Chaucer's heavy dependence on Christian apocalyptic concepts to further his ideas, especially the apocalyptic elements developed in the *Commedia* and its models, works such as *Revelation* and the *Visio sancti Pauli*. These concepts, expressed in Book 3 through both structural parallels and iconography, are operative mainly as parts of the complex analogy Chaucer draws between the workings of earthly fame and the process of Christian judgment: the events in the palace of Fame are to narratives what the Last Judgment is to souls. A related analogy involves the narrator's own role as participant in the action: seeing the literary afterlife of stories ("tydyngs") is as relevant to this cloistered reader's personal interests as seeing the afterlife of souls would be to a theological poet's concerns. (And here we might keep in mind, for the purposes of comparison, the kind of poet-narrator that Dante creates.) Thus, each kind of poet records (actually creates) the sort of vision most appropriate to his vocation and self-definition as a writer; if one is a reader and writer rather than an active participant in life (Chaucer's persona), one will be more directly interested in finding out the secrets surrounding literary afterlife (fame) than in learning about those that relate to the afterlives of real people. Throughout Book 3, Chaucer develops these analogies, always keeping earlier visionary materials before him as he shapes his poem in their image.

Allusions to previous apocalyptic texts are liberally scattered in Book 3, beginning with the invocation, which, as scholars have long recognized, comically adapts Dante's majestic language from the opening of the *Paradiso* to Chaucer's humbler project. Also, when Chaucer's narrator makes the arduous climb up Fame's mountain of ice, he encounters "famous folkes names fele" (1137) graven on its side, some beginning to melt away in the sun's heat—a detail that recalls Paul's experience before the gates of Paradise, where he finds the names of the righteous inscribed.[16] The biblical Apocalypse is openly alluded to in lines 1381–85, where Chaucer draws a comparison between Lady Fame and the beasts "that Goddis trone gunne honoure / As John writ in th'Apocalips." And B. G. Koonce, though he fails in his attempt to make Chaucer's poem into a Christian allegory, has collected an impressive number of parallels between images in Fame's court and the apocalyptic imagery in *Revelation*, including the physical positioning of the minstrels and singers, the ordering of Chaucer's catalogues, the description of the hall, and other miscellaneous symbolic details and actions.[17]

Yet Chaucer's "heavenly Jerusalem," though carefully constructed with other medieval and early Christian sources in mind, is a city with distinct idiosyncrasies, all of them created with the purpose of making this vision refer to its dreamer's artistic—and quite nonreligious—interests. The awe-inspiring architectural wonder that is Fame's castle, for

example, with its gargoyles, pinnacles, niches, tabernacles, and numerous windows (1188–94) seems to be a secularized version of a Gothic
cathedral, that is, an earthly image of the Celestial City.[18] But as a castle
rather than a church, Fame's dwelling exists at a level two large analogical steps away from the real Heavenly Jerusalem that St. John saw in his
vision, being merely an image of an image of the Heavenly Jerusalem.

In interpreting certain details of Fame's environment, however, it is
useful to keep the idea of a cathedral in mind. On the outside of the
castle walls, Chaucer sees "sondry habitacles" (1194) or niches in which
perform famous harpers who, as W. W. Skeat and B. G. Koonce have
noted, correspond in position to the "saints of lesser glory" who are
often seen carved into the "niches on the pinnacles and buttresses of the
Church."[19] But Chaucer's harpers, all pagans when named, are singing
songs about fame, the secular equivalent of Christian salvation. They are

> mynstralles
> And gestiours that tellen tales
> Both of wepinge and of game
> Of al that longeth unto Fame.   (1197–1200)

And as if to reproduce the angelic hierarchy believed to be present in the
Celestial City, whereby each order of angels imitates and learns from the
orders above them who are closer to the reality of God,[20] the lesser harpers sit under the great harpers

> in dyvers seës,
> And gunne on hem upward to gape,
> And countrefete hem as an ape
> Or as craft contrefeteth kynde.   (1210–13)

The lowest group of artists, some hardly classifiable as anything more
than noisemakers or image-mongers who rely on illusion for their art,
occupy positions behind this tableau, completing a scene that imitates
the ordered celestial hierarchy, with the higher orders closest to the truth
their art represents and the lower orders dependent on what those above
them have chosen to convey. But what is important to note here is that
Chaucer has restricted his mock-religious imagery to the basic theme of
art. The poem has little to do with life or the judgments on it that will
be rendered at Doomsday; rather, it refers only to artistic representations of life, to visual/verbal constructions of reality, not to reality itself.
Artists imitate other artists, as this tableau suggests, and The House of
Fame is very much a poem in which "kynde" (or reality) practically dis-
appears as a useful concept.[21] With "kynde" written out of this highly
text-centered vision, Chaucer, in a potentially deconstructive argument,

subverts the mimetic claims of visionary poetry, foregrounding the absence that echoes within them.

Also in keeping with this theme of textual eschatology are the Muses who sing in Fame's hall (1395–1406), replacing the heavenly choirs of angels in the Celestial City. Even the narrator participates in the apocalyptic action here, for according to Christian doctrine, on Judgment Day each individual's conscience will be opened to him like a book, and he will "recall to memory all his own works, whether good or evil, and shall mentally survey them with a marvelous rapidity, so that this knowledge will either accuse or excuse conscience."[22] Although our narrator's conscience is not opened to reveal his sins in this textual version of the apocalypse, he definitely experiences a moment of self-judgment, applied—as we might expect—to his art:

> "I wot myself best how y stonde;
> For what I drye, or what I thynke,
> I wil myselven al hyt drynke,
> Certeyn, for the more part,
> As fer forth as I kan myn art."   (1878–82)

And just as St. Paul hears *arcana verba* in his rapture that he cannot disclose, so Chaucer hears a tiding "that shal not now be told for me" (2136).[23]

But most important to Chaucer's poetic eschatology are the seven pillars that line each side of Fame's dwelling, upon which stand the great narrators of Jewish and classical history. Josephus, Statius, the tellers of the Trojan tales, Vergil, Ovid, Lucan, and Claudian are obviously the great men of literary history responsible for maintaining and disseminating in their works the fame of non-Christian narratives. Yet their symbolic function is more complex than this. Here, they are secular stand-ins for the Old Testament patriarchs and prophets that one would normally find represented on columns in the great European cathedrals, Chartres being a fine example.[24] The taletellers of pre-Christian narrative, then, take on a mock-figural meaning—that is, these great writers are to poetic salvation history what the patriarchs and prophets are to the real salvation history defined by the Christian tradition. Just as the twenty-four elders of *Revelation,* who stand for the Old Testament, are seen in heaven with the Christ they prophesied and prefigured, so these old writers, the Old Testament of poetry, serve to adumbrate Lady Fame. They, after all, disseminated fame in a fashion that Lady Fame will vastly improve upon, for if Vergil and Ovid spread defamatory or contradictory stories about the pagans of their time (remember poor Dido in Book 1) and if the Trojan talebearers can argue about who among them is lying

(1475–80), then Lady Fame exists to go one step further. She has come not to destroy the Old Law but to fulfill it.

At this point the complete symbolic function of Venus's Temple in Book 1 begins to emerge. It too participates in the typology of poetic history, for the fame-spreading texts of Vergil and Ovid—both represented there—prefigure Lady Fame's operations in this later stage of the vision. Indeed, the Temple of Venus is an "Old Testament" version of Fame's "cathedral." In it

> ther were moo ymages
> Of gold, stondynge in sondry stages,
> And moo ryche tabernacles,
> And with perre moo pynacles,
> And moo curiouse portreytures,
> And queynte maner of figures
> Of olde werk, then I saugh ever.   (121–27)

As an analogue of Scripture, then, Chaucer's poem demonstrates the scriptural technique of figuralism, whereby Venus's temple foreshadows Fame's "church," much as the Temple of Solomon was defined as the type of the Christian church and the Heavenly City of Jerusalem for which it stood.[25] Yet here we are seeing the salvation history of poetry alone, a kind of private typology designed to make sense out of one particular reader's experience with his ancient and sometimes contradictory books, the "olde werk" of the poets who lived and wrote before him. Such an interpretation of past poetic history is extremely clever here, but it is not original with Chaucer. Dante, in the *Commedia*—a poem also designed by its author to be read in the manner of Scripture—handled classical texts and their writers in this typological fashion, and it is likely that Chaucer is imitating him here, with subversive designs. For what Chaucer exposes in his poem is not the virtue and proto-Christian significance of the classical poets (a task Dante sets for himself in the *Commedia*), but rather their tendency to be as irresponsible as any human being in the manner in which they disseminate news.[26]

Lady Fame's own questionable judgments, of course, form the lion's share of Book 3, and Chaucer develops, at length, nine different examples of her irrationality, partly to show how much more perverse she is than any of the "Old Testament" fame-bearers who prefigure her. The supplicants (or rather their embodied words) enter, making known their conditions and desires relative to fame, and the deity pronounces a judgment that—in every case—seems to us to run counter to any true standard of fairness or Christian merit. Good people, for example, who ask for and deserve good fame, receive bad fame or oblivion. One group of exceptionally meritorious folk who want no fame at all, arguing that their deeds were done for "Goddys love" alone (1697), get what they desire, even though such exemplary virtue actually deserves to be perpetually admired by Christians. Another similar group, however, receives good fame in spite of their earnest hope to avoid "renoun" (1709), showing beyond any doubt that Fame's decisions do not conform to any consistent or rational conception of merit. In addition, bad people who want good fame sometimes receive it and sometimes do not, depending on Lady Fame's whims at the moment. And even some bad people who desire bad fame are provided with what they want, although they admit that they performed their treachery with precisely the goal of achieving notoriety in mind; in a world controlled by some discernible principle of justice, these people would be denied any fame at all.

In sum, Lady Fame is incapable of acting with any comprehensible sense of fairness. As Paul Ruggiers has noted, her injustice "is to Chaucer's poem what the impenetrable mystery of God's justice is to the *Divine Comedy*"[27]—in fact, one might want to see her, in Dantean terms, as a master of the "anti-*contrapasso*."[28] Moreover, her trumpets, Cler Laude and Sklaundre, clearly suggest salvation and damnation, the former with its accompanying odor of roses (1685–87), the latter with its stench like "the pit of helle" (1654). But we must be sure to remember that Lady Fame's judgments extend only to reputations, not to the afterlives of souls—and appropriately so, for we are only hearing texts speak, not the reality they claim to be representing. Unlike Dante, Chaucer refuses to determine the ultimate culpability or virtue of human beings, because he knows that such assessments, like Lady Fame's, are in effect merely assessments of texts, not "truth."

With the House of Rumor, Chaucer further adds to his developing cosmology of narrative, for in this final vision his narrator witnesses the origin of the stories that ultimately receive Fame's judgment. Although Chaucer takes much of the detail for this scene from Ovid's account of Fama's dwelling (*Metamorphoses* 12.39–63), he situates his own House of Rumor so that it serves as a kind of birthplace and temporary storehouse for the narratives upon which Lady Fame (*cum* Christ the Judge) will render judgment. In doing so, Chaucer suggests that his House of Rumor is more than just a pagan image of earthly gossip—somehow it fits into the Christianized scheme he has been building on since the beginning of his dream.

At first it would seem that the House of Rumor makes sense best as an image of the world. Its natural building materials, twigs, and its chaotic noisiness and disorder certainly suggest this view, as does the narrator's description of its teeming population:

> But which a congregacioun
> Of folk, as I saugh rome aboute,
> Some wythin and some wythoute,
> Nas never seen, ne shal ben eft;
> That, certys, in the world nys left
> So many formed be Nature,
> Ne ded so many a creature.   (2034–40)

Sheila Delany, in fact, sees the House of Rumor as an image of worldly experience, where "originate the events which fame either commemorates or condemns to oblivion."[29] Koonce agrees, noting that in Christian mythography, the labyrinth of Dedalus—to which the House of Rumor is compared (1920–23)—was a symbol of the maze of this world.[30] Moreover, if Chaucer's journey is structurally comparable in any way to Dante's, then it would be appropriate for it to culminate in an awe-inspiring vision of the place of origin of all stories (the world), just as Dante's ended with a glimpse of the place of origin of Love (Heaven).

A further reason for seeing the House of Rumor as the world (or at least as a highly stylized analogue of it) is suggested by the fact that the "tydings" there have "lives" just as people do on earth, and the longer they exist the more likely it is that their truth or "goodness" will be corrupted. Interestingly, in fact, the condition of the tidings exactly imitates the categorizable states of human souls; a few are wholly good ("sad soths"), a few are wholly bad ("lesyngs"), but the majority of them end up being "fals and soth compouned" (2108), just as the majority of human souls were deemed, in medieval times, to be mixtures of good and evil, *bonum conjunctum malo*, at death.[31] In Chaucer's text, this understanding is closely applied to the "lives" and ultimate "deaths" of tidings, for we see how the world's conditions make it impossible to separate their truth from their falsity by the time they "die":

> And somtyme saugh I thoo at ones
> A lesyng and a sad soth sawe,
> That gonne of aventure drawe
> Out at a wyndowe for to pace;
> And, when they metten in that place,
> They were achekked bothe two,
> And neyther of hem moste out goo
> For other, so they gonne crowde,
> Til ech of hem gan crien lowde . . .

"We wil medle us ech with other,
That no man, be they never so wrothe,
Shal han on [of us] two, but bothe
At ones. . . ."
Thus saugh I fals and soth compouned
Togeder fle for oo tydynge.   (2088–2109)

Yet in spite of its likeness to the world, the House of Rumor is not really a picture of the earth, experience, or life as most humans know it. The people there are important only to the extent that they affect the state of tidings—by uttering them, enlarging on them, and spreading them about. Nothing actually happens in the House of Rumor, for "reality"—that is, what really occurs and why—is again totally absent in Chaucer's vision, and appropriately so, for he has told us earlier that he knows next to nothing about real experience, spending all his waking hours immersed in his books. His House of Rumor absolutely confirms this fact, showing what the world might look like from the standpoint of one who has relied on stories about it for his information, never having witnessed what the stories represent. It is thus a very textualized vision of the world, depicting a place that is chock-full of narratives but devoid of the events that occasioned them. As a result, we have many people's versions of what "really happened," but no accurate or disinterested perspective on any "truth" of human history itself. With this final scene, then, we have arrived at the last and perhaps the best manifestation of how the content of this bookish narrator's dream is ridiculously circumscribed by his limited contact with life. His vision is so thoroughly delimited and defined by his individual consciousness that it is incapable of yielding any verifiable "truth" at all.

It might seem at first that Chaucer's persona as a cloistered reader in *The House of Fame* has restricted his potential range and greatness as a poet, since it has radically narrowed the scope of his vision to exclude the subject of life itself. But examining more deeply what *The House of Fame* suggests, we can see that his persona has actually empowered Chaucer to make some very astute observations on the fundamental nature of art. His text-centered vision in *The House of Fame,* seemingly so myopic when compared to the grander vantage points of Dante and other medieval visionaries, in fact allows him to get at a kind of truth ignored—perhaps even avoided—by his glorious predecessors. He frankly admits, as he did in *The Book of the Duchess,* that the substance of his vision comes from books, and books, after all, are merely some fallible human being's questionable version of the "truth," thoughtlessly sanctioned by the capricious Lady Fame. To destabilize matters even further, the very choice of books one makes, and the ways in which one decides to interpret those books, will be governed by personal, idiosyncratic and often self-interested reasons, as Chaucer openly demonstrates through his narrator's visit to the Temple of Venus. So, by candidly refusing to assert any authority or truth and by demonstrating the inevitable personal slant in all human visionary discourse, *The House of Fame* subtly reveals the dubiousness (and pretentiousness) of other poets' claims that they are recording revelatory or historical reality objectively.

Chaucer is also launching a much more specific critique in this poem, one that strikes at the very heart of Dante's self-characterization as both historian and prophet of judgment in the *Commedia*. If we cannot ever accurately judge the truth of stories that we read and hear, then how can we possibly presume to assess the actual lives of the people whom these stories inaccurately represent? More specifically, if the *Commedia* is constructed out of other people's reports, and if the degree of truth of those reports is always indeterminate (as the House of Rumor confirms), then it follows that the truth of the *Commedia*'s judgments is dubious at best—in spite of its author's claim that he is, in some sense, recording God's own Truth. After all, like Lady Fame, Dante assigned people he had never met to heaven and hell, and his method of determining their merit was as limited as Fame's—all he had were garbled tidings gleaned from books and unreliable tales. His judgments about people, therefore, are in effect as irrational as her own, and, like hers, should be viewed only as a form of reputation-mongering rather than as a just assessment of the worth of human souls. In function, then, Dante resembles Lady Fame; he is a "New Testament" Christian dispenser of undeserved reputations, foreshadowed by the pagan poets of old.[32]

Chaucer's professed inability to talk about reality itself is a powerful narrative device, both here and in his other poetry, for not only does it allow him to explore the deficiencies of those who claim to know life's ultimate truths, but it also reflects certain important dimensions of his own self-definition as a poet. At the risk of incurring Chaucer's curse on those who "mysdeme" him (94–108), let us extrapolate a bit on the issues raised in *The House of Fame* and recognize that, contrary to the poem's insistent disclaimers, it really is in some sense about life, and about the deceptiveness of the writers who claim to reflect it. Throughout his works, Chaucer's careful avoidance of judgment in his own narrator's voice—a hallmark of his style—contrasts, sometimes rather comically, with the poetic strategies of other ambitious medieval writers. But in choosing to avoid a rigorous moral stance, Chaucer is arguing that writers must admit to a degree of incompetence in the impossible task of assessing final human worth. Few medieval writers were willing to confess to this limitation, for to do so was to admit that human art was incapable of capturing the traces of God that they thought to be manifest in his creations. But Chaucer saw that his poetry could be no less "true"—and certainly no less ambitious—even when it confronted its author's own fallible human judgment. Indeed, Chaucer may be implying that his poetry is truer than that of the visionaries, for his narrator—the sequestered figure whose expertise is limited to books and the tidings they are based on—has, at the request of his creator, peered into the hidden otherworld of all human knowledge and authority, and has seen *facie ad faciem* its unspeakable flaws.

CHAPTER THREE

"Making" in *The Parliament of Fowls*

‌ᴖᴥ T‌he critical history of *The Parliament of Fowls* has been marked by nearly as much debate and indecision as Chaucer's avian parliament itself. But the most persistent problem facing critics throughout the last century, when the search for a work's "unity" was still a common new critical goal, was that the poem failed to reveal any unity of structure, any clear organizational plan. If *The Parliament of Fowls* is about love, as it seems to be, then why does Chaucer take so long to get to his subject, and why does he close with the comic parliament scene, which forces us to attend to the conflicting discourse of the birds rather than to any doctrine of love? If the poem is not about love, but about politics, Christian philosophy, the literary tradition, or whatever, then why does it spend so much time digressing on the subject of love? Indeed, no matter what subject critics selected as the governing idea behind the poem's complex action, there were still sections of the work that eluded even the most determined of the unity-seekers among them. *The Parliament of Fowls* presented such readers with a massive critical problem, one made even more difficult by the bewildered dreamer in charge of its narration.

The search for underlying unity, now abandoned, has been replaced with arguments that the poem's disunity points to the incoherence of the very tradition within which Chaucer is working, or to precepts visible in medieval aesthetic theory, which valued the linear juxtaposition of elements over unitary structural models. John P. McCall, for example, though he thinks the *Parliament* is a "harmonious" poem, believes that it should finally be seen as an "interweaving of conflicting elements."[1] H. M. Leicester, Jr., argues that "Chaucer's traditional and authoritative materials fail to cohere," and that the poem shows a "delight in the display of learning for its own sake, the recreative verbal play of imitation *qua* imitation, with minimal concern for the expressive value, objective content, or wider relevance to the poem of the forms imitated."[2] David Aers, in responding to Leicester's argument, notes that the *Parliament* is "utterly subversive of all dogmatizing fixities and finalities" and "finely resistant to authoritative and dogmatic closures of all kinds."[3] And Robert M. Jordan argues at length that the poem "lacks the single unifying impulse, the continuous development, and above all the economy of means that would ensure tightness of structure and the relevance of all parts."[4] There is much in all of these positions, especially Leicester's and Aers's, that we cannot ignore. Clearly, Chaucer has somehow chosen and arranged his traditional materials in an unconventional manner, one that encourages readers to see the conflict and irresolution discernible in the textual tradition itself. Moreover, as Leicester and Aers have shown, there is a profound subjectivity in this poem, visible, for example, in the narrator's repeatedly turning our attention to his own problems and to the ways in which his reading and dreaming reflect them.

Indeed, the kind of subjectivity that Leicester and Aers have begun to define in the *Parliament* deserves greater scrutiny. Although Leicester rightly notes that "the materials of the dream become meaningful primarily as projections of various elements of [the dreamer's] consciousness" and Aers remarks that the poem exhibits a "continuous self-reflexivity,"[5] neither critic sees how profoundly this narratorial subjectivism provides the *Parliament* with not only a way to talk about reading and writing as subjective, destabilized activities, but also a strategy to critique visionary, authoritative discourse in general. For if we see the *Parliament* as a poem that represents the anxieties of the narrator as he tries to write a poem, the work's subversive intertextuality begins to gain in force.

To understand how this principle works in *The Parliament of Fowls,* we must pay close attention to the poem's opening stanza, where Chaucer associates the language of love with a proverb relating to the difficult craft of writing poetry:

> The lyf so short, the craft so long to lerne,
> Th'assay so hard, so sharp the conquerynge,
> The dredful joye, alwey that slit so yerne:
> Al this mene I by Love. (1–4)[6]

Although readers have rightly pointed out that the proverb of line 1 refers to the time-consuming process of learning to write poetry and that lines 2 and 3 may be a continuation of that idea (writing is difficult, a "dredful joye" to its practitioners), they usually take line 4 as an an-

nouncement of the new topic of Love. That is, what critics do not generally recognize in this important first stanza is that Chaucer is setting
up an analogy that will continue to work throughout the rest of the
poem: like love, writing poetry is a frustrating enterprise whose ultimate
reward—the finished poem—is as difficult to win as a lover's elusive
lady, even after very hard work.[7]

To paraphrase line 4 in a new way, "writing" is what Chaucer means
by "Love" in *The Parliament of Fowls,* and if we extend this correspondence throughout the work, rather than simply limiting it to the frame
or envelope that surrounds the poem, we will discern a kind of internal
logic in the *Parliament*: love is merely a vehicle for the narrator's most
immediate concern, which is to describe his own struggle with poetic
composition. That this approach is reasonable can be seen by examining
two other passages occurring early in the poem, one in which our narrator reminds us that he is not a lover "in dede" (8), and the other in
which he prays to Venus for help with writing instead of with the amatory activities she would usually be expected to sponsor (113–19). In
other words, it is reasonable to assume that whatever "dredful joye" this
nonlover is likely to experience will not be tied up with the wooing of an
actual woman, but rather with courting the coy lady of his art.[8]

If one is a medieval poet, then one's "courtship" of a poem begins
with reading (for out of old fields comes the new corn), an activity that
Chaucer's narrator describes as a form of labor. He does not read idly
(though reading brings him pleasure), but rather he searches his books
with a purpose in mind, a "certayn thing to lerne" (20). As in *The Book
of the Duchess,* reading is here represented as hard work for a poet, a
kind of "besynesse" (86) that exhausts him at the end of the day. Lest
we fail to note the laboriousness of this preliminary work that poets do,
the narrator underscores it in the following lines:

> But fynally my spirit at the laste
> For wery of my labour al the day,
> Tok reste, that made me to slepe fast.   (92–94)

Later, Affrican too calls the narrator's reading a kind of "labour" (112),
and even sees fit to reward the poet for his toil.

As we saw in *The Book of the Duchess,* however, hard work does not
ensure success—neither for poets nor for lovers. The narrator's arduous
reading of the text of Scipio's dream fails to provide him with whatever
it was he was seeking, a state of affairs that Chaucer records in two of
the poem's most perplexing lines: "For bothe I hadde thyng which that

I nolde / And ek I nadde that thyng that I wolde" (90–91). The subject
of much tortuous commentary, these lines are often allegorized or sup-
plied with interpretations that seek to make the poet's reading experience cohere with the amatory details of his dream. But a more
appropriate understanding of these lines is, I think, a literal one: reading
about Scipio's vision did not supply the narrator with any matter useful
to his current daytime project. Rather, his long day of difficult reading
ends in a failure to get started on the poem at hand, a situation that
squares with what our narrator recorded about poetry's elusiveness in
the opening lines.

Just as the narrator's reading is unsuccessful, so is his dream. This
judgment is encouraged by a variety of details, most notably the lines in
the last stanza of the poem, in which the narrator apologetically states
that he hopes to read—and then dream—with greater success in the future (695–99). But we are also given even stronger evidence that this
particular nocturnal vision should be seen as a trivial one, that is, as a
response to our dreamer's anxiety rather than as an example of any
"newe science," in the narrator's comments on the genesis of his dream.
There, the narrator notes that dreamers tend to relive their daytime concerns in the nighttime hours:

> The wery huntere, slepynge in his bed,
> To wode ayeyn his mynde goth anon;
> The juge dremeth how his plees been sped;
> The cartere dremeth how his cart is gon;
> The riche, of gold; the knyght fyght with his fon;
> The syke met he drynketh of the tonne;
> The lovere met he hath his lady wonne.   (99–105)

Chaucer's source for this passage is the preface to one of Claudian's pan-
egyrics. In a section Chaucer does not use in his text, Claudian extends
the central idea of these lines by saying that he, as a poet, dreams about
successfully completing his poems, an extension that serves as a key to
our understanding of Chaucer's own dream.[9] Poets, too, inevitably return during sleep to their daytime preoccupations, and the poet's dream
we are about to witness will be no exception to Claudian's general rule.

We must also remember that Macrobius himself "raughte nat a lyte"
about dreams such as this one; he calls them *insomnia* and writes that
they have "no importance or meaning." They are "caused by mental or
physical distress, or anxiety about the future: the patient experiences in
dreams vexations similar to those that disturb him during the day. As
[an] example . . . we might mention the lover who dreams of possessing

his sweetheart or of losing her." An *insomnium*, then, has little or no real significance, and, according to Macrobius, is "not worth interpreting."[10]

Given these remarks and Chaucer's own diffidence about the content of his dream, it would be a mistake to seek out any grand new doctrine—amatory, political, philosophical, or whatever—in Chaucer's vision of the park, the temple, and the parliament. In fact, by unmistakably identifying his dream as one of the least significant types, Chaucer hopes to steer us away from too serious an assessment of the events and images he records within it. Moreover, as Leicester, Aers, Ferster and others have rightly shown, Chaucer's dream presents us with no new knowledge about anything; instead we are presented with a seemingly chaotic array of styles, images, and perspectives (mainly on love), drawn from the narrator's reading experience. In contrast to Scipio's vision, Chaucer's provides no theodicy; nor does it even furnish us with much satisfying narrative action, since nothing happens in the temple or garden, and the parliament scene comes to a halt with inadequate closure, no decision being rendered in the eagles' marriage suit. Yet the dream makes a kind of provisional sense if we read it as the *insomnium* Chaucer identifies it as, a reflection of its dreamer's daytime anxieties. Approached from this angle, every one of the major dream sequences can be seen to dramatize the narrator's desire to write a poem—and his failure, at least on one level, to do so. This important idea, then, not only relates the dream to its prefatory material, but also provides the dream with a unity of its own.

The dream begins with Affrican guiding the dreamer to the gates of the park. The gate itself, with its expanded oxymoronic inscription, not surprisingly reflects nothing more than the conflicting feelings that the narrator was experiencing before his dream began. The "dredful joye" of line 3, for example, should probably be seen as the primary inspiration behind the dream-gate's antithetical message. Moreover, the gate's first inscription, "Thorgh me men gon into that blysful place" (127), seems to pick up on the "blysful place" (83) reported by Affrican in the narrator's reading of Cicero, and the dreamer feels "astoned" (142) by the gate in precisely the same way that the subject of love "astonyeth" (5) him in the poem's first stanza. Love's cruel "strokes" appear both in the beginning of the poem (13) and in the dream-gate's second inscription (135), and the dreamer's paralysis and indecision in front of the gate (143–51) simply dramatize the confusion he feels as he writes the poem's opening stanza (6–7). It is safe to say that the dream's early imagery, the description of the gate, does not introduce any new knowledge

to the dreamer, but instead merely reflects his daytime beliefs and uncertainties; whatever the dreamer formerly believed to be true is confirmed by the content of his vision, which ends up being a reshuffling of
old information rather than a window on new truth.[11]

Affrican's dramatic appearance further demonstrates how the narrator's dream is wholly shaped by the dominant preoccupations of the
poem's opening lines. Since the narrator's chief anxiety relates to his
inability to write, it is not surprising that the main character from his
bedtime reading, one who was so helpful to Scipio in a time of need,
shows up in the dream offering aid to the frustrated writer. Just as Af-
ricanus showed Scipio the reward of eternal life he would receive if he
lived—and loved—properly, so Affrican shows Chaucer the garden of
eternal creativity that would be his if only he "haddest connyng for t'en-
dite" (167). That is, the "successful living and loving" recommended in
Cicero's text are reduced here to "successful writing," solely because
such a reduction makes Cicero's text relate better to the narrator's selfish
concerns. Neither a Roman citizen nor a lover—"for thow of love hast
lost thy tast, I gesse" (160)—the narrator imaginatively adapts the circumstances found in his reading material to suit his own psychological
and literary needs.

The same can be said of the Edenic garden the narrator visits with
Affrican's help. Just as Scipio saw in his own dream the "hevene blisse"
(72) promised to worthy Roman citizens, so our narrator—in his role as
a writer—sees the future bliss appropriate to his particular calling: a
garden of perfectly realized artistic creativity. Loosely derived from the
locus amoenus tradition of medieval love poetry, this blissful garden
contains examples of ideal artistic achievement, comparable to God's
own flawless and eternal creative output.[12] The music in the garden, for
example, manifests an impeccable harmony:

> Of instruments of strenges in acord
> Herde I so pleye a ravyshyng swetnesse,
> That God, that makere is of al and lord,
> Ne herde nevere beter, as I gesse.   (197–200)

Made up not only of instrumental music "in acord" but of natural sound
as well, including bird song and the rustle of leaves on the trees, the perfect music our narrator hears—probably inspired by Scipio's hearing the
melody of the spheres—constitutes the artistic wish-fulfillment only
possible in dreams.

Even the trees seem to have been created with art in mind, for each is
either described as the raw material for some future craftsman's project

or assigned a conventional symbolic meaning such as might be useful to
a poet or a painter:[13]

> The byldere ok, and ek the hardy asshe;
> The piler elm, the cofre unto carayne;
> The boxtre pipere, holm to whippes lashe;
> The saylynge fyr; the cipresse, deth to playne;
> The shetere ew; the asp for shaftes pleyne;
> The olyve of pes, and eke the dronke vyne;
> The victor palm, the laurer to devyne.   (176–82)

In addition, the garden contains suggestions of continual fertility with
its green leaves, blooming flowers, productive "welle-stremes, nothyng
dede" (187), and its birds who "besyede hem here bryddes forth to
brynge" (192). Such fertility is the exact antithesis of the narrator's poetic barrenness; but Affrican, who knows that what "thow canst not do,
yit mayst thow se" (163), hopes that such a vision will motivate the poet,
as it presumably did Scipio, to "loke ay besyly thow werche" (74) toward
a more productive life. The narrator, however, is not destined to spend
his whole night happily viewing himself amid the heavenly comforts of
perfected creation. After all, the gate had warned him that periods of
artistic sterility were inevitable, too. (Scipio also saw "peyne" in his vision, not just bliss.) Therefore, the narrator's frustration as a writer, his
failure to capture the poem that eludes him, is also bound to appear in
his nighttime dream, and it does so in the temple of Venus, described in
the poem's next major section.

Borrowed almost wholesale from Boccaccio's *Teseida*, the description
of Venus's temple is appropriate in one major way to the narrator's inability to write: although there is much active preparation in and around
the temple for the physical act of love, the act itself fails to occur during
the narrator's visit there. That is, just as our narrator is not successful
in his "making about love," so there is no active love-making in or near
the temple he encounters. Chaucer has added to Boccaccio's description
of the temple the "pilers greete of jasper" (230), jasper being a gem that
was traditionally held to restrain lust.[14] Also, Cupid's bow, "al redy"
(213) lies at his feet instead of actually being used in any amatory hunt.
Wille, his daughter, is busy tempering arrowheads, but her task is merely
in anticipation of some future need.[15] The allegorical characters in lines
218–29, including the appropriately "disfigurat" Craft, are static, not
interacting with one another or with any human lover (as one might see
in the *Roman de la Rose*) but rather waiting idly for some action in which
to take part. Even the potentially arousing dance of the "dishevele"

women (235) is described by the narrator as if it were part of a weari-some routine: "That was here offyce alwey, yer by yeere" (236). And although Peace and Patience are taken directly from Boccaccio's original text, Chaucer adds the "hil of sond" (243) upon which the latter sits, a detail that underscores the narrator's own eroding patience in the face of his failure to write.

More telling, however, are the characters the narrator sees in the temple itself. Priapus, with his erection in full display, stands in one of the temple's most prominent places:

> The god Priapus saw I, as I wente,
> Withinne the temple in sovereyn place stonde,
> In swich aray as whan the asse hym shente
> With cri by nighte, and with hys sceptre in honde. (253–56)

By showing Priapus at the very moment he is thwarted from achieving the sexual fulfillment for which he was adequately armed, Chaucer presents us with a fitting comic analogue to his narrator's lack of success: he is ready but finally unable to follow through with the "sexual act" of writing that would end this period of unfulfilled "desire." And in the next lines, significantly altered from Boccaccio's original text, Chaucer alludes further to the connection between failed sex and failed writing:

> Ful besyly men gonne assaye and fonde
> Upon his hed to sette, of sondry hewe,
> Garlondes ful of freshe floures newe. (257–59)

Try as they might, Priapus's attendants cannot garland this thwarted lover, just as the thwarted writer receives no laurel crown.[16]

Venus, too, is far from suggesting the sexual action she should normally inspire. Hidden away in a "prive corner" (260), she can scarcely be seen by the narrator because of the temple's darkness, a condition that contrasts markedly with the "cler day" (210) of the artist's paradise left behind. Lying idly on a bed, she passes her whole day, "Til that the hote sonne gan to weste" (266), conversing lightly with her female porter Richesse, a situation that is far from erotic in nature. And although she is naked from the head to the waist, her sexual organs are veiled: "The remenaunt was wel kevered to my pay" (271).[17] Her companions, Bacchus and Ceres, sit quietly beside her. (*Lascivia,* present in Boccaccio's original text, has been omitted from Chaucer's version in order to de-eroticize Venus's environment even further.) Also, in a detail original to Chaucer, two young supplicants are in Venus's presence, begging her for aid:

> amyddes lay Cypride,
> To whom on knees two yonge folk ther cryde
> To ben here helpe.   (277–79)

As analogues of the narrator's own psychological condition, these two hopefuls seeking amatory success stand in for our narrator himself, who, we should remember, similarly begged Venus for aid before his dream was underway: "Be thow myn helpe in this, for thow mayst best!" (116). Finally, on the walls of Venus's temple hang the symbol of her past accomplishments, the broken bows of former virgins who at one time "gonne here tymes waste" (283) in Diana's chase but ultimately joined the ranks of the loving. In this scene, the narrator is again faced with an image of his own anxiety; like Diana's servants, he has wasted time in his retirement from loving/writing.

Moreover, the stories of adulterous and incestuous lovers on the temple walls (285–94) confront him with the perversions that were traditionally thought to result when Venus becomes lazy; as Alain de Lille says in *The Complaint of Nature*, "the unproductiveness of sloth is wont to form its abundance of misshapen offspring," and the idle Venus "has denied the hammers the association of their proper anvils, and condemned them to the adulterous anvils."[18] Clearly, while the narrator visits this temple, Venus and her many attendants are between engagements; though they may be ready for proper amatory action, our narrator never sees any, since his dream is shaped to reflect only his own *poetica interrupta*.

The parliament scene also dramatizes the narrator's specialized anxiety, although with a different cast of characters and a social setting that appropriates the values of the upper-classes in order to demonstrate how, as in *The Book of the Duchess*, the formidable rigors of composition might delay the production of a literary work. Back in the ideal garden of creative fertility (295), the narrator meets Lady Nature, an artist figure of great accomplishment whose success in giving form to God's creative intentions is in direct contrast to the narrator's recent failures. By tradition, Lady Nature is an *artifex* whose achievements cannot be matched by the labors of human craftsmen; Macrobius, Alain de Lille, Jean de Meun, and others characterize her as an ideal creator much to be envied by her struggling earthly counterparts.[19] In the *Parliament*, Nature appears as the "vicaire of the almyghty Lord" (379), whose creatures, numerous and perfectly formed, press around her, exemplifying the happy results of her hard work. A successful artisan, one "that hot, cold, hevy, lyght, moyst, and dreye / Hath knyt by evene noumbres of acord" (380–81), Lady Nature takes special pride in her finest creation, the noble formel eagle "so wel iwrought" (418):

> A formel egle, of shap the gentilleste
> That evere she among hire werkes fond,
> The moste benygne and the goodlieste.
> In hire was everi vertu at his reste,
> So ferforth that Nature hireself hadde blysse
> To loke on hire, and ofte hire bek to kysse.   (372–78)

A perfectly formed artistic creation, the formel eagle is appropriate to this particular *locus amoenus,* for she is Nature's analogue of what Chaucer the narrator hopes to achieve in his daytime labors as a poet—a perfect work of art.

Remembering that *The Parliament of Fowls* consistently depends upon the analogy between loving and writing, we can see that the elaborate avian courtship scene also works well when viewed as yet another dramatization of the narrator's failure to win the analogical "lady" that is his poem. To make this point clear, Chaucer manipulates the analogy very skillfully here by arranging a mating contest between three noble suitors, all of whom strive arduously but fail to win the formel eagle, Nature's best work of art. Even among the lesser birds a mating competition is at work, and Nature favors only those who "sigh the sorest" for their love:

> "But which of yow that love most entriketh
> God sende hym hire that sorest for hym syketh!"   (403–404)

Only the three worthiest strivers, the tercels, however, are given space in this poem to demonstrate their "besy cure" (369) as wooers. Although there are minor differences in their tones and in the length of time during which they say they have been courting their lady, all three noble eagles are obviously earnest suitors, willing to serve their sovereign lady faithfully and to argue their case laboriously throughout the daytime hours:

> Of al my lyf, syn that day I was born,
> So gentil ple in love or other thyng
> Ne herde nevere no man me beforn—
> Who that hadde leyser and connyng
> For to reherse hire chere and hire spekyng;
> And from the morwe gan this speche laste
> Tyl dounward went the sonne wonder faste.   (484–90)

As poet-figures, these courtly birds are analogues to the narrator in his role as the writer/suitor of his art.[20] Working, like them, all day to get "his lady," he nonetheless goes unrewarded for his labor—at least for the time being. The tercels are doomed to wait and "serveth" (660) a year until the coy and unready formel agrees to accept a mate, just as the narrator, in a comparable situation, will have to read and dream some more before his poem can be won.

The lesser birds, impatient with the extended courtship of the tercel eagles, do not understand the complex conventions—and hard work— that surround the amatory (and poetic) behavior of upper-class lovers/ poets. Much of their discourse is marked by the comic spontaneity that one might expect to encounter in the uninitiated, those who are unfamiliar with the high standards set by a refined courtly culture. As a group, the lesser birds are more concerned with completing the act of sexual pairing than with the quality of the whole production:

> The noyse of foules for to ben delyvered
> So loude rong, "Have don, and lat us wende!
> . . . Com of!" they criede, "allas, ye wol us shende!
> Whan shal youre cursede pletynge have an ende?"   (491–95)

Especially impatient are the wormfowl and the waterfowl, both of whom waste no time in establishing their preference for haste in the mating game. The cuckoo plays on the double meaning of "spede," saying, "For comune spede, take on the charge now" (507), as do the waterfowl later (559), who spend very little time in conference together, taking only a "short avysement" (555). Their representative, the goose, says, "I love no taryinge" (565), and the cuckoo announces later that his advice is a "shorte lessoun" (609), advanced only so that the debate will end sooner, leaving him to have his "make in pes" (605). Expedience personified, the wormfowl and the waterfowl clearly represent the uncomprehending laity who can't understand why a lover—or a poet—might need extra time to carry out the duties of his office. As the tercelet remarks to the duck, "Thy kynde is of so low a wrechedness / That what love is, thow canst nouther seen ne gesse" (601–602). Yet in spite of their comic impatience, the narrator clearly feels a measure of admiration for these lesser birds, for they are able to get their "making" done without the worrisome delays to which the nobler "makers" are susceptible. Indeed, the ease with which they complete their Valentine's Day duty (both mating and "making," since they compose the light roundel with which the dream concludes) is downright enviable in the eyes of the thwarted artist who is recording this vision. Were it not that it would compromise his art, the dreamer could himself be among the satisfied fowl who actually finish their appointed task.

The seedfowl, on the other hand, take a different attitude toward the laborious courtship of the noble eagles, primarily because their representative is the "turtle trewe" (577). She advocates constancy and continual service in the quest for one's chosen mate, and her elevated rhetoric approximates that of the noble tercels themselves:

> "Nay, God forbede a lovere shulde chaunge!"
> The turtle seyde, and wex for shame al red,
> "Though that his lady everemore be straunge,
> Yit lat hym serve hire ever, till he be ded.
> Forsothe, I preyse nat the goses red;
> For, though she deyede, I wolde non other make;
> I wol ben hires, til that the deth me take."   (582–88)

Patient and idealistic by nature, the turtledove argues that even "straunge" ladies, those whose coyness or emotional distance makes courtship of them difficult, should be actively served in spite of lack of success in gaining them. Arguing a position that Chaucer's narrator will take in the "courtship" of his poem as described in the *Parliament*'s closing lines ("and thus to rede I nyl nat spare"), the turtledove chastizes the other birds for their restlessness, asking them to "abyde a while yet, parde!" (509).[21] Then, with a modesty characteristic of Chaucer's narrator, she makes a point that Chaucer himself is indirectly advancing in this poem: it is not the office of those who fail to understand the political, social, and formal complexities of a high-class poet/lover's project to criticize him for taking a long time to complete it:

> "I am a sed-foul, oon the unworthieste,
> That wot I wel, and litel of connynge.
> But bet is that a wyghtes tonge reste
> Than entremeten hym of such doinge,
> Of which he neyther rede can ne synge;
> And whoso hit doth ful foule hymself acloyeth
> For office uncommytted ofte anoyeth."   (512–18)

That is, those unfamiliar with the arduous labor required to produce a literary text are in no position to carp at the slow progress of a hardworking poet.

Nature's parliament finally comes to a close without success, either for the lovers or for the poet. The young formel eagle requests a year as "respit for to avise me" (648); she is not ready to love actively, wishing to serve neither Venus nor Cupid "as yit" (653). Needing extra time to consider her options, she wants more than the mere "suffisaunce" (637) that would result if she quickly chose the royal tercel, as Nature urges. Not surprisingly for a poem in which every major character so far has somehow shown similarities to the troubled narrator, the formel eagle too mirrors in her behavior the narrator's state of affairs. Serious poets need time to "lerne the craft," and the best of them will avoid the speedy "making" of their inferiors. Electing to remain chaste and therefore unproductive for a time, the formel eagle sticks to a plan that will provide for the best possible result, even though it wreaks havoc on Nature's deadlines.[22] But Nature, as a hard-working artist herself, does not quarrel with this delay. Instead, she quickly acquiesces to the formel's request: " 'Now, syn it may non otherwise betyde'; / Quod Nature, 'heere is no more to seye' " (654–55). Thus the failures of the amatory parliament and the narrator's long day of reading are exactly parallel, as J. A. W. Bennett has noted: "[Just] as Chaucer has been busy all day over Macrobius, with no apparent result, so the 'business' of these debating birds has brought them 'nevere the neer' (619) by sundown."[23]

In spite of the poetic failure that the narrator's dream details, however, the conclusion of The Parliament of Fowls ends up calling attention to a curious kind of success. For even though the narrator awakens from his dream in the same unproductive state as when he had fallen asleep, he *has* gotten his poem done, by recording the anxiety-ridden dream of his aborted attempt to write.[24] And the poem we are left with, though not exactly conforming to what an aristocratic audience might expect of a love poem for St. Valentine's Day, manages, by adapting some of the aristocrats' own conventions, to say a great deal about Chaucer and his poetics. This comic "failure" of a poem, for example, shows us that Chaucer is deeply aware of how dreams—and poems—are products of authorial anxiety and need, which are themselves defined by the special role that the institution of patronage creates for court poets. Rather than being disinterested glimpses of new or impersonal truths, poems (even very good ones like The Parliament of Fowls) reflect the immediate concerns of their individual creators, and they are drawn from—and inspired by—other works of literature, points that Chaucer is surely making even about the visionary materials he uses as his sources. Scipio, Dante, Boccaccio, and Alain de Lille, all of whom wrote visions of their own, should not be viewed as poets with any truer perspective than that adopted by our Chaucerian dreamer. The difference between Chaucer and his models, however, is that Chaucer foregrounds the unconditional textuality of his dream, and thus his poem, making no claim that it captures external, authentic or impartial truth; rather, it is a self-interested construct pieced together out of other people's books.

It is right, then, to note that the Parliament is interested in debunking its narrator's own naive claim about poetry's ability to convey "al this newe science that men lere" (25). But it would be wrong to see the poem as incoherent and lacking unity, for Chaucer has shaped each scene and each character from his sources in order to force upon us his larger point about the selective, political, and highly personal nature of all poetic texts. As we see in the *Parliament*, poets use and alter sources to suit their own local and particular needs, and those needs are certainly not consistent with the task of conveying impartial revelatory truth to readers. In fact, it is precisely because poets are not gifted with genuine otherworldly knowledge that they have to plow those "olde feldes" as much as they do. In the absence of supernatural poetic aid, they are doomed to a life of hard work. Sometimes, for example, they read all day (as Chaucer's narrator did) and still fail to find the specific things they need to make a poem work exactly right. On the other hand, even though Chaucer wants us to recognize that his poems are the fruits of intense and often frustrating toil, carried out to meet a patron's deadline, we should remember that the central analogy of *The Parliament of Fowls* suggests to its courtly audience that this hard work is, after all, in part a labor of love.

CHAPTER FOUR

The Rhetoric of Reading in
Troilus and Criseyde

I

꘠ The issues raised in *The House of Fame* and *The Parliament of Fowls*—the impossibility of objective judgment, the sociopolitical production of meaning, and the inevitable personal slant visible in all writers' versions of the "reality" they aim to reflect in their works—are again brought before us in *Troilus and Criseyde*. In addition, the *Troilus* is another nonreferential work in the sense that its fictional premise is that the text faithfully reproduces another text, which in turn supposedly reflects historical events (whose "truth" turns out to be unrecoverable). But in this longer and more ambitious work, Chaucer presents his case in a different—and much more elaborate—way. Here, through the action and speech of the narrator, Chaucer's strategy is to show his readers, before their very eyes, the slow but certain movement away from any claim to objectivity in storytelling—in spite of the storyteller's early professed desire to be absolutely faithful to the "matere" that serves as his referential base and in spite of his claim that he has no preconceptions or biases that might interfere with his record of the truth, as it is putatively represented in Lollius, his fictional source. Moreover, in adapting Boccaccio's *Filostrato* to suit his own purposes, Chaucer added, expanded upon, and embellished certain incidents within the story itself to show his characters' subjective and social constructions of reality at work, suggesting that he wanted to foreground hermeneutic and epistemological issues in general and explore them fully in his poem.

That the narrator of the *Troilus* believes himself to be an objective recorder of his narrative material is everywhere visible in his proems, textual interjections, and offhand remarks about his source. It is not hard, he implies throughout, to present his audience with an accurate reproduction of Lollius's text; such a task merely involves careful translation, with—of course—scholarly "footnotes" that point out how customs and language have changed since Lollius's time or that speculate about what Lollius's narrative fails to include about the historical events it is representing. Each reader of the *Troilus* probably has a favorite Lollius-as-source passage; mine appears in Book 3, where the narrator interrupts the action to apologize for not being able to record every word, look, and sound that actually occurred. He's sorry—that sort of thing just doesn't seem to be done in stories, and besides, his author simply didn't get it all written down:

> But now, paraunter, som man wayten wolde
> That every word, or soonde, or look, or cheere
> Of Troilus that I rehercen sholde,
> In al this while unto his lady deere—
> I trowe it were a long thyng for to here—
> Or of what wight that stant in swich disjoynte,
> His wordes alle, or every look, to poynte.
>
> For sothe, I have naught herd it don er this
> In story non, ne no man here, I wene;
> And though I wolde, I koude nought, ywys;
> For ther was som epistel hem bitwene,
> That wolde, as seyth myn autour, wel contene
> Neigh half this book, of which hym liste nought write.
> How sholde I thanne a lyne of it endite?   (3.491–504)

Several of the narrator's deluded assumptions about storytelling are exposed in this single address to the reader. We can see, for example, that our naive narrator clearly believes there is little or no difference between people's versions of what "actually happened" and the historical events themselves. He trusts his author completely in the matter of objectivity: Lollius simply deleted some of the facts because it would take too long to record them and because—for some reason that escapes the narrator—it appears to be conventional to leave out such things from stories: "I have naught herd it don er this / In story non." What the narrator does not seem to realize is that writers always shape their narrative material to suit their purposes, and, more importantly, that even if their purposes were to record history accurately, there is no privileged perspective on the "truth" that could be said to be free from some bias or ideological preconception, visible in either the selection or the arrangement of the historical material itself. But our narrator clearly believes, at this point anyway, that Lollius was only transcribing truth in his work and that he, as translator of Lollius, is merely yet another impartial vehicle in which this truth may be transported from one generation to another. Such an unexamined view of Lollius—and of his own narration—

persists in the *Troilus,* well after we and perhaps, to some extent, even the narrator himself have come to realize its patent falsity.[1]

We will return to analyze more of the narrator's revealing editorial comments later, when we discuss his handling of the story proper. But first it is important that we examine his opening remarks, in which he sets forth what he sees as his own purpose in undertaking this project. The first stanza of the *Troilus* flatly announces the nature of the task the narrator hopes to carry out:

> The double sorwe of Troilus to tellen,
> That was the kyng Priamus sone of Troye,
> In lovynge, how his aventures fellen
> From wo to wele, and after out of joie,
> My purpos is, er that I parte fro ye.   (1.1–5)

Though very general, this "purpos" certainly seems neutral enough, and Chaucer hopes to increase our initial confidence in his narrator's neutrality by having him feel little if any emotion about this story at its outset, needing help from Tisiphone to provide him with the "sory chere" (14) he feels to be the appropriate visage for the teller of a sad tale. Though his verses "wepen" (7), he does not—he is merely the "instrument" (10) that will help others to feel genuine emotion. And from the lovers in the audience he asks for special aid in the form of prayerful intercession:

> And ek for me preieth to God so dere
> That I have myght to shewe, in som manere,
> Swich peyne and wo as Loves folk endure,
> In Troilus unsely aventure.   (1.32–35)

Further evidence of the narrator's belief in his objectivity is visible in his autobiographical remarks concerning his unsuccessful love life:

> For I, that God of Loves servantz serve,
> Ne dar to Love, for myn unliklynesse,
> Preyen for speed, al sholde I therfore sterve,
> So fer am I from his help in derknesse.   (1.15–18)

Though some timidity is visible in these lines (he is *afraid* to ask for help from the God of Love in his writing project), the narrator is nonetheless certain that his "unliklynesse" as a lover will not have a negative effect on his story. Any emotion necessary to the tale's success, he believes, can just as easily come from the audience as from the author—and that is precisely the way in which the narrator envisions his poem achieving its impact:

> But ye loveres, that bathen in gladness,
> If any drope of pyte in yow be,
> Remembreth yow on passed hevynesse
> That ye han felt, and on the adversite
> Of othere folk, and thynketh how that ye
> Han felt that Love dorste yow displese. (1.22–27)

Without committing himself at all to an authoritative position on the joys or sadnesses of human love, he delegates all such responsibility to actual lovers, asking them to pray for others' amatory success and for lovers' relief from any despair occasioned by the failure of love affairs.[2] Clearly, all of these complex matters of love are seen to occur at some distance from the detached narrator, applying not in the least to his own life. His perspective on the story, then, would seem to be uniquely "objective," unlike that of the emotionally involved lover-narrators of previous amatory verse.

What *does* apply to the narrator's life, however, is his hope to improve the condition of his soul in the course of writing his poem about Troilus:

> For so hope I my soule best avaunce
> To prey for hem that Loves servauntz be,
> And write hire wo, and lyve in charite,
>
> And for to have of hem compassioun,
> As though I were hire owne brother dere. (1.47–51)

Here, the narrator, still so sure that he is uninvolved in his characters' sad predicament and far from the condition of loving that precipitates it, ends up adopting what might be seen as a superior moral tone, for he suggests that in his detachment he can easily achieve the state of Christian "charite," feeling compassion for his poor benighted brothers but avoiding the actual involvement with love that has brought them their "wo."

The picture of the narrator projected in the *Troilus*'s opening lines, then, is basically one of an objective bystander—by necessity. He obviously wishes that he were closer to his subject matter (close enough to serve his poetic aims), but even without that closeness, he feels he can handle his amatory material by adopting the role of the good Christian commentator, the compassionate but simultaneously detached recorder of the sad truth about the "peyne and wo" suffered by Love's folk. However, though the narrator doesn't realize it, the role of good Christian commentator does not entirely suit him. If examined carefully, his lines about love show that from a Christian perspective he is distinctly confused. In spite of his insistence that he is not a lover, there is a strong suggestion that he would like to be one and if the God of Love were friendlier to him, he would gladly accept Love's aid; he merely "dares not" (16) ask because "so fer am I from his help in derknesse" (18).

Moreover, using religious terminology (as he does throughout this section), he says that lovers like Troilus can be brought "in hevene to solas" (31) and those who are "despeired out of Love's grace" should be mercifully put to death by the Christian God (40–42). And finally, in a passage that comically shows utter ignorance of Christian priorities, the narrator says:

> And biddeth ek for hem that ben at ese,
> That God hem graunte ay good perseveraunce,
> And sende hem mysht hire ladies so to plese
> That it to Love be worship and plesaunce.   (1.43–46)

Remarkably, the Christian God is here being asked to help provide for the worship of the God of Love, leaving no question about whether Cupid's or God's "religions" more fascinates the narrator. Although he doesn't conflate the two gods into one (as he will later), he nonetheless sees no problem in believing in them both, asking the one to help the other.

Our "objective" narrator, then, ends up having some unstated and oddly paradoxical hidden biases from the very start of his poem, and they will affect his narration throughout. He is determined to advocate the seeking of erotic love (partly because erotic lovers constitute his audience, as we realize in lines 19 and 20), yet he also thinks that he can advance his soul by taking a more distanced Christian view of his subject. Obviously, since these views are, at bottom, in conflict, he is in for some very problematic moments as the teller of the tale that follows, and he will finally come to be deeply troubled by the difficulties inherent in wanting to serve both his audience's happiness and his soul's bliss. But here, in his opening remarks, he blithely harmonizes these two perspectives—and it is quite likely that the audience he addresses is willing to overlook the problem, too: after all, the lovers to whom he directs the poem, "Ye . . . that bathen in gladnesse" (22), would surely find it in their own self-interest to avoid complicating their happiness by having to come to terms with its possible falseness, transitoriness, and danger to their souls.

Thus, whatever objectivity the narrator thinks he has is already being called into question even before the poem gets underway, for he clearly has purposes other than mere translation—and when his source fails to advance these purposes, he will end up trying to force it to do so. His own desires and those he perceives in his audience will both become factors in the production of his text; moreover, the narrator's two de-sires—to encourage *eros* and to save his soul through charity—are inev-itably going to conflict, resulting in the need for him to engage in some painful rethinking of his proem's unexamined position.

These complexities, troublesome as they make our experience of read-ing the *Troilus,* are in fact a major part of what Chaucer has to teach us in his poem. To insure that the difficulties attending any belief in objec-tivity and those arising from conflicting purposes are witnessed clearly, Chaucer develops them not only through his narrator but also in the love story itself. Troilus, Pandarus, and Criseyde, like him, face situations in which the things that they want to achieve are in conflict with each other, or, more interestingly, with the actual represented truth about events and others' motivations. In this sense, the characters often seem to be mirror images of the narrator himself, a situation which critics have al-ready noted to some extent in the case of Pandarus and Troilus.[3] But the argument could—and should—be extended to Criseyde, too, for the narrator comes to her defense in part, I think, because her final betrayal is the direct result of a situation exactly paralleling his own, an inability to come to terms with conflicting desires and a failure to see how one's own desires and one's own social situation determine (largely uncon-sciously) one's actions. Thus, when the narrator opens Book 1, he has no idea just how much he already is his characters' "owne brother dere" (51); like them, he innocently drifts into experiences that force him to act, resulting in self-deception and, sometimes, betrayal.

II

The narrator's confidence in his own and his source's objectivity is established very early in Book 1. By telling us that his book does not say whether Criseyde had any children or not, for example, he projects the image of a scholar, one who refuses to alter the facts as he has found them:

> But wheither that she children hadde or noon,
> I rede it naught, therfore I late it goon. (1.132–33)

Likewise, he believes that the "Troian gestes," the martial facts of the Trojan story, can be found in "Omer, or in Dares, or in Dite" (146) ex-actly "as they felle" (145), suggesting that, unlike the narrator of *The House of Fame,* he has not yet come to realize the contradictory and un-trustworthy nature of Trojan source material, or indeed any historical narration. His immediate source, Lollius, is also blindly trusted as an accurate, unbiased recorder of Troilus's words exactly as they were originally uttered in the *Canticus Troili*:

> And of his song naught only the sentence
> As writ myn auctour called Lollius,
> But pleinly, save oure tonges difference,
> I dar wel seyn, in al, that Troilus
> Seyde in his song, loo, every word right thus
> As I shal seyn.   (1.393–98)

Foolishly assuming that he has Troilus's actual language before him in spite of "tonges difference" and the very long span of time that separates the event from the versions that record it, the narrator, rather presumptuously (yet with innocence and naiveté), is claiming the truth of his narrative and that of the writer upon whom he relies.

The narrator's assured sense that he knows the truth is especially visible in his treatment of Troilus's falling in love in the early sections of Book 1. Yet it is also here that the narrator's own subjective interpretation begins to emerge quite clearly. When Troilus is struck by Cupid's arrow, the narrator haughtily remarks, "kaught is proud, and kaught is debonaire" (214), taking a condescending tone that is continued in his comparison of Troilus to an arrogant and willful horse, beaten back into submission by the lash of the driver's whip (218–24). At this point in his story, the narrator feels so secure with his material and so superior to it that he interrupts the action to draw a moral he thinks will please his audience of lovers, to whose special interests he is pandering already. His moral—that love is too strong to overcome, and besides, it is a desirable thing (231–59)—is definitely not organic to the story as we have it so far, seeming rather to be heading toward a position exactly opposite to the one that is generally visible in what Chaucer is asking us to surmise about "Lollius's" version of these events.

Lollius's narrative (to the extent that we can discern its general trajectory in this double-voiced work) seems to suggest that Troilus, in his pride, is headed for a fall, but it nowhere suggests that the love he is about to become ensnared in is a better alternative to remaining free, or that love is a "thing so vertuous in kynde" (254), as the narrator says, that we should accept it without question. In fact, the story the narrator is telling suggests just the opposite, that Troilus is in for an abrupt and unpleasant comeuppance in the form of future pain and suffering. But the narrator, interpreting the story in a manner markedly different from the way in which his source text does, fails to see that he is reading (and moralizing) self-interestedly, ignoring Lollius's purposes in order to advance his own. Instead, like the supercilious Troilus before his own coming to knowledge, the narrator merely acts as if he might be saying, "Loo! is this naught wisely spoken?" (205) In this single digression, then, which Chaucer added to his Boccaccian source, we see our self-styled objective narrator already engaged in falsification of his *matere,* partly because he wants to cater to the special interests of his audience of lovers.

In determining Chaucer's position on the inevitable kinds of falsification that poets, such as our narrator, are continually susceptible to, it is useful to introduce the example of Pandarus, who, as critics have rightly noted, is an artist figure and an analogue to the narrator himself. Pandarus's "creation" is, of course, the love affair of Troilus and Criseyde, and his medium is "not words but people," as E. Talbot Donaldson remarked some time ago.[4] But Chaucer has taken great pains to underscore Pandarus's role as a poet figure in general by representing his activities in language borrowed from well-known treatises on the poetic art. While advising Troilus on how to write his first love letter, for example, Pandarus quotes from Horace's *Art of Poetry* (2.1041–43). In addition, his careful plans for bringing about the consummation of the affair are presented in Geoffrey of Vinsauf's words, drawn from the *Poetria Nova* (1.1065–71). Chaucer's having Pandarus read a book "for countenance" while the lovers engage in sex might also be present to stress the idea that Pandarus's activity all along has been to complete his "book," which finally reaches closure when the lovers unite. He himself calls their affair his "tale" (3.769).[5]

Pandarus's social functions resemble a poet's too: he is the intermediary between a story and its audience (when, for example, he represents Troilus's views to Criseyde and vice versa)[6]; he is a rhetorician aiming to persuade an audience of a particular view (as he manipulates Troilus and Criseyde into accepting positions they did not hold at first),[7] and he is the repository and promoter of authoritative wisdom, with his constant stream of proverbs and folk knowledge, ready "for the nones."[8]

In his role as an artist, Pandarus indeed shows some general similarities to the narrator of the *Troilus* (and perhaps to Chaucer the artist himself). But there are some more specific similarities between Pandarus and the narrator that are important to this poem as well: both are unsuccessful in love; both are well-intentioned in carrying out their projects, wanting to please the friends they address; and both think that love is "blessed" in converting lovers (compare 1.308 and 998–99), believing that it is absolutely natural to all human beings (compare 1.238 and 977–78). Also Pandarus's lines to Troilus near the end of Book 1 echo uncannily the narrator's opening address to lovers (compare 1.19–21 and 1042–43).

But there are some important distinctions between Pandarus's and the narrator's understandings of the nature of art. Unlike the narrator, Pandarus, from the moment we meet him, seems to understand thoroughly the basic Chaucerian principle that an artist's purposes and an artist's audiences always govern the arrangement of his material and that his representation of "reality" is going to be selective, showing everywhere signs of certain purposes being worked out before specific audiences. This principle is what makes Pandarus so successful at completing his "narrative" of love; it is also the principle that Chaucer chooses to highlight from Geoffrey of Vinsauf's treatise: before the artist begins building his "house," Pandarus thinks to himself, he must determine how his project may best be constructed, "alderfirst his purpos for to winne" (1.1069). Thus Pandarus is a self-conscious and sophisticated "narrative artist," one who knows how to manipulate his material to achieve his goals in the most successful manner possible. His opening speech confirms this view, for his words to Troilus are said to be spoken not out of sincerity but only "for the nones," to anger Troilus into changing his mood.

The narrator, however, is blithely unaware that stories—either his own or his source's—have purposes, some of them hidden, and that those purposes affect the way the teller's material is presented. As late as the proem to Book 2, even after watching Pandarus's obsessively purposeful behavior for quite a while and hearing his words on the importance of purposes to the successful completion of projects (1.960–66), the narrator still believes that his own role as the teller of Lollius's tale is an uninvolved one. He invokes Clio, for example—the muse of history—presumably because he perseveres in thinking that he is faithfully recording what really happened. His opening metaphor is revealing, too, for he says that he is scarcely able to steer the boat of his "connyng" (2.3–4), conveying the distinct sense that he genuinely believes his material is controlling him rather than the other way around. His remarks about his poem continue in this vein: he asks for Clio's help only in finding rhymes, for "me nedeth here noon other art to use" (!) and he apologizes to the experienced lovers in his audience for not having any emotion of his own:

> Forwhi to every lovere I me excuse,
> That of no sentement I this endite,
> But out of Latyn in my tonge it write.   (2.12–14)

Once again claiming to be following his "auctour" slavishly, he asks for his audience to excuse his own limited contribution to the project, for, as a nonlover, he is at a disadvantage: "A blynd man kan not juggen wel in hewis" (2.21).[9]

But what the narrator is most blind to is his own and Lollius's purposeful behavior as actively involved—not passive—tellers of their tales. He observes in a scholarly fashion that languages and customs change over time and differ from one culture to another, a passage that is traditionally cited as a remarkable example of Chaucer's own awareness of cultural and historical difference, of his almost "unmedieval" interest in historical relativity. To be sure, that kind of authorial sensitivity is present in these lines; but we should not forget that the narrator (not Chaucer) speaks them and that they are serving to characterize more fully his attitudes about his narrative. Noting that "In sondry londes, sondry ben usages" (28) and that "Ecch contree hath his lawes" (42), the narrator is arguing here, once again, that his version of the story is the absolute historical truth. Worried that some members of his audience might think Troilus's wooing took a form quite different from their own and therefore the story they are hearing is unrealistic or actually unreal, the narrator claims that in some times and places other than fourteenth-century England the game of love would have been ruined, "If that they ferde in love as men don here" (39). That is, the narrator is suggesting that he has not modernized his story at all, but rather has reproduced the facts exactly as he received them, even though such historical fidelity might confuse his modern audience. In a further attempt to defend his belief in his story's absolute truth, he asks his audience to see that, although lovers everywhere have a variety of amatory methodologies that differ from person to person, all have basically the same goal—to win their ladies:

> Ek scarsly ben ther in this place thre
> That have in love seid lik, and don, in al;
> For to thi purpos this may liken the,
> And thi right nought; yet al is seid or schal;
> Ek som men grave in tree, some in ston wal,
> As it bitit.   (2.43–48)

This stanza and those right before it also inadvertently show us something more about the narrator's progress as a storyteller. His argument about the past's similarity to the present is clearly motivated by two specific desires: to preserve his pagan story exactly as he thinks it occurred, and to have it relate closely to the tastes and interests of the present-day lovers in his audience. So far, this dual purpose has been manageable (although it necessitated a pro-love digression in Book 1). But here, the fact that the narrator feels he must argue away the problem of historical difference suggests that he senses a growing incompatibility between Lollius's story and the tastes of his modern audience. His claims that lovers always have the same purpose is fairly convincing on the surface, yet the nervousness clearly visible in the proem's last two lines, "But syn I have bigonne, / Myn auctour shal I folwen, if I konne" (2.48–49), suggests that the narrator is starting to feel the strain of having to serve two masters—Lollius and his own audience.

The narrator's ignorance of the ever-present purposefulness behind narrative art of all ages (including that depicted by his "auctour") becomes demonstrably clear when one compares his naive assumptions with Pandarus's more sophisticated ones. In Book 2, as we watch Pandarus work on his own audience—Criseyde—we can see just how well he has mastered the subtleties involved in distorting truth to suit his own purposes and to sway his audience into believing what are at bottom little more than lies. At one point, he actually tells Criseyde about this process (partly to capture her trust!):

> How so it be that som men hem delite
> With subtyl art hire tales for to endite,
> Yet for al that, in hire entencioun
> Hire tale is al for som conclusioun.   (2.256–59)

One stanza later, we learn more about Pandarus's artistic principles, this time receiving a lesson on how one must manipulate one's tale to suit the audience:

> Then thought he thus: "If I my tale endite
> Aught harde, or make a proces any whyle,
> She shal no savour have therin but lite,
> And trowe I wolde hire in my wil bigyle . . .
> Forthi hire wit to serven wol I fonde—"   (2.267–73)

By successfully "serving Criseyde's wit" throughout this encounter—by flattery, fear tactics, and persuasive but skewed reasoning—Pandarus finally manages to bring her around to his way of thinking.

Yet Pandarus could not have been so successful, Chaucer implies, if Criseyde had not been ready to accept his flattery or his direct appeals to her reputation and future welfare, that is, to those things that have been established from the beginning as very important to her. Troilus, too, is manipulable, for once he decides that he wants Criseyde, "N'yn him desir noon other fownes bredde, / But argumentes to his conclusioun"

(1.465–66). Pandarus, knowing this, works on precisely that obsessive personal interest which he knows governs Troilus. The general point being made here is that when audiences are faced with the task of accepting or rejecting a poet's arguments, they generally tend to accept what is consonant with their hopes or current beliefs and to reject all that might conflict with them. Reading, in other words, is just as purposeful an activity as writing, and self-interest can often be counted on to influence a reader's construction of a text (and, of course, "reality"— as we later sadly see when Troilus mistakes a "fare-cart" for Criseyde).[10]

III

In order to develop the idea that readers tend to interpret texts in a self-serving fashion that often has real consequences, Chaucer has added some scenes of his own invention and modified some of his Boccaccian material to highlight the subtle processes at work in readers' minds as they respond to texts. One of his original scenes occurs in Book 2, when Criseyde, at a crucial moment in her decision-making process, hears Antigone's song. This song expresses its writer's deeply felt contention that love produces virtue and is the source of perfect happiness. Since the subject of the song bears so directly on Criseyde's personal situation, she is very much interested in its content and also in the real-life circumstances of its composition. Hoping to learn more about love's operations in actual life, she asks Antigone: "Who made this song now with so good entent?" When Antigone reports that its author is an honorable and happy woman of "gret estat" in Troy, she inadvertently gives Criseyde exactly what she needs to hear to be fully persuaded of love's worth. Desiring honor, happiness, and "gret estat" herself, Criseyde now sees no conflict between these conditions and loving Troilus; thus, the writer of the song has—without knowing it—served as a kind of pander, since Criseyde, an unforeseen "reader," is about to apply the argument of the song to her own life.

Instead of seeking to learn more about this song's vague praise of love, Criseyde—because she is at this point predisposed to love Troilus—is clearly susceptible to, and uncritical of, its argument. When Antigone is through explaining the song's genesis and major position on love, we learn that Criseyde has been extremely attentive:

> Every word which that she of hire herde,
> She gan to prenten in hire herte faste,
> And ay gan love hire lasse for t'agaste
> Than it dide erst, and synken in hire herte
> That she wex somwhat able to converte. (2.899–903)

In fact, by this time she has so thoroughly been "converted" to the idea of love that when she overhears a nightingale's song later that evening, she is willing to believe, without knowing the language of birds, that it is singing a "lay of love" (2.921–22). So impressive an example of self-interested interpretation is surely nowhere else to be found in this poem.[11]

To develop further the central concept of misreading in his poem, Chaucer significantly adds to the letter-writing activity of the two lovers. Receiving Criseyde's first letter, which coolly refuses to "make hireselven bond / In love" (2.1223–24), offering only to please Troilus as a sister might, Troilus finally interprets this document as evidence of some success on his part—even though on first reading he definitely sees the equivocal nature of Criseyde's message. At first, the letter alternately makes his "herte glade and quake" (2.1321); after reflecting on it a bit, however, Troilus decides to read the letter selectively, finding in it only what he wants to hear[12]:

> But finaly, he took al for the beste
> That she hym wroot, for somwhat he byheld
> On which hym thoughte he myghte his herte reste,
> Al covered she tho wordes under sheld.
> Thus to the more worthi part he held.   (2.1324–28)

In Book 5, Criseyde's last letter—a letter which, if read carefully by an uninvolved party, shows many signs of her unwillingness to return—is ultimately read by Troilus in the same benign way, in spite of his real knowledge that the letter is "straunge":

> But fynaly, he ful ne trowen myghte
> That she ne wolde hym holden that she hyghte;
> For with ful yvel wille list hym to leve
> That loveth wel, in swich cas, though hym greve.   (5.1635–38)

And even though Criseyde's hidden purpose here is probably to keep Troilus from knowing of her decision to stay with the Greeks, it is ironic that in this very letter she tries to gain his good will by warning him to discern carefully the letter's intention: "Th'entente is al, and nat the lettres space" (5.1630). Yet Troilus, unwilling to know the truth about Criseyde's decision, is determined to place the most positive construction possible on this revealing letter.

Dreams, too, the interpretation of which serves throughout this poem as an analogue to the interpretation of texts, are foregrounded by Chaucer to illustrate the human tendency not only to create self-serving fictions but also to interpret dream narratives generally in subjective ways.

Donald Howard has persuasively demonstrated that Criseyde's dream of the heart-exchanging eagle is wholly fabricated out of her specific expectations, fears, and hopes.[13] Troilus's dreams, too, reflect, at one point, nothing but his own specific anxieties (5.246–54). In fact, if this were all the evidence we had, we might be content to accept part of Pandarus's skeptical argument that dreams routinely proceed from an individual's physical or emotional discomfort, and that to bother with their interpretation is foolish: "A straw for alle swevenes signifiaunce" (5.362). Yet even Pandarus, when confronted with the task of interpreting Troilus's boar-dream (perhaps the one dream in all of Chaucer's work, besides Chauntecleer's, that actually points, however vaguely, toward the future),[14] shows himself to be a creative and socially adept interpreter. To help alleviate Troilus's fears, Pandarus quickly comes up with an alternative reading of the dream's portentous imagery: the boar that Criseyde kisses is only her father (5.1282–88). Finally, it takes Cassandra, with her divinely-inspired knowledge, to articulate the truth of Troilus's dream, and though she reports it undiplomatically (she is neither socially nor politically motivated, as are Pandarus and the narrator), we are still surprised to see how unwilling Troilus is to believe her—even though by now he has had plenty of independent evidence confirming her view.

Other scenes scattered throughout the *Troilus* are designed to remind us of the impossibility of escaping from the hermeneutic circle of self-serving interpretation, even when one knows it is a danger. Troilus and Pandarus together, for instance, in order to avoid seeing Pandarus's role as that of an unseemly pimp, manage to manipulate accepted cognitive categories until they have convinced themselves that he falls within the category "friend" (3.253–420).[15] Also, very early in Book 1, Troilus cynically remarks (without foreseeing how he himself will be implicated) that there is inevitable misreading in lovers' communications:

> that ye loveres ofte eschuwe,
> Or elles doon, of good entencioun,
> Ful ofte thi lady wol it mysconstruwe,
> And deme it harm in hire oppynyoun. (1.344–47)

And Criseyde—who knows very well that people are often misconstruers (her obsession with her reputation proves it)—argues at one point that she will be able to convince her father that his selfish cowardice "Made hym amys the goddes text to glose" (4.1410).

In short, all the major characters in the *Troilus* realize at some point in the narrative that interpretive acts are complex, that things can be, and are, read in different ways, especially when the interpreter has a personal stake in the outcome of the interpretation. Yet this realization in no way forearms Chaucer's characters or prevents them from falling victim to the inevitable trap themselves, for even as late as the end of Book 5, all three are still relying on convenient, self-satisfying constructions of themselves and their surroundings, avoiding the more painful but truer constructions still available for consideration. Troilus, for instance, governed so thoroughly by his vain hopes in Book 5, pathetically mistakes the "fare-carte" (1158–62) for Criseyde long after the more objective (only because less self-involved) Pandarus sees it for what it really is.

Even though Chaucer has skillfully arranged it so that, godlike, we have foreknowledge of what the future holds for the doomed lovers, our reaction to their misinterpretation tends to be one of pity rather than detached contempt. Furthermore, those characters within the represented world of the poem who do see the truth early and accurately are by and large those who do not have our good will—the traitorous Calchas, the cold Cassandra, and the scheming Diomede. Calchas and Cassandra, because their readings of present and future events are shaped by supernatural knowledge, are immune to normal human interpretive failings. Diomede, whose very first appearance shows him already to have perceived the truth about the hidden relationship between the lovers, "as he that koude more than the crede / In swich a crafte" (5.89–90), also conveys the tone of a cold-hearted prophet, as he tells Criseyde in detail what will happen in the future to the doomed folk of Troy (5.883–917).

Even Pandarus, often a sympathetic character, seems to fall in our estimation once we realize that he knows Criseyde will not return. Twice in Book 5 Pandarus feigns in front of Troilus, hiding the truth from him even as he articulates it clearly to himself. The first time occurs early in Troilus's waiting period:

> And to hymself ful softeliche he seyde,
> "God woot, refreyden may this hote fare
> Er Calkas sende Troilus Criseyde!"
> But natheles, he japed thus, and pleyde
> And swor, ywys, his herte hym wel bihighte
> She wold come as soone as evere she myghte.   (5.506–11)

Much later, in answer to Troilus's mistaken conviction that Criseyde will arrive that very evening, Pandarus deceitfully says:

> "It may be, wel ynough,"
> And held with hym of al that evere he seyde.
> But in his herte he thoughte, and softe lough,

And to hymself ful sobreliche he seyde,
"From haselwode, there joly Robyn pleyde,
Shal come al that that thow abidest heere.
Ye fare wel al the snow of ferne yere!"   (5.1170–76)

Those in the poem who for one reason or another have knowledge of what the future will bring are portrayed as insensitive and coldly removed from the action. With this strategy, Chaucer creates the conditions for a complex response to his erring protagonists: though they cannot apprehend what is "right" or "good" or "true," they are represented as having little control over the interpretive strategies they end up adopting. Not only do their own fears and expectations (known or unknown) influence their reading of texts and the represented world they inhabit, but so do the selective, purposeful, and therefore heavily mediated configurations of both events and texts offered up by others, who are themselves purveyors of hidden agendas, whether consciously or not. Authoritative interpretation of any sort is thus shown to be impossibly difficult for the unprivileged characters in this poem, a fact that Chaucer works steadily to prove in scene after scene of *Troilus and Criseyde*.

IV

Perhaps Chaucer's most convincing demonstration of what is at stake in any act of interpretation is his narrator, who, as we have seen, reflects every one of the interpretive failings of his characters, from having unrecognized personal and social purposes that interfere with his reading of the tale he retells, to cheerfully believing that he can be "objective" in his treatment of the "objective" story that faces him. Thinking that he is exempt from the epistemological complexities that affect his characters, or perhaps not seeing these complexities at all, he continues to interpret Lollius's story in a manner that caters to his own and his audience's love interests well past Book 1, failing to perceive clearly either the origin or the result of such readings. In Book 2, for instance, he again adopts the neutral scholar's stance—"how it was, certeyn, kan I nat seye" (2.492ff.)—and, when he perceptively realizes that some members of his own audience are likely to misread his narrative in self-serving ways—"Now myghte som envious jangle thus: / 'This was a sodeyn love.'" (2.666–67)—we are surprised that he does not apply this insight into the nature of subjective reader-response to himself. But he does not; in fact, as critics have convincingly shown, the narrator is such an obvious advocate of the lovers throughout Book 3 that he is unable to maintain any moral distance at all on their amorous involvement, seeing their love affair mainly through Troilus's eyes, as the Proem to Book 3 suggests.[16] There, Chaucer gives to his narrator lines in praise of love (1–39) that Boccaccio had written for Troilo, a bit of artistic manipulation that reveals quite clearly Chaucer's desire to show the extent of this teller's personal engagement with (and spirited defense of) the love affair.[17]

The engagement has, of course, begun even earlier: in Book 2 the narrator intrudes at one point during the process of Criseyde's falling in love to say:

> To God hope I, she hath now kaught a thorn,
> She shal nat pulle it out this nexte wyke.
> God sende mo swich thornes on to pike!   (2.1272–74)

Yet the narrator, in the middle of his proem to Book 3, still blindly believes in his objectivity, for he asks Venus ("whos clerk I am") to provide him with the "sentement" he thinks he lacks (43) and he asks his muse, this time Calliope, to lend her "vois" (45) to help him achieve epic grandeur. However, he needs the aid of neither, for the stanzas he has just written demonstrate both passion and loftiness. In addition, these stanzas continue to reflect devotion to both *caritas* and cupidity at once, a problem that has been visible with the narrator from the poem's opening lines. Like Pandarus and Troilus, who conveniently decide to ignore the differences between the concepts of "pimp" and "friend," the narrator—in order to sanction erotic love in his poem and in its audience—fails to make any distinction at all between the love that originates in God (3.8–12) and that which inspired Jove's rapes (3.15–21).[18]

The narrator, however, although he remains unaware of the effects of his own subjectivity, social situation, and conceptual confusion on his telling of Books 3 and 4, does come to an awareness of how such conditions affect the lives of his characters. Those critics who are quick to condemn Criseyde's willingness to be alone with Troilus in Pandarus's bedroom, for example, need to be reminded both of the persuasive lie about Horaste that brought her there and of the narrator's convincing assessment of how and why she yielded:

> This accident so pitous was to here,
> And ek so like a sooth at prime face,
> And Troilus hire knyght to hir so deere,
> His prive comyng, and the siker place,
> That though that she did hym as thanne a grace,
> Considered alle thynges as they stoode,
> No wonder is, syn she did al for goode.   (3.918–24)

To some, this passage might be interpreted as the first in a series of inef-
fectual and unreasonable defenses of Criseyde, launched by the personally involved narrator. To be sure, the narrator here still shows himself
to be an advocate of the lovers; thus, it would not be inconsistent for
him to begin seeking arguments to support his particular stance. But if
we read the reported dialogue between Pandarus and Criseyde carefully,
we can see—here at least—that the narrator seems only slightly over-
zealous in his defense of Criseyde: Pandarus's lie *was* "like a sooth at
prime face." The narrator, in other words, witnesses quite clearly in this
episode how easy it is for even prudent people to be led astray when
faced with choices that involve personal desire and interpreting evidence
whose degree of truth they cannot ultimately judge. Criseyde believes
Pandarus's lie, she loves Troilus, and she sees no threat to her reputation
in being with him that night (in fact, Pandarus has suggested to her that
not seeing Troilus immediately might lead to the loss of both her lover
and her honor, the two things dearest to her). Indeed, the narrator shows
some insight here, in addition to the compassion we have come to expect
from him. But he still does not see just how closely he himself resembles
Criseyde in sharing the same vulnerabilities.

One of the ways in which the narrator most consistently resembles
Criseyde is his inability to discern with any accuracy who (or what) is
responsible for certain occurrences in the poem's plot—even when his
narrative source is clear on the matter. In the section of Book 3 just referred to (which Chaucer added to his Boccaccian source), we see the
perceptual limitations of both the narrator and Criseyde worked out in
tandem, making certain remarkable parallels between them visible: in
both cases, they blame Fortune for events that Pandarus brought about.
When Criseyde is told of the rumors concerning her and Horaste, the
very lie that looks "like a sooth" to her, she delivers a Boethian speech
on "mannes joie unstable" (3.820), categorizing her state as an example
of a general philosophical principle, namely, that earthly happiness is
"fals felicitee" (814). Not knowing that Pandarus is at the root of her
problem, she is left only with the vague sense that the world is governed
by unidentifiable malignant forces. Likewise, the narrator—with much
less excuse—blames Fortune for something wholly attributable to Pandarus's machinations. First reporting that Pandarus carefully planned
the time of consummation to fall on a dark and rainy night (3.546–53),
the narrator later seems unaccountably surprised at the weather, blaming Fortune for the rain that forced Criseyde to tarry at Pandarus's
house:

> But O Fortune, executrice of wierdes,
> O influences of thise hevenes hye!
> Soth is, that under God ye ben oure hierdes,
> Though to us bestes ben the causez wrie.
> This mene I now: for she gan homward hye,
> But execut was al bisyde hire leve
> The goddes wil, for which she moste bleve.   (3.617–23)

Almost as humorous as Chaucer's Monk blaming Fortune for Lucifer's fall, this assessment shows quite clearly the way in which the narrator's incomplete grasp of what he is relating is comparable to (but much less excusable than) Criseyde's own limited evaluations of the facts before her.[19]

In his proem to Book 4, the narrator continues to blame Fortune for events that will prove to have more adequate explanations. Here, in fact, we get the distinct sense that Fortune has become a convenient scapegoat for the narrator, one that he uses in order to avoid having to attribute guilt to any of his characters. After opening Book 4 with a stanza about Fortune's cruelty, the narrator goes on to describe Criseyde's upcoming betrayal in terms of Fortune's wheel:

> From Troilus she [Fortune] gan hire brighte face
> Awey to writhe, and tok of hym non heede,
> But caste hym clene out of his lady grace,
> And on hire whiel she sette up Diomede.   (4.8–11)

Then, for the first time, the narrator's struggle against the substance of his source-text is made overt. Whereas earlier he had defended Lollius's story from its possible detractors, now his advocacy of Criseyde causes him to doubt the veracity of his source's account:

> For how Criseyde Troilus forsook—
> Or at the leeste, how that she was unkynde—
> Moot hennesforth ben matere of my bok,
> As writen folk thorugh which it is in mynde.
> Allas, that they sholde evere cause fynde
> To speke hire harm! And if they on hire lye,
> Iwis, hemself sholde han the vilanye.   (4.15–21)

By suddenly calling into question the objectivity of his sources at the very moment they begin to narrate events personally disagreeable to him, the narrator is also inadvertently calling attention to his own biases about the subject matter of the story. That is, as long as Lollius's version of *Troilus and Criseyde* basically accords with the narrator's own perspective on it—that love is a great thing, that both lovers are worthy and good, that if not for Fortune, lovers' affairs would run smoothly, and so on—the narrator is willing and able to be faithful to it. But as soon as the obvious purpose of his source, in this case, to portray Criseyde's lack of "trouthe" in love, conflicts with the narrator's hopes and preconceptions about this love affair, the narrator refuses to believe unequivocally in the truth of his source text. Because he is now so involved in his story—his heart "gynneth blede" (4.12) and his pen "quaketh for drede" (4.13) at the thought of narrating the end of this love affair—he cares less about Lollius and the history that he previously believed Lollius to be representing than he does about making sure that his own and his audience's beliefs are confirmed. As much as the narrator wants to be like the "true Troilus" of his story by being absolutely faithful to Lollius even when such fidelity goes well beyond normal expectations, he in fact resembles Criseyde much more, for he discovers that, like her, he is torn between conflicting desires that show themselves to be ultimately incompatible. A closer look at Criseyde's governing purposes and how they sponsor the choices she makes will reveal how similar her betrayal is to the narrator's, for both spring from the same desire to maintain a difficult balance between irreconcilable goals.

V

As for Criseyde, her life is represented as proceeding comfortably as long as being with Troilus does not interfere with her very deeply felt fear of losing her honorable reputation, a loss that would, indeed, threaten her well-being as a citizen of Troy. Criseyde's fear, as C. S. Lewis and others have shown, influences much of her decision-making, being attributed to her the very first time she appears in the poem (1.94–95, 108).[20] Moreover, much of Pandarus's success in bringing Criseyde into the arms of Troilus rests on his skill at convincing her that maintaining her honor and security is not incompatible with having a love affair:

> "I am thyn em; the shame were to me,
> As wel as the, if that I sholde assente
> Thorugh myn abet that he thyn honour shente." (4.355–57)[21]

Throughout the course of the love affair, Criseyde finds herself juggling the twin desires of pleasing Troilus and preserving her honor and thus her protected role in society. This is shown both in her earliest inclinings toward the idea of love—"wol I fonde, / Myn honour sauf, plese hym from day to day" (2.479–80)—and also in her private deliberations later about whether or not to accept Troilus's favors, where the conflict becomes a major factor:

> "Now sette a caas: the hardest is, ywys,
> Men myghten demen that he loveth me.
> What dishonour were it unto me, this?   (2.729–31)
>
> And though that I myn herte sette at reste
> Upon this knyght, that is the worthieste,
> And kepe alwey myn honour and my name,
> By alle right, it may do me no shame."   (2.760–63)[22]

Moreover, since Antigone's song, as we have seen, provides Criseyde with a "real-life" illustration of both honor and love existing harmoniously in an actual woman's life, it is deeply persuasive for Criseyde, offering her a pleasant vision of her own two desired states peacefully coexisting in a single individual's experience. When we consider how and why Criseyde agrees to see Troilus, once at Deiphebus's house and once in Pandarus's bedroom, we should note that she is drawn there primarily out of concern for her honor; Pandarus's fictions about Poliphete and Horaste are both designed to suggest that people are talking about Criseyde behind her back.

By Book 3, it becomes clear that Criseyde's controlling purpose in life is to preserve her good name. All that she agrees to do she does if, and only if, it does not conflict with this all-important concern. "Myn honour sauf," she remarks, "I wol wel trewely . . . Receyven [Troilus] fully to my servyse" (3.159–61), showing here that although she is certainly willing to love Troilus back, she never ceases to hold as her first principle the retention of her name.

Pandarus sees very clearly that if Criseyde's reputation is threatened in any way as a result of the love affair, the affair is over: it is for this reason that he nags Troilus at such length about keeping it secret (3.265–336, 1625–38), not because he genuinely wants to protect his niece's good name (or her actual chastity, for that matter).[23] Trusting Pandarus, however, and showing what comes first among her priorities, Criseyde says to him:

> "So werketh now in so discret a wise
> That I honour may have, and he plesaunce:
> For I am here al in youre governaunce."   (3.943–45)

Indeed, for a while, love and honor coexist without conflict in Criseyde's life, partly because Troilus (at Pandarus's request) sees to it that the two never oppose one another. For example, when Troilus hears of Criseyde's impending exchange for Antenor,

> than thoughte he thynges tweye:
> First, how to save hire honour, and what weye
> He myghte best th'eschaunge of hire withstonde. (4.158–60)

Very quickly, however, he realizes that these two propositions are mutually exclusive:

> "Thus am I lost, for aught that I kan see.
> For certeyn is, syn that I am hire knyght,
> I most hire honour levere han than me
> In every cas, as lovere ought of right.
> Thus am I with desir and reson twight:
> Desir for to destourben hire me redeth,
> And reson nyl nat; so myn herte dredeth." (4.568–72)

And when he decides to consult Criseyde on the matter, what we see is a woman faced with a "kandekort" indeed, for the love she feels for Troilus is now indisputably in direct conflict with maintaining her honor. Though it is never clear that she is fully aware of the nature of her dilemma, two of her proverbs in this section express it quite concisely:

> "Lo, Troilus, men seyn that hard it is
> The wolf ful and the wether hool to have;
> This is to seyn, that men ful ofte, iwys,
> Mote spenden part the remenant for to save." (4.1373–76)

> "Whoso wol han lief, he lief moot lete." (4.1585)

Using these proverbs with reference to her father, Criseyde is represented as not seeing how very precisely they apply to herself.

Predictably, Criseyde's paralysis in the face of this dilemma slowly gives way to some certainty in the form of a decision that provides for protection of her name. Unlike Troilus, she never once considers opposing the action decided on by the parliament, because it would cause a scandal; instead she merely assumes that she will go as they have decreed. Her own solution—to return to Troy at a later date and under contrived circumstances—not surprisingly attempts to preserve a difficult balance, one that will both retain her honor *and* keep the love affair alive: "May ye naught ten dayes thanne abide / For myn honour . . .?" (4.1328–29). When she argues at length against Troilus's suggestion that they run away together, Criseyde further makes her conflict visible, for although she swears sincerely to be true to him in three emotional stanzas, she spends equal time expressing her concern for their reputation (4.1562–82). Indeed, the exchange plot itself is an analogue of the kind of conflict at work in Criseyde. Troy can have either Antenor or Criseyde, but not both; one or the other is going to have to be relinquished. Yet, characteristically, Criseyde's plan forms part of a fantasy wherein both can end up in Troy: "And thanne have ye both Antenore ywonne / And me also" (4.1315–16).

In attempting to sort out the reasons behind Criseyde's betrayal of Troilus, we must always keep in mind her need to maintain in harmonious balance desires that are inevitably, at some point, going to clash. At the Greek camp, when considering her narrowing options for the last time, she delivers a speech about her position that very openly demonstrates this conflict. In it, she realizes that by failing to meet Troilus on the appointed day, her reputation, in *his* eyes, will be destroyed:

> "My Troilus shal in his herte deme
> That I am fals, and so it may wel seme."   (5.697–98)

However, if she does attempt to escape to him, she may be apprehended and "be hold a spie" (5.703). To her mind, then, in either case someone is going to think her dishonorable and say untrue things about her, destroying her good name. Therefore either action—staying or leaving—becomes reprehensible to her, given the importance she places on honor and the social acceptance that comes with it. And even later, when she decides to attempt the escape, to hold strictly to "this purpos" (5.754), her reputation so concerns her that she vainly searches for convincing arguments about why one need not pay attention to "wikked tonges janglerie" (5.755–63).

Once we recognize her obsession with her honor, we can see more clearly why Diomede succeeds as well as he does in enlisting Criseyde's affections. Diomede's very first line of dialogue shows him striking (probably unwittingly) at Criseyde's weakest spot, for he alludes to her honor:

> "Iwis, we Grekis kan have joie
> To honouren yow as wel as folk of Troie."   (5.118–19)

Later, he brings in love:

> "And thenketh wel, ye shal in Grekis fynde
> A moore parfit love, er it be nyght,
> Than any Troian is.   (5.918–20)

Here, and at other "love and honor" moments in his seductive speeches, Diomede convinces Criseyde that her honor is not in conflict with love, that in this new relationship she can have again the kind of synthesis of the two that has become impossible in her previous one. Indeed, once Criseyde comes to believe this proposition, her betrayal of Troilus is inevitable. In other words, she falls in love with Diomede for exactly the same reason that she fell in love with Troilus; the only difference is that Diomede is his own Pandarus.[24]

We cannot deny, of course, that in the final analysis Criseyde is untrue to Troilus. Yet the questions of moral agency raised by the text, those involving the extent of Criseyde's guilt and the role of her will in this tragedy of betrayal, are never clearly answered by its represented action. To be sure, the narrator believes in Criseyde's sincerity at all times, and the reader is never led to question her good intent when the love affair is proceeding smoothly.[25] But our narrator is decisively untrustworthy after Book 3, especially on the subject of Criseyde. It is nonetheless worth asking the following questions: Is Criseyde ever represented as knowing that she is, to a large extent, at the mercy of social forces larger than herself? Does she ever come to apprehend that her decisions are governed by her need for an unworkable synthesis of love and good reputation, the latter a crucial prop in maintaining her respected social identity?

Though she may enter into the relationship with Troilus with a vague understanding of her dual role as lover and respected widow, it is by no means clear that she is able to point to it with any precision. When she is alone, trying to come to terms with her own treason, she never arrives at a clear understanding of how and why she ended up in the situation of "falsing" a worthy man she thought she loved. The most convincing evidence of her confusion on this issue occurs during her two attempts to rationalize her betrayal, that is, to avoid the pain of full self-incrimination. In these two speeches, Criseyde does indeed strenuously seek out explanations for her behavior, yet she fails to assign the blame where it would most effectively free her from guilt. In her first speech she attributes her mistakes to her lack of knowledge about the future (5.744–49), a defense that is unconvincing, since everyone is at the mercy of the same limitation. In her second meditation, she openly confronts the fact that she has been false, but she is still seeking arguments (none of which looks sound) to explain away the betrayal:

> [Women] wol seyn, in as muche as in me is,
> I have don dishonour, welaway!
> Al be I nat the first that dide amys,
> What helpeth that to don my blame awey? (5.1065–68)

If Criseyde were aware of how Pandarus and then Diomede had entrapped her by working on her desire to have both love and honor simultaneously, she would surely articulate it here, for she is obviously quite ready to grasp at any straw that will exculpate her. Yet this, her best defense, is never used, because it is unavailable to her; she clearly does not understand how her own longing to maintain the conflicting social roles of lover and honorable widow profoundly affected her choices and made her vulnerable to the "paynted processes" of Pandarus and Diomede. Her two desires are innocent enough when considered apart, but when—as her eyebrows are described—they are "joyneden yfeere," they become a fatal "lak" (5.813–14).

To some readers, Criseyde's overriding concern for her reputation might itself seem to be a character flaw. But the arguments against this position are strong. First, as those critics who have examined the evidence regarding Criseyde's social position in the poem have noted, her precarious status in Troy as the unprotected daughter of a despised traitor would certainly have demanded that she take care to preserve whatever honor she had (and rightfully had, we might argue, since we are given no reason to believe when we meet her, that she deserves otherwise). Second, every lady in Chaucer's medieval Christian audience would certainly have agreed that one's honor (whether deserved or not) is of utmost importance to one's well-being in society. Criseyde's concern for it is hardly unusual; not only is it a courtly cliché in amatory literature, but Chaucer himself also seems to assume that the actual ladies in his court audience share the same concern, for he makes one of Criseyde's worst fears the idea that women of the future will feel that the honor of their whole gender has been damaged by her betrayal.

Finally, Criseyde's identity as a pagan makes her honor and her reputation extremely important. Lacking any other concept of an afterlife, pagans—according to medieval tradition, at any rate—considered their reputations to be their way of achieving immortality after death.[26] A good reputation was a kind of salvation; a bad one tantamount to damnation. Thus, when Criseyde laments the loss of her reputation,

> "Allas, of me, unto the worldes ende,
> Shal neyther ben ywritten nor ysonge
> No good word, for thise bokes wol me shende.
> O rolled shal I ben on many a tongue!
> Thoroughout the world my belle shal be runge!"   (5.1058–62)

she is lamenting something very dear not only to herself but to pagan culture in general, something analogous to salvation for Christians. Criseyde is forever damned by the standards of her society, a fate so sad to the narrator that he feels great pity:

> Hire name, allas, is publysshed so wide
> That for hire gilt it oughte ynough suffise.

And if I myghte excuse hire any wise,
For she so sory was for hire untrouthe,
Iwis, I wolde excuse hire yet for routhe.   (5.1093–99)

VI

   However much readers might feel compelled by this text to contem-
plate the extent of Criseyde's innocence or guilt, it is more important
that they discern the larger point about the social and institutional bases
of hermeneutic behavior that Chaucer is making through her—and simultaneously through his narrator, whose behavior is exactly parallel to
Criseyde's throughout the course of the poem. Like Criseyde, the narrator unknowingly enters into his project with two absolutely conflicting
social roles: he not only wants to support and encourage erotic love
(since his immediate audience is made up of lovers), but he also hopes
to save his soul and to remain in favor with the dominant Christian community of which he is a part. Desiring somehow to remain in the good
graces of these two at times incompatible audiences without ever having
to choose between them, the narrator (as we have already seen) willfully
distorts his source text when it doesn't allow for the kind of balance he
so ardently desires. He misreads self-interestedly, he places benign constructions on events that clearly have dark or threatening implications,
and he adds his own material to his source whenever he believes the
source does not sufficiently promote the perspectives he thinks his audience likes: "at Loves reverence," he notes at one point, "[I have] in
eched for the beste" (3.1328–29). But he is most like Criseyde when he
begins his betrayal of Lollius, slowly but definitively abandoning the
"true" text to which he was previously quite sincerely committed.
   The signs of this betrayal are visible as early as the Proem to Book 4,
where we discover, for the first time, that the narrator is aware of other
versions of the story he is telling and that he has begun to consult them
in the hope of finding one that does not "lie" about Criseyde, a "lie"
being defined as any view of her that differs from the narrator's own:

Allas, that they sholde evere cause fynde
To speke hire harm! And if they on hire lye,
Iwis, hemself sholde han the vilanye.   (4.15–21)[27]

Casting around for other sources that will supplement Lollius by im-
proving Criseyde's image (notice his use of the plural "they" in line 20),
the narrator shows his "slydyng of corage" here and in a variety of other
passages that allude to authors other than Lollius alone. The narrator
consults Juvenal, for example, to help support his passionately held belief

that the parliament did the wrong thing in attempting to get Antenor
back (4.197–201). Later, when he intrudes to comment favorably on
Criseyde's intention to return to Troy, he alludes to more than one
authority:

> And treweliche, as writen wel I fynde
> That al this thyng was seyd of good entente,
> And that hire herte trewe was and kynde
> Towardes hym, and spak right as she mente,
> And that she starf for wo neigh whan she wente,
> And was in purpos evere to be trewe;
> Thus writen *they* that of hire werkes knewe.
>
>   (4.1415–21, emphasis mine)

He may be right here, but it is nonetheless clear that there is enough uncertainty in Lollius's record of the dialogue to send the narrator franti-
cally to other versions of the story, written by those who (he claims, in
his positivist voice) actually knew Criseyde's deeds. Now crediting these
other unnamed sources with more authority than his Lollius, the narrator is shifting his allegiance before our very eyes.

In Book 5, the same behavior is visible. The narrator's first reference
to his source material shows again that he has more than one author in
mind:

> And trewely, as men in bokes rede
> Men wiste nevere womman han the care,
> Ne was so loth out of a town to fare.   (5.19–21)

Similarly, when the narrator stops the action to provide us with his curious portraits of the three principal actors in Book 5, it is clear that he
has just recently come across this information—it seems truly out of
place so late in the action—and that it derives from a variety of sources:
"as bokes us declare" (799), "som men seyn" (804), "they writen that
hire seyn" (816), "in storye it is yfounde" (834).

The effects of his independent research are even more clearly evident
when he has to confront the fact of Criseyde's betrayal, an event whose
unpleasantness obviously drove him to seek out every possible version
he could find in the hope of discovering one or more that would alleviate
her guilt. He is overjoyed, for example, to discover that the books leave
out some information, the omission of which will allow him to construe
Criseyde's actions in a more sympathetic light:

> But trewely, how longe it was bytwene
> That she forsok hym for this Diomede,

Ther is non auctour telleth it, I wene.
Take every man now to his bokes heede,
He shal no terme fynden, out of drede.
For though that he bigan to wowe hire soone,
Er he hire wan, yet was ther more to doone.　(5.1086–92)

He finds "ek in stories elleswhere" (1044) that Criseyde was compassionate in that she wept for Diomede's wounds, and "trewely" (1051) that she was sorry for her infidelity to Troilus. But when the stories confront the betrayal coolly and squarely, the narrator again casts doubt on their veracity by refusing to include his own "authoritative" voice in the chorus of negative opinion: "Men seyn—I not—that she yaf hym hire herte" (5.1049).[28]

Indeed, the treason of Criseyde and the treason of our narrator occur at the same time and for roughly the same reasons. Both desperately want their conflicting social roles to be lived out in complete harmony, and so they both—with "good intent" throughout—end up as faithless betrayers. Sadly, neither arrives at a full understanding of their social selves; neither seems to see very clearly what makes them so vulnerable to the "slydyng" that results in their actions. But the narrator, whose compassion for Criseyde is in part the result of his seeing in her (and others) how easy it is for interpreters to be led astray by their own self-deception, by the "processes" of others, and by the tangled social forces in whose complex mechanisms they are trapped, does grope toward a kind of limited philosophical understanding that the lovers never achieve.

As the poem's plot comes inexorably to its close, with Criseyde's permanent disappearance becoming clearer and clearer to the grieving Troilus, the narrator begins to reflect more actively on what Lollius—and his own experience—have demonstrated about the nature of deception. When Criseyde answers Troilus's inquiring letter with rhetoric designed to comfort him rather than provide him with the truth, the narrator responds, "Thus goth the world" (4.1434). Though one might be tempted to see this remark as yet another attempt to deflect blame away from Criseyde (as we saw the narrator do with Fortune in the Proem to Book 4), by this point in the poem the narrator has fully earned the right to say, with some comprehension, that "the world works like this," an insight he repeats again toward the end of the poem (5.1748–50). For by now his poem has begun to teach him that human beings have the capacity to avoid telling—and accepting—the truth when that truth does not conform to their own purposes, desires, or larger social identities, the two lovers being particularly apt examples of this precept. Yet in spite of having arrived at the beginning of insight, the narrator is still not quite ready to apply this view to himself.

Well into the concluding sections of his poem, the narrator blindly continues to pursue his conflicting purposes, with the familiar result that his epilogue is at times schizophrenic, contradictory, and awkward in its service of two masters.[29] Both God and the God of Love have roles in the narrator's concluding remarks, as he struggles to represent both of them, attempting (but failing) to keep their opposing worlds in some kind of harmonious balance. In his address to the women in the audience, for example, he once again becomes a version of Criseyde (see 5.1065–68), worrying aloud that women will think badly of him for demonstrating a woman's unfaithfulness:

> Bysechyng every lady bright of hewe,
> And every gentil womman, what she be,
> That al be that Criseyde was untrewe,
> That for that gilt she be nat wroth with me.   (5.1772–75)

In further imitation of Criseyde, he claims that he was not the first to "do amys" (see 5.1067) in showing female fickleness: "Ye may hire gilt in other bokes se" (5.1776). Here, therefore, he is still concerned about keeping his audience of earthly lovers happy (keeping his reputation, as it were, in good shape), still hoping to be able to claim (if not in this particular poem) that earthly love is worthy of our praise and our service: "And gladlier I wol write, yif yow leste, / Penelopeës trouthe and good Alceste" (5.1778).

Continuing to take a woman's view of things by moralizing—a bit too strenuously—about the guile of men who betray innocent females, the narrator implicitly defends Criseyde again, this time by supplying us with the argument about entrapment that she herself could not see:

> N'y sey nat this al oonly for thise men,
> But most for wommen that bitraised be
> Thorough false folk—God yeve hem sorwe, amen!—
> That with hire grete wit and subtilte
> Bytraise yow. . . .
> Beth war of men, and herkneth what I sey!   (5.1779–85)[30]

In effect, our narrator has now covered all the superficial moral bases available by saying "Beware of women" and "Beware of men." Though both of these morals are, with qualifications, organic to his story, the narrator does not yet see that in taking these positions, he is, in fact, by clear implication, warning his audience against earthly love—a stance he certainly does not want to assume, since his audience is made up of lovers whose authority he dares not contradict and whose involvement he envies. Thus, like Criseyde and Troilus both, he is so blinded by both social pressures and his own desires that he fails to discern the Christian implications of his story, even as he is expressing them. Were he not so intent upon pleasing the lovers in his audience (and perhaps the God of Love, too), he might have been able to see that Lollius's story very powerfully shows the tragic effects, on both sexes, of "feynede loves."

But not surprisingly, when the truth about human misinterpretation applies to issues that do not threaten to undermine, but rather confirm, the narrator's own desires, he is willing to see it—at least to some extent. In his envoy, he addresses his poem with these words:

> So prey I God that non myswrite the,
> Ne the mysmetre for defaute of tonge;
> And red wherso thow be, or elles songe,
> That thow be understode, God I biseche!   (5.1795–98)

Realizing, "for the nones," that people distort texts to suit their own selfish purposes, the narrator here tries to protect his own poem from future mutilation and misreading. But there is no small irony here: this comes from a man who has mangled, misread, and finally abandoned Lollius's text—and all because his source didn't give him what he wanted to find.

The long Christian ending of the poem, which represents the other half, as it were, of the narrator's dual purpose, has struck many readers of the poem as inorganic, insincere and inappropriately shrill at times in its rejection of the love affair and of the world in general.[31] To be sure, we would hardly expect our advocate of earthly love—the one who, in the beginning, asked the Christian God to help lovers please their ladies better—to be capable of adopting the impassioned voice of the Christian moralist, a voice heard more often from the pulpit than from one of Cupid's supplicants. But we must realize that the narrator's sudden shift to a strongly Christian perspective is not undertaken until he has had the chance to record and reflect upon Troilus's death. From his privileged position in the heavens, Troilus reports that our earthly desires are but vanity, that they inevitably blind us to the truth of the world's wretchedness:

> And in hymself he lough right at the wo
> Of hem that wepten for his deth so faste,
> And dampned al oure werk that foloweth so
> The blynde lust, the which that may not laste.   (5.1820–24)[32]

Fully despising "this wrecched world" (1817), Troilus harshly rejects earthly love, and, by implication, the poem that has so warmly reflected it. And however much we—and the narrator—might wish to believe the contrary, we cannot deny that, given this poem's medieval contexts, Troilus speaks a certain truth. But it is the truth as it might be seen in the cold hard light of eternity, unmixed with any human compassion or any human tenderness, for Troilus is not human anymore. But we are; and therefore we find ourselves surprised at his callousness. (How could he laugh at those who are mourning his death?) Indeed, we now react as he once did in the presence of cold Cassandra; though he suspected she was telling the truth, he could not bear to receive it.

These stanzas, then, place the narrator "at dulcarnoun" indeed. If he rejects Troilus's doctrine of *contemptus mundi* so that he will not have to abandon his advocacy of earthly love or contradict the desires of the "interpretive community" of lovers that constitutes his audience, he knows he will be making an error that his own poem (and his own dominant Christian culture) very vividly warns him against. However, if he accepts Troilus's doctrine, he will have to surrender his dearly held commitment to *amor* and come to terms at last with his text's representation of the severe limitations of erotic love, possibly insulting his audience of lovers at the same time. As he realizes now, he can no longer easily have it both ways; he cannot please God at the same time that he is working for Cupid.

His resolution of the problem, announced perhaps overexcitedly, in a moment of frantic negotiation, no longer requires him to juggle contraries in a precarious balance, yet it nonetheless still manifests a faintly divided view. He takes as his first and only governing principle the safe, medievally correct, view of the "false worldes brotelness" (1831). He definitively cuts his ties to the "corsed olde rites" (1849) of Jove, Apollo, and Mars (we might add Venus and Cupid, too), but his deep compassion for erring human lovers—both Christian and pagan—remains, and well it should, since he now poignantly sees how much he is their "owen brother deere."[33] His dilemma is no different from his characters' dilemma—and it is no different from the dilemma he now sees as inevitably arising in his audience as well:

> O yonge, fresshe folkes, he or she,
> In which that love up groweth with youre age,
> Repeyreth hom fro worldly vanyte . . .
> . . . and thynketh al nys but a faire,
> This world that passeth soone as floures faire.   (5.1835–41)

The sympathy he extends to his audience of "yonge, fresshe folkes," who—like himself—consider the world as attractive as "floures faire," is clear in the gentle admonitory rhetoric of this stanza. The narrator identifies very profoundly with their attachment to the world, and he understands their natural desire to have both lovers and salvation.

But the concepts of love and salvation cannot easily be united in any workable synthesis, unless it is the one employing Christ's radical redefinition of love:

> And loveth hym the which that right for love
> Upon a crois, oure soules for to beye,
> First starf, and roos, and sit in hevene above;
> For he nyl falsen no wight, dar I seye,
> That wol his heste al holly on hym leye.
> And syn he best to love is, and moste meke,
> What nedeth feynede loves for to seke?   (5.1842–48)

With his act of redemption, Christ embodied both love and salvation in a perfect union, making it possible for those who love him back to partake of that union in its only unfeigned form. But this is certainly not what the narrator's audience expected (or wanted) to hear when they began listening to the story of Troilus and Criseyde—and it is also not what the narrator, our advocate of *eros,* envisioned as the conclusion of his tale.

The difficult rhetorical situation in which our narrator now discovers himself actually sends him in search of a new audience, one that will appreciate the Christian perspective with which his tale ends; he now asks the moral Gower and the philosophical Strode to "correcte" (1858) his book, no longer directly seeking the advice of the lovers in his immediate courtly audience, those who, in Book 3, were asked to provide "correccioun" (1332) where they saw fit. Needing to abandon his original audience if he is going to adopt the rigorous Christian views that the "true" Troilus himself urges, the narrator comes to realize that art's place in the community is defined by its social dimensions; it is shaped perhaps less by independent moral agency than by the larger ideologies (often in conflict) of the audiences for whom it is written. For although the authoritative voice of Christian truth predictably wins out in the final stanzas of the *Troilus,* it does so only after intense narratorial suffering over the conflicting pressures exerted from powerful, opposing ideological camps.

VII

By focussing our attention on interpretive issues in *Troilus and Criseyde,* and on the ways in which a poet's audience influences his treatment of his material, we have been able to address anew many of the poem's classic difficulties: the problem of the two loves; the false issue of Criseyde's goodness or badness; the narrator's character and involvement in his story; the apparent disunity of the epilogue; and the principle behind Chaucer's alterations of or additions to his Boccaccian source. Indeed, Chaucer's rhetorical strategy of representing his narrator as one who shares the weaknesses of the pagan characters he writes about even though his status as a Christian would seem to render him superior to them in many crucial ways also works to sustain much of the poem's power as a statement about the impossibility of capturing historical "truth," since history is always interpreted and transmitted by social beings in social contexts. For in the *Troilus,* we see "history" being interpreted and transmitted in a social context that has genuinely altered it, and we are faced with the strong implication that each version of the story written before the narrator's source was also a socially constructed document with the results of its own (now hidden) social negotiations embedded within it.[34]

Thus, instead of "pulling rank" on his characters, Chaucer painstakingly sustains a series of analogies that underscores the similarities between his narrator's experience as a writer and his characters' lives as lovers: he is a Troilus in his blending of *eros* and *caritas*; he is a Pandarus in his role as purposeful artist, the intermediary shaping force between his story and its audience; and he is a Criseyde in the betrayal of his source and in his desperate attempt to maintain some viable balance between conflicting social roles. And like all of his characters, he is a self-interested or socially determined interpreter of both texts and events, unaware of the hermeneutic circles that enclose us all when we are confronted with untangling the complexities of life and the art that claims to reflect it. Moreover, faced with a literary predestination exactly comparable to the predestined lives of his pagan characters, the narrator lives with them through the horror of feeling powerless to change the tragic events fated to occur.[35]

By creating a narrator who must struggle with the same problems that his limited protagonists confront, Chaucer accepts and even heatedly argues for the fact that poets are not exempt from the epistemological traps that have, at all times in human history, frustrated the search for ultimate answers. His complex assessment of the inevitable limitations of textual authority was no doubt partly prepared for by his own experience as a poet. For as a poet—and therefore an incessant reader of other people's poetry—he would have repeatedly confronted the problem of authority in a number of important medieval texts. His own source for the *Troilus,* Boccaccio's *Filostrato,* shows a marked interest in exploring the interpretive behavior of self-interested readers, for its own narrator, like Chaucer's, misreads his source in an undisguised effort to relieve personal sorrow.[36] Identifying closely with the suffering Troilo and hoping to convince his lady, through Troilo's woes, to return to him, Boccaccio's short-sighted narrator fails to see how definitively his source text condemns the unregenerative erotic love that destroys its young hero. The story's Christian message eludes this love-struck narrator, just as Chaucer's narrator fails to discern how closely his characters' errors, developed by Lollius, mirror his own. Thus, Chaucer's project is very close to Boccaccio's (with many incidental differences, of course) in that both poets are well aware of poetry's diminished ability to instruct its recalcitrant and self-indulgent readership. But since poets cannot be writers until they too have been readers, poets themselves are susceptible to this trap, for in the making of their art, in the act of advancing purposes to suit their own social and personal situations, poets manipulate source material, thus perpetuating the uncertain truth-value of all human art.

In his *Filostrato* Boccaccio is questioning, at times very directly, the claims advanced by Dante's *Commedia,* a work that implicitly presents itself as an unerring record of God's own truth.[37] Though Boccaccio deeply admired Dante's achievement in that poem, it is clear that he did not share his master's confidence either in the ability of fallible human artists to know the truth or in the ability of fallible human readers to receive it when it was there to be had.

Chaucer definitely followed Boccaccio's lead in this matter; in fact, before he finished the *Troilus* he had already expressed much of his skepticism about Dante's access to ultimate truth in his own *House of Fame,* and he would continue to do so in *The Legend of Good Women,* discussed in the next chapter. In the *Troilus,* Dante's influence is noticeable throughout, often extending beyond Boccaccio's own imitations of the *Commedia.* As scholars have noted, Chaucer independently added to his work numerous Dantean adaptations and allusions, culminating in the poem's last lines, which closely render Dante's prayer to the Trinity in *Paradiso* 14.[38] Indeed, both Dante and Chaucer have related aims in writing their large and ambitious poems; both hope to explore the relationship between *eros* and *caritas,* the major issue—the cutting edge, as it were—for writers of thirteenth- and fourteenth-century courtly verse. As Elizabeth Kirk has written, Chaucer "makes the poem not simply a love story but an analysis of 'courtly love' in the sense in which it had been central to the development of medieval poetry. . . . *The Divine Comedy* and *Troilus* are the two great retrospective analyses of 'courtly love' and its meaning in the larger universe of Christian revelation."[39]

Moreover, both poems are designed to allow their narrators active involvement in learning about the tensions between *eros* and *caritas*. On this point, Winthrop Wetherbee notes:

As Dante, astray amid false images of good, is rescued by being made to experience imaginatively the fates of "the lost people," so Chaucer's narrator can be liberated from his perilous involvement with the fate of Troilus only by living it through to the end. Like Dante, vicariously experiencing damnation on the shores of Acheron or swooning out of sorrow at the story of Paolo and Francesca, he will abandon all rational and spiritual perspective in his identification with the lovers. . . . But as for Dante, so for Chaucer the imaginative experience constitutes an artistic as well as a spiritual progress, a symbolic and practical exercise in the creation of high poetry. Both poets attain a sense of profound affinity with the vision of the greatest of the *antichi spiriti*, even as they are led to a rejection of that vision.[40]

These parallels between the *Commedia* and the *Troilus* are demonstrably present, and there are others, too; as Wetherbee goes on to argue, for example, at times Pandarus functionally resembles Dante's Vergil, and Troilus's experience in love can be profitably compared to that of Dante the pilgrim.[41]

Recognizing these parallels is central to an adequate grasp of the *Troilus,* for if we ignored them we would not have a context in which to interpret Chaucer's larger aims, both those that affiliate him with the medieval tradition and those that set his individual achievement apart from the work of the great love poets before him. By calling our attention so often to the *Commedia* (through language, plot, character, and so on), Chaucer, like Boccaccio, hopes to encourage his audience to notice how much his own poem actually differs from the *Commedia*—in its treatment of love, in its narration, and in its final "solution" to the problem of the two loves. Elizabeth Kirk argues compellingly that Chaucer's poem never achieves a vision of the continuity of earthly love and divine love so central to Dante's poem. Rather, the *Troilus* shows the difficulty of sustaining such a view in the face of the clear conflicts between divine and human values represented throughout the poem and its epilogue.[42] Karla Taylor, too, shows that "Chaucer uses the *Com-*

media itself to react against Dante on grounds of deep concern to both poets: the social effect of literature." Noting that Dante used the "same language to describe both human and divine love," Taylor argues that for innocent and uninformed readers, this illusory connection is "misleading and destructive"—even potentially responsible for the actual damnation of readers who are led to believe in its truth. The *Troilus*, she notes, demonstrates the problems with—and the possible destructive potential of—Dante's poetic experiment.[43]

These arguments are supportable with evidence from Chaucer's text, especially when we consider some of the negative effects that Chaucer imputes to clever but irresponsible artists, of whom Pandarus is his prime example.[44] As a poet figure with well-planned purposes and the organizational skills to carry them out, Pandarus ends up acting out the negative role of the love poet who is heedless of the effects he has on people with whom he is in contact. As Criseyde points out very early in Book 2, Pandarus, as her uncle and protector, should be keeping her away from the dangerous entanglements of love—not encouraging her to enter into them:

> "Allas, what sholden straunge to me doon,
> When he that for my beste frend I wende
> Ret me to love, and sholde it me defende?" (2.411–13)

In addition, Pandarus's activity at the end of Book 2, in which he choreographs the crowd at Deiphebus's house so that Helen and Deiphebus find themselves alone together in the garden, constitutes a kind of pimping (though of an unintentional sort), for, as the Trojan histories tell us, Helen and Deiphebus end up later running away together.[45] In this instance, Pandarus the artist has inadvertently served as the couple's go-between, not foreseeing the effect of his machinations on those only marginally involved. And when faced with the grieving Troilus in Book 4, Pandarus is such a "for the nones" kind of artist that to please Troilus (his audience, as it were), he tries to cheapen his love for Criseyde by suggesting that Troilus simply forget her and find a different woman:

> Thise wordes seyde he for the nones alle . . .
> He roughte nought what unthrift that he seyde. (428–31)

In Chaucer's view, poets must not say "unthrifts" in their attempts to serve the "nones"; they have more to lose than just their "speche," as Diomede remarks (5.798), for their words can—and do—have effects on their readers, sometimes beyond what they themselves predict. And here we might recall Antigone's song, the author of which "pimps" for Criseyde without realizing it. Moreover, the song is a sort of miniature pagan version of Dante's *Commedia*: earthly love is, by analogy, compared to the heavenly sun, too bright for mortal eyes (2.862–65). Yet even Antigone, the singer of the idealizing song, knows that distinct kinds of love can easily be confused by undiscerning people:

> "But wene ye that every wrecche woot
> The parfit blisse of love? Why nay, iwys!
> They wenen all be love, if oon be hoot.
> Do wey, do wey, they woot no thyng of this!"   (2.890–93)

In other words, the author of Antigone's song is, in some sense, responsible for advertising what could, in the wrong hands, be a dangerous product. But she did not intend to do so, nor, presumably, is she guilty of misrepresenting her own ennobling experience. Artists, even the best intentioned of them, must realize that their art may be misapplied, used inappropriately by unknown, unskilled, or differently situated readers hoping to find confirmation of the rightness of their love. That love poets and their art often function as deleterious panders is something that Dante knew well himself, for Francesca in Hell makes the point abundantly clear: "Galeotto fu'l libro e chi lo scrisse" (*Inferno* 5.137).[46] But that even Dante's own good, didactic, and religiously orthodox love poem could function likewise is something that Chaucer and Boccaccio see as possible. As Chaucer's narrator remarks, "Man maketh ofte a yerde / With which the maker is hymself ybeten" (1.740–41).

Chaucer's response to Dante in *Troilus and Criseyde* is thus a complex one indeed. Recognizing the greatness of the *Commedia* as a love poem, Chaucer must have admired the skill with which Dante so brilliantly reconciled the poetry of erotic love with "the love that moves the sun and other stars." But he also questioned some of the fundamental assumptions that made possible the *Commedia*'s greatness. Dante's claim that he is the scribe of God and thus that his poem records the truth is tested, in a way, by the narrator of the *Troilus*, who, likewise, claims that he is an objective recorder—although of Lollius's truth, not God's. Yet even with this more limited and seemingly much easier task, of rendering a human text whose subject is neither mysterious nor new, Chaucer's narrator proves how unlikely it is for any scribe to remain uninvolved in the work at hand; the inevitable result will always be a transcript riddled with the transcriber's personal and often idiosyncratic beliefs. And if even a nonlover cannot keep himself out of his record of another's love affair, Chaucer implies, then imagine the problems that arose when Dante-the-lover, one fully committed to the purifying nature of his love for Beatrice, tried to write objectively about himself, his own lady, and God's unknown realms!

If we add to these complexities the problem of the poet's necessary artistic concessions to his audience, what we end up with is far indeed from any "truth." The *Troilus*, then, raises several profound questions about texts and their creators. Can human poets validly claim that they present an unbiased record of the truth when other agendas—such as their hopes, their beliefs, and their desires to please an audience—are liable to interfere with such a project? Even if objective truth is possible, can one be certain that it will be received, undistorted, by audiences, whose own hopes, beliefs, and social contexts are likely to affect their constructions of the work at hand?

The *Troilus* boldly raises these questions, which Chaucer was to raise again, with respect to Dante, in his *Legend of Good Women* and in *The Canterbury Tales*. And although the *Troilus* does not directly answer the important questions it confronts, it definitely reflects Chaucer's skepticism about the success achievable in any poetic transaction. For by means of his earnest but erring narrator, Chaucer creates a poem that confesses openly to the inescapable obstacles facing any poet whose project is to instruct or inform an audience. Looked at in this way, the *Troilus* is (somewhat paradoxically) one long error that leads us to the truth—not, perhaps, the Truth of God that Dante ambitiously tried to convey, but rather the truth about people in search of it.

This major difference between the *Commedia* and the *Troilus*, however, should not obscure the essential way in which the two poems agree: both Chaucer and Dante felt that love poets had the responsibility to guide their readers to an awareness of Love as it is manifest in the Trinity. After all, Chaucer concludes his *Troilus* by speaking in Dante's lyrical voice, drawn from the *Paradiso*:

> Thow oon, and two, and thre, eterne on lyve,
> That regnest ay in thre, and two, and oon,
> Uncircumscript, and al maist circumscrive.
> (5.1863–65; compare *Paradiso* 14.28–30)

Both poets fix their last gaze on heaven, bringing their poems to closure only after attaining the Christian perspective they know their readers should adopt. But they have achieved their similar purposes with contrasting poems. As Chaucer's narrator says about the shared goals and different methods of lovers, "som men grave in tree, some in ston wal"

(2.47). Though they have arrived at a common destination, they have without question taken different routes. To quote the *Troilus* once more:

> every wight which that to Rome went
> Halt nat o path, or alwey o manere.   (2.36–37)

Rome can be reached by different paths indeed.

CHAPTER FIVE

The Legend of Good Women:
Chaucer's Purgatorio

T o many readers (myself among them), the opening
lines of the Prologue to *The Legend of Good Women,* in which Chaucer
remarks that there is no one living "in this contree / That eyther hath in
hevene or helle ybe" (F,G 5–6),[1] seem to contain a veiled allusion to
Dante.[2] Certainly, Dante's claim that he had actually witnessed (and to
some extent experienced) the joys of heaven and the pains of hell before
he sat down to describe them was interesting to Chaucer at this stage of
his career, for, as we have seen, in poems such as *The House of Fame*
and *Troilus and Criseyde,* he was struggling with a basic question that
Dante's claim unavoidably raises: can texts ever be trusted to provide
something other than a socially, politically, or personally biased record
of "reality," either earthly or divine? Chaucer's attitude toward the textual tradition was marked by deep skepticism; in his view, Lady Fame
never took into account a text's truth before assigning it a permanent
place in the literary tradition. But Dante had seemed, at first, to offer
hope to the truth-starved reader, for here was a poet who had "seen it
all" (or so he claimed) and then had faithfully "recorded" his experience
in the *Commedia.*

In *The House of Fame,* however, Chaucer had implicitly denied
Dante's authority as a poet of reality, showing that the *Commedia's* reliance on books and the inevitably inaccurate reports contained in human tidings severely undermined the poem's claim to be telling the truth.
In *The Legend of Good Women,* Chaucer once more asks important
questions about textual truth, and he does so again with reference to
Dante. If the *Commedia,* as Dante had claimed, is the record of an eye-
witness observer of God's invisible realms, can it therefore be trusted?
Does it provide, by implication, significant support for what the naive
narrator of the *Legend's* opening lines so strenuously asserts, that books

can and indeed should be believed, since they are all that homebound readers have to rely on when their experience is limited—when, in other words, they "han noon other preve" (F,G 28)?

This argument is not openly addressed again in *The Legend of Good Women*, nor is the example of Dante developed in any overt way. But both of these subjects—textual truth and Dante's *Commedia* as a possible example of it—are, by implication and subtle allusion, raised throughout the rest of the poem. The prologue, for instance, dramatizes for us how poets end up lying in spite of their best intentions to record the historical truth. And the individual legends, which, like the *Troilus*, start out as part of a seemingly neutral project to render the "naked text" (G 86) of classical authors into the English vernacular, end up being unfaithful to "reality" in a variety of ways, misrepresenting (among other things) men, women, classical texts, pagan eroticism, and Christian *caritas* (as I have argued elsewhere).[3] Most important to this essay, however, is the way in which the *Legend* advances Chaucer's developing argument about textual unreliability. His vehicle is Dante's *Commedia* (the implied "true text" of the *Legend*'s opening lines), which has systematically governed Chaucer's selection of imagery (suns, stars, dazzling light, and so on), his development of plot and character (Alceste and the God of Love interacting with the poet figure), and his choice of subject matter for the legends themselves (a synthesis of secular and Christian love). But what results from Chaucer's close dependence on the *Commedia* is a critique—not an approval—of Dantean poetics, much as we have seen in *The House of Fame*. That is, while writing his own comic mini-version of Dante's majestic poem, Chaucer calls into question the *Commedia*'s reliability and its claim to be anything but a tissue of biases, about both historical and present events.

The *Commedia*'s influence on the *Legend* has only in part been documented. It has been clearly established, for example, that Chaucer used material from the *Convivio* and the *Inferno* in his construction of the *Legend*.[4] But Dante's influence is sometimes visible in Chaucer's poetry in ways other than verbal correspondence alone; Winthrop Wetherbee, R. A. Shoaf, and Glending Olson (among others) have recently made compelling cases for the claim that Dante's influence on Chaucer's poetry extends to plot, character, structure, and subject matter as well.[5]

As we examine these elements of the *Legend*, we can see (even in a preliminary and somewhat superficial comparison) similarities between Chaucer's poem and the *Commedia*—especially the *Purgatorio*. In plot, for example, both the *Purgatorio* and the *Legend* depict artist-narrators doing penance for past transgressions. Both poems also contain female figures (Beatrice and Alceste) who act as helpful—even necessary—mediators between the poets and the judgments of an angry god. These female intercessors—portrayed as apotheosized versions of their narrator's ladies—wear allegorical costumes, have handmaidens to accompany them, display attributes that liken them (in mediative function) to Christ and Mary, and are said to have their origins in the real world. Finally, in terms of structure and subject matter, both poems are organized around the general theme of love. As readers of Dante will remember, his Purgatory is constructed to reflect the idea that sin is merely love gone wrong; its inhabitants, Dante included, are there to cleanse their souls of errors in desire committed during their lives on earth.[6] For Chaucer, too, love is the subject, for in the *Legend* we learn that the poet will do penance for his supposed heresy against the amatory laws of the God of Love.[7]

The *Legend* and the *Purgatorio* are more importantly alike, however, in that both attempt, in similar ways, to articulate and defend certain poetic principles held by their respective poets. One of the most important principles, in both cases, relates to how the writing of secular love poetry can be justified in a Christian world. Is passionate love continuous or compatible with the love that is God? How can a poet who wishes to preserve earthly love as a subject for his art (and thus also to preserve the classical poetic tradition) synthesize *eros* and *caritas* in a workable union? That Chaucer's *Legend* is about this issue I have argued at length elsewhere, but I will return to those arguments here. That the *Purgatorio* is concerned with this issue has been repeatedly confirmed in the large body of criticism devoted to this poem, especially those sections that feature Dante the pilgrim engaged in autoexegesis, explaining himself and his poetry to the inhabitants of the purgatorial realm—and thus ultimately to his readers.[8] The famous Bonagiunta episode (*Purgatorio* 24.49–63), to which I will return later, is certainly one of the most important of these scenes, for there Dante is identified as a proponent of a new kind of poetry in the *dolce stil nuovo*, a style that had made possible the synthesis of earthly and heavenly love in a vernacular love poetry deriving from the secular tradition.[9] The *dolce stil nuovo* was itself made possible, however, by Dante's creation and use of the "idea of Beatrice," whose purpose is, I believe, exactly comparable to that of Chaucer's Alceste.

It is impossible to understand Beatrice's full import without consulting the work in which Dante constructs her out of his experience and his imagination, the *Vita Nuova*. As Charles Singleton has argued so persuasively, in that work Beatrice becomes the "solution which Dante has brought to the conflict between love of woman and love of God."[10] Attempting to discover meaning in his own actual veneration of this Florentine lady, Dante finds in Beatrice's life a deep Christian significance, which he expresses by means of several startling analogies and much suggestive detail. For example, her name is said to signify her nature ("she who brings beatitude"), and her death—the central event of the *Vita Nuova* and of Dante's life as it is described there—is made analogous to that of Christ both in its function (it brings beatitude to the one who loves her) and in its surrounding detail (Dante imagines her as participating in a scene that resembles the Crucifixion and Resurrection). Beatrice, then, is like Christ for the worshiping Dante, and through her mediation he is able, at least imaginatively, to reconcile his love for an earthly creature with his striving for heaven.[11] Most important, however, is that she is Christlike in a literary sense, too, for she redeems much of the secular love poetry Dante wrote to her and to other women before the *Vita Nuova*'s composition. When choosing poems to include in his new work, Dante consciously adjusts their previous significance to suit a Christian purpose, so that they themselves have a "new life" comparable to Dante's own.[12]

This process, whereby nonreligious poetry is revisionistically made to conform to Christian truth, is continued and expanded in the *Commedia,* where Dante partially redeems his beloved Vergil by making him Beatrice's deputy and by having Statius claim that the *Aeneid*—read in a way different from its author's original intent—actually converted him to the Christian faith (*Purgatorio* 22.64–93).[13] And when both Dante the pilgrim and the *Purgatorio*'s angels use lines from the *Aeneid* in referring to Beatrice (30.48, 30.21), we are clearly seeing "dead poetry rise again" (*Purgatorio* 1.7), for Vergil's original language—here being used in a prophetic sense to refer to Beatrice—is made comparable to the words of the Old Testament prophets that foretold Christ's arrival. In both cases, of course, the original lines must be distorted and taken out of context, but the happy result of such distortion is that they (and their authors) are made servants of Christian truth. Beatrice, then, does for Vergil what Christ does for the Old Testament; she makes literary salvation possible for Vergil's *Aeneid*. Though she eclipses his light with her greater truth, Vergil is at least shown to be her important precursor on the road to the poet-theologian's salvation.[14]

Turning now to Chaucer's *Legend,* we can observe that Alceste shows many striking similarities, both in construction and significance, to Dante's Beatrice. Chaucer's lady, like Beatrice, has a meaningful name— at least in her pre-apotheosized identity as his beloved flower. She is, "by reson," called a daisy, says Chaucer, "or elles the 'ye of day'" (F 183–84). That is, her name means *sun,* a heavenly body with Christian significance, especially in Dante's universe, where it symbolized the light of God.[15] Moreover, this daisy—the proto-Alceste—is an "erthly god" (F 95), one to whom the narrator devotes many lines of religious love language (as Dante did to Beatrice in his attempt to praise her adequately). But most important, it is Alceste's death, described in the vision proper, that serves to bring her close to Beatrice, both in function and ultimate meaning. Chaucer clearly struggled to find a female classical figure in his books whose life pattern could, like Beatrice's, be brought into general conformity with the life of Christ—and he found one in the story of Alcestis, who chose to die in place of her husband in order to save him from hell. This story, alluded to in the *Legend*'s prologue (F 513–16, G 502–504), tidily recapitulates the general pattern of Christ's self-sacrifice for humanity in the same way that Dante makes Beatrice's death comparable to that central Christian event. Moreover, both Alcestis and Beatrice, like Christ, are resurrected after their charitable acts, Alcestis by Hercules on one of his visits to the underworld.

Both Alceste and Beatrice have special properties that make them Christlike agents of mediation between their poets and heavenly reality. In the Christian scheme of things, such mediation is necessary, of course, because divine realities are much too profound for limited human perception, and both poets use the common Christian analogy of sunlight to express this idea. Dante is repeatedly dazzled by God's light throughout the *Purgatorio,* as in these lines from Canto 17: "the sun . . . oppresses our sight, and veils its own form by excess" (52–54).[16] Chaucer, too, when faced with the bright God of Love, finds his sunlike visage difficult to behold; in the G Prologue, for example, we read, "For sikerly his face shon so bryghte / That with the glem astoned was the syghte" (163–64).[17] What both poets obtain from their ladies is a means by which to view divine light without being overwhelmed by it; that is, they are given a version of divine transcendence specially attuned to the limited capacities of the human mind. For Dante, Beatrice is a "light between the truth and the intellect" (*Purgatorio* 6.45); she provides him with a glimpse of the sun by "shading its visage and tempering the vapors" so that "the eye [could sustain] it a long while" (*Purgatorio* 30.25–27). Later he is actually able to see the shining Griffin of Christ, but only as it is reflected in Beatrice's eyes, "as the sun in a mirror" (*Purgatorio* 31.121).[18] In an ingenious adaptation of these ideas, Chaucer attributes to his daisy/Alceste exactly the same function. As a daisy, she gives off a gentle "lyght" to guide the poet in his dark world (F 84–85);

she allows him a glimpse of the sun through her sunlike crown and her heliotropic rising and setting (F 60–65; G 51–54); and as Alceste she mirrors the crown and costuming of the God of Love.

The mediative power of Alceste and Beatrice, however, goes beyond their abilities to moderate bright light. Also important to the action of both the *Legend* and the *Purgatorio* is the mediation they offer their sinning poets in the presence of an angry god, a function that again shows the identification of these ladies with Christ—this time in his role as advocate for fallen humanity. Indeed, both the *Legend* and the *Purgatorio* (especially its last four cantos) enact what is basically the same scene: the poet-narrators, guilty of some transgression against Love, are shown the way to purgation by their ladies.

Before comparing these scenes more closely, we must be aware of a major difference between them—besides the obvious contrasts in tone (Chaucer's poem is highly comic; Dante's is sober and dignified). Whereas Dante is doing penance for his life, Chaucer suggests that he is merely doing penance for his art. In other words, though Chaucer has elected to use Dante's terms and concepts, he has eliminated any suggestion that, in this new context, they apply to life. Rather, repeating the secularization of Dante that he had employed in *The House of Fame,* Chaucer uses the concepts of the *Commedia* to apply strictly to art, resulting not only in a foreshortened *Purgatorio,* but also in a secularized one that describes the penance of a sinner in his poetry alone.

For example, whereas Dante's Purgatory cleanses errors in love, Chaucer's "purgatory" cleanses errors in love poetry, Chaucer's narrator being commanded—by a literary deity, not a real one—to perform sociopoetic penance, to make up for his fictional treatment of women by writing laudatory things about them in a new work of art. Similarly, Chaucer's narrator—not a lover himself, as he repeatedly claims, but only a writer about it—has appropriately chosen for his apotheosized lady a character from books, not a human being as Dante's Beatrice was.[19] Moreover, whereas Beatrice sternly reviews Dante's error-ridden love life for him in Canto 30 of the *Purgatorio,* Alceste (also sternly, but less so than her exemplar) reviews Chaucer's error-ridden art by listing those poems that may have offended the God of Love (F 417–30, G 405–20). Both ladies believe that some kind of penitence is in order (even though they are strong advocates of their lovers), and they both sponsor restitutional acts: Beatrice makes Dante do penance, and Alceste outlines the penitential legends that Chaucer is to write.[20]

Another major difference between the *Purgatorio* and the *Legend* bears precisely on this issue of guilt and advocacy. In Dante's work, the poet admits he is guilty as charged; he answers in the affirmative when Beatrice asks him to concur with her assessment of his mistakes in love (*Purgatorio* 31.5–15). However, in Chaucer's comic version of this scene, the situation is much less clear. The narrator never once admits his guilt, but instead feebly tries to defend his poems before the God of Love. Even Alceste herself expresses uncertainty about whether he has actually done anything wrong: "I not wher he be now a renegat" (G 401). In fact, when viewed as a whole, the dialogue between Alceste and the God of Love makes clear that in this case it is the deity who is wrong, not the poet. Alceste's job is largely to convince the angry god not to "wreke hym on a flye" (F 395, G 381). This hilarious reversal of the *Purgatorio*'s closing scene suggests that Alceste is there as a "way to placation," not salvation (as Dante envisaged Beatrice) and that the God of Love is a sorry version of the just Christian God who provides Dante's life—and poem—with structure and significance.

Before discussing the meaning of Chaucer's God of Love and his possible Dantean origins, we must note one more connection between Beatrice and Alceste. We have seen that Beatrice, acting as the object of Dante's desire, comes to embody a powerful synthesis whereby earthly love and Christian *caritas* are both achieved in the same act of loving. That is, in loving Beatrice Dante decides that he is loving an image of Christ. Consequently, as a happy result of Beatrice's synthesizing properties, Dante is able to redeem his early secular love poetry to her, finally extending this redemption, in the *Purgatorio,* to his favorite classical text, Vergil's *Aeneid.* In other words, Beatrice gave Dante (and by implication Dante's poetry) the power of salvation, because she was able to save the classics by providing classical literature with a new signifier: herself as an embodiment of Christian truth.[21] Chaucer's Alceste, in a function exactly comparable to this one, provides a mechanism whereby classical love poetry could be seen to signify Christian truth, for the pattern of her Christlike life story is imposed upon the classical narratives of Chaucer's legends as a kind of archetypal plot. This imposition is not the brainchild of Chaucer the narrator, but comes entirely from the God of Love. He tells the poet to use Alceste's virtuous life as a model, or "kalendar" (F 542, G 533), for the other classical narratives, with the strange result that these pagan lovers end up being oddly redeemed; they are all made to appear as martyrs for love, and their stories are made to conform to the generic requirements of Christian hagiography.[22]

Such a synthesis between paganism and Christianity is clumsy and contrived. What we have in Chaucer's legendary is a series of elaborate and very funny lies, stories so unfaithful to their classical sources that

we are forced to conclude that the poet intended them to be examples of
a poor and unconvincing pagan/Christian synthesis. Yet we cannot deny
that they behave in the same way as Dante's classics; distorted and excised from their pagan contexts, they are made to look like types of
Christian truth through the saving power of a woman whose life is
shown to be Christlike, one who, as the God of Love says, "taught al the
craft of fyn lovynge" (F 544, G 534). Thus Beatrice, "la gloriosa donna
della mia mente" (*Vita Nuova*, 1) and Alceste, "the maistresse of my
wit" (F 88), both end up as saviors of classical poetry, but Alceste's com-
ical results undeniably seem to parody Dante's serious experimentation
with his lady's power to redeem the pagan *auctores*.[23]

The Legend of Good Women, however, is not working as a critique of
the female characters, whose lives are given a Christian significance they
should not be asked to bear. Rather, its attack is directed toward those
male poets who, through narrative "rape," steal what they want from
the women's life stories and abandon what remains. These ladies (one
real, one a character from books) are merely innocent vehicles by means
of which their poets advance certain points necessary to their larger
theorizing. Beatrice's life story, for instance, was plundered for only
those details that were appropriate to Dante's Christian purposes; the
rest of her history, not being useful to his plan, was neglected and thus
forgotten. In other words, to use a line from Chaucer's *Legend of Hyp-
sipyle*, Dante "tok of hir substaunce / What so hym leste" (1560–61),
and let the rest pass unremarked—an unfair, and, in some ways, a very
selfish act, in Chaucer's view. It may have provided for Dante's religious
salvation, but it certainly did nothing for the real Beatrice herself, beyond
lending her the same kind of purely literary afterlife that Chaucer pre-
tends to provide for his pagan ladies.[24]

In Chaucer's *Legend*, Alceste's life is also exploited (as are the lives of
the ladies in the legends), this time by the God of Love, not the poet.
Desiring a tidy synthesis of Christian doctrine and pagan poetry, the
God of Love sees that Alceste's life story can advance this goal; indeed,
his praise of her shows little beyond self-interest: "To me ne fond y better
none than yee," he remarks to her (F 445–46, G 435–36).[25] Moreover,
Alceste's genuine humility (F 535–36, G 523–24), which contrasts
markedly with the God of Love's arrogance, wins our esteem and prevents us from seeing her as an object of Chaucer's satire. In fact, the
Legend implies that, before the God of Love appeared on the scene,
Chaucer's narrator had actually benefited from the daisy/Alceste's inspiration; she is intended in part to represent (in a Dantean way) some
of the poetic principles to which Chaucer was committed.[26] The real ob-

ject of the poet's satire, then, is Chaucer's fatuous deity, the one whom Chaucer the narrator must please in order successfully to pay back the "debt of love-poetry" he is said to owe in this purgatorial vision.

There is, of course, no direct model for Chaucer's God of Love in the *Commedia*. Since Dante was mainly interested in describing Christian reality, there was no place for a Cupid figure in his final representation of things. But it seems clear that Chaucer's comic deity nonetheless has roots in Dante's thought, especially in Dante's conception of love as it appears in the *Vita Nuova* and, more subtly, in the *Purgatorio*. In the former work, Dante does indeed employ a god of love, one who is self-consciously described as a figure of speech, a poetic device with attributes and functions resembling those of the Christian God. A Christianized Cupid, he serves to aid Dante in transforming troubadour love poetry into deeply religious verse, especially in the early chapters of the *Vita Nuova* where he conveys to the poet, in words and images, the Christian significance of the beloved Beatrice.[27] Later in the work, however, once the god of love has shown the poet this new synthesis of love of woman/love of God, he is deemed superfluous, disappearing from the narrative as a used-up simulacrum of the truth, whose heuristic function has been superseded by Beatrice herself. She is real, but the god of love is not—and her powers and abilities to bring Dante to God are judged to be greater than those of this merely literary vehicle. "Beatrice resembles me," the deity remarks, and with that observation he transfers to her all the authority of love.[28]

Chaucer's God of Love seems to bear a close resemblance to the Amore of the *Vita Nuova*, both in appearance and in function. For example, both deities seem to represent the poetic tradition and its readership as these influenced the poets' new literary creations. Dante uses his Christianized Cupid to personify the old troubadour tradition as it was starting to be elevated into a new life-giving religious mode; Chaucer (comically, of course) uses his God of Love to personify a new extreme in the literary conflation of erotic love and Christian *caritas,* one which he saw visible in Dante's verse and possibly in other European poetry indebted to Dante's precedent. Like Dante's Amore, Chaucer's god is not real; he is an artificial creature constructed out of pieces drawn from both classical and Christian sources, so that although he resembles Cupid with his wings and arrows, for instance, he also makes Christian pronouncements about heaven, hell, salvation, and penance. He calls his mother "Seynt Venus" (F 338, G 313) and he awkwardly conflates pagan and Christian ideals in several of his observations about poetry:

"Ek al the world of autours maystow here
Cristene and hethene, trete of swich matere."   (G 308–309)

Moreover, because he sees little difference between classical amatory verse and hagiography, he likes the idea of erotic saints' lives, the new poetry that Chaucer wishes us to see as a burlesque of the Dantean synthesis of earthly and heavenly love.[29] Finally, just as Dante's deity resembles Beatrice, the lady he accompanies, so Chaucer's god resembles (literally!) Alceste, for both wear daisy outfits and have sunlike crowns.

We should note here that Dante and Chaucer both ultimately reject their deities as models for their art, finding that their ladies achieve a more useful synthesis of earthly and heavenly love. In Chaucer's case, Alceste's synthesis is more credible than the God of Love's, because she unites the real world (in her humble origin as a daisy), classical literature (in her identity as Alcestis of Thrace), and the moral virtue that is compatible with Christian doctrine (in the *caritas* of her self-sacrifice and faithfulness as a wife). Thus, although the deities of Chaucer and Dante show similar functions, we should not overlook the humor visible in Chaucer's version. His God of Love is a witty parody of Dante's sublime Amore and is surely designed in part to represent the powerful readership that desired (in Chaucer's case ordered) poets to deal in a new and exciting way with the subject of love, to make their poetry flexible enough to accommodate secular love as well as the ideals of the Christian faith. To borrow Jauss's term, the "horizon of expectation" among fourteenth-century readers of courtly verse certainly included the synthesis of *amor* and *caritas*; the fictional audience of the *Troilus* itself bears witness to this expectation in Chaucer's own courtly readership.

That Chaucer is also indebted to Dante's *Purgatorio* for his God of Love, however, not just to the more theoretical *Vita Nuova,* will become clear if we keep the *Legend*'s action in mind as we examine several of Dante's important purgatorial scenes. In the final cantos of the *Purgatorio,* for example, we find what is probably the main source for the ritualized arrival of Chaucer's God of Love and Alceste—the scene describing Beatrice's appearance as the herald of the Griffin of Christ. In a kind of proto–beatific vision, the Griffin's presence here allows Dante to see the dual nature of Christ (both God and man) through the creature's seamless fusion of the eagle and lion, that is, through its identity as "one person in two natures," as Dante writes (*Purgatorio* 31.81). It is at this point that Beatrice provides the greatest mediation, for only through the reflection in her eyes (like the sun in a mirror) can Dante see "the two-fold animal gleaming there within, now with the one, now with the other bearing" (*Purgatorio* 31.121–23). Both Beatrice and the Griffin join earth and heaven in a remarkable synthesis, but Beatrice does so as an apotheosized human, and the Griffin in a more supernatural way, reproducing through an unnatural creature's form the dual identity of Christ. The God of Love in Chaucer's *Legend* acts as a counterpart to Dante's Griffin, for both creatures appear as the main figures in the beatific visions of which they are a part. Both are also creatures that attempt complex syntheses, and both require, as we have seen, that their power be tempered or reflected for mortal intelligences by the ladies that accompany them. The single major difference between them, however, is that Chaucer's deity does not attempt his synthesis in any theological sense (he is not a serious Christ figure like Dante's Griffin), but has his power restricted to the social realm of art.[30]

This purgatorial scene shows other similarities to Chaucer's poem, especially in its evocation of certain typological schemes. Both Beatrice and Alceste, clad in green mantles, arrive on the scene with much ritualistic fanfare involving songs of praise and symbolic attendants. Beatrice has, among other escorts, twenty-four elders preparing her way who wear lily crowns and sing a hymn of praise to her, "Blessed art thou among the daughters of Adam" (*Purgatorio* 29.82–87), a song that alludes clearly to Mary as bearer of Christ. These elders, who stand for the twenty-four books of the Old Testament,[31] present in their devotion to Beatrice an analogue to the Christian belief in the truth of Old Testament prophecy; that is, the elders make explicit the idea that within each book of the Old Testament one can discover foreshadowings or figures of Christ's (Beatrice's) existence on earth. This elaborate allegorical episode is constructed in part to demonstrate further that Beatrice's function is a kind of justification of history, whereby she provides an essential link between the old life of Adam (and Dante) and the new life of Christ, just as Mary (as mother of Christ) was instrumental in exposing the coherence of the Old Testament and the New.[32]

This essential doctrinal point is imitated in Chaucer's poem, but again with the change in focus that consistently distinguishes these two works: Chaucer alters the scene just enough to make it refer to poetics alone. To correspond to Beatrice's elders, Alceste has a small group of ladies attending her, dressed in regal attire. They (along with other women present) venerate her, not with a Latin hymn, but with a secular *balade* in the G Prologue and a song about "figuring" in the F version:

> Heel and honour
> To trouthe of womanhede, and to this flour
> That bereth our alder pris in figurynge!   (296–99)

Later, we learn who these women are—they are pagans whose stories are available in books and who will serve as subjects for Chaucer's classical legends. It is not the Old Testament signified here, but rather (as in *The House of Fame*), the exact counterpart to it from a poet's perspective—that is, classical (pre-Christian) narrative. Chaucer suggests that the stories of these classical ladies and their truth in love prefigure Alcestis's life of perfect *caritas* and self-sacrifice, just as the Old Testament (Dante's elders) prefigures Christ's life of charity (as symbolized by Beatrice). As a natural link between pagan erotic love and pagan love that approximates Christian charity, Alceste represents in Chaucer's purely literary vision what Beatrice meant to Dante.[33]

Finally, the large crowd of faithful women, "the thridde part, of mankynde, or the ferthe" (F 287, G 190), who follow Alceste and venerate her along with the regal ladies, also seems to have its counterpart in Dante's conception of things. Just as the idea of Beatrice is in part an attempt to redeem the female nature and elevate it in status to a vehicle for salvation, so Chaucer's Alceste clearly stands as a prototype of faithfulness in love, by means of which all true women, represented here by the crowd of women, hope to achieve "salvation"—with the major difference that the salvation suggested here is metaphorical and not real. Only the women's literary reputations are at stake in the *Legend*'s fiction, not their souls; Chaucer will only have the power to redeem (and in a distorted fashion, at that) their *fame*.[34] About such serious issues as real salvation Chaucer remains wisely silent here, and his calculated avoidance of addressing ultimate things in the *Legend* constitutes one of the most significant differences between this poem and its Dantean ancestor.[35]

The last purgatorial scene that I wish to address in this chapter is the famous Bonagiunta episode, which is central to an understanding of Dante's poetics and may well have contributed to Chaucer's construction of the God of Love in the *Legend*. In Canto 24 of the *Purgatorio*, Dante is recognized by Bonagiunta as the great poet who wrote in the *dolce stil nuovo*. In response to Bonagiunta's further questioning, Dante identifies himself as the "one who, when Love inspires me, takes note, and goes setting it forth after the fashion he dictates within me" (*Purgatorio* 24.52–54). Love, briefly personified here as the one who guides Dante's verse, is further defined as the *dittator* of Dante's style a few lines later, when Bonagiunta notes that "your pens follow close after him who dictates" (*Purgatorio* 58–59).

One of Dante's intentions here, of course, is to set forth his own artistic conviction that poems about love must be informed directly by the experience of love. But, as Teodolinda Barolini notes, this passage also articulates the central strategy of the whole *Commedia*, for in taking Love's dictation Dante is also setting himself up as the secretary of God, Love being none other than God himself in the Christian scheme that Dante adopts. Thus, this passage (by analogy) "results in a license to write the world, in fact to play God unchecked,"[36] for it simultaneously allows Dante complete freedom *and* absolute divine authority in his project, an ideal situation for earthly poets. Dante reminds his readers of his role as God's scribe in the *Paradiso* (10.27); there, as here in the *Purgatorio*, this identity is clearly central to his poetics. By adopting the role of God's recorder, he can claim to be the humble imitator of reality at the same time that he takes whatever liberties he needs to with his *materia* to achieve his larger social and personal purposes.

In Chaucer's poem, Love dictates, too, but what is written is against the artist's will and has disastrous results—the legends themselves. Thus, the liberation made possible for Dante by his self-justificatory role as scribe is countered in Chaucer's poem with a vision of artistic bondage, because Chaucer the narrator, in being pressured to make his poetry conform to the purposes of the God of Love, is being denied the chance to complete his original project (to be an accurate "scribe" or translator of his classical texts) in the faithful manner he had intended. Instead of being granted the power to "write the world" (as Dante was), Chaucer the narrator is being forced to write (rather rewrite) the world of classical texts as an act of subjection to Love's ill-designed dictates. Yet I believe that Chaucer nonetheless wants us to see that the results of Dante's freedom and the results of Chaucer the narrator's bondage are in some ways comparable, for both situations produce texts that lie.

If we stop for a moment to analyze what Chaucer is saying by his use (and alteration) of Dante's terms and concepts, we can see that through a series of elaborate ironies Chaucer is letting us know that he is aware of certain kinds of fabrication that result from Dante's ambitious desire to tell God's Truth. That is, Chaucer suggests that Dante could not have recorded "reality" objectively in his *Commedia* (in spite of his disingenuous claim that he had) because one of his purposes (the one Chaucer embodies in his legends) was to demonstrate that earthly love (especially Dante's own and that of his readers) is commensurate with Christian *caritas*. In Chaucer's eyes, this purpose—identical with the God of Love's—forced Dante to be relentlessly subjective rather than faithful in his recording of history, because history, viewed without the distorting lenses of poetic transfiguration, would never reveal such a purpose on its own. That is, the *Legend* implies that Dante lied about reality, both past and present, to the same extent and for the same reason that Chaucer's narrator lies about classical texts in his legends; once a purpose (in this case, to synthesize *eros* and *caritas*) is imposed upon one's *materia,* then the *materia* will perforce be distorted to conform to the purpose (a point that the *Troilus* had made as well).

Dante knew this, of course; his selectivity is what allowed him to be a great poet, although he achieved his expression of the big, important Truth at the expense of the less significant truths that clutter the world. But if he had admitted to this distortion, he would have undermined the effectiveness of his entire poetic corpus, since the full success of his works hinges on the illusion that they are deeply rooted, at all times, in the facts of the actual world and in God's construction of these facts. As Singleton has noted, "the fiction of the *Comedy* is that it is no fiction,"[37] and Dante's artistic brilliance in discovering this strategy is what freed him to create that one version of reality that could best tie together, in the extravagant poetic vision of the *Commedia,* all the strands of medieval life and thought.

But the success of Dante's poem does indeed depend in an important way on the reader's belief that Dante's particular version of the world (including Beatrice's life story, his own life story, and the lives and texts of Vergil and Statius, for example) is the one that is "really true." His selectivity, though it makes possible what is perhaps the greatest medieval poem ever written, nonetheless must be seen as a personal and highly subjective view of the truth, for in creating a world of signs out of mundane reality, he had to suppress those parts of it that did not fit into his overall scheme. Let us remember that Chaucer does the same thing with his legends; in an attempt to force the lives of the classical women into a Christian pattern, he boldly suppresses those details that cannot be tidily accommodated in a Christian framework. Thus, suggests Chaucer, something is lost in Dante's ambitious attempt at monistic world-making, and only a naive reader (such as Chaucer's narrator in the *Legend*'s opening lines) would treat Dante's book as one worthy of our "feyth and ful credence" (F 31, G 33). It may be great poetry, to be sure, but, like any other book, it cannot—and should not—be read as an unbiased record of God's truth.

What, then, can we finally conclude about Chaucer's heavy involvement, in his comic little *Legend,* with Dante's *Commedia*? The key to this question lies in an analysis of some of the important contrasts in the narratorial strategies of the two poets. Where Chaucer deviates most from his Italian *auctor* is in the characterization of his persona. Whereas

Dante claims to be recording what he knows about love from the "book of his experience" (to borrow the opening figure from the *Vita Nuova*), Chaucer's persona, who has no experience in love, records what he has learned about love from his experience with books. Moreover, by systematically reducing Dante's theological poetics to poetics alone, Chaucer repeatedly calls attention to the epistemological limits he wishes to impose on the subject matter of his art. There is thus a massive difference between the two poets in the range and scope of the material they claim to record in fulfilling their roles as scribes of the truth, and it is a difference that is crucial to Chaucer's entire career as a poet.

Like Dante, Chaucer wishes to have the authority to write what he chooses, but unlike Dante, he has opted to restrict his *materia* to what other people have dubiously claimed as the truth, not to what is necessarily God's Truth itself. That is, Chaucer's fiction is that he has no truth to tell, a poetic self-definition that is pervasive in his works: in the dream-visions his persona is an observer of his own self-reflecting dreams; in the *Troilus* he is a biased and socially pressured translator; and in *The Canterbury Tales* he is the timid scribe of other people's lies. Never claiming (as Dante did) to have any authority in love, but merely identifying himself as familiar with other people's claims about it, Chaucer frees himself from being accountable (as Dante was) for the ultimate truth of what he "recorded." Yet his abilities as a love poet were in no way inferior to Dante's, for his narratorial strategy made available to him *everyone's* recorded perspective—Dante's included—as raw material for his art. Moreover, his role as recorder of other people's records allowed him to foreground a variety of epistemological and social issues, none of which required any obvious lying to be propounded.

There are thus several rich ironies that Chaucer achieves by repeatedly forcing Dante's works to our attention during the *Legend*'s action. Chaucer wanted his readers, even in the poem's opening lines, to be thinking of Dante's claim to be telling the truth; then, as the *Legend* proceeded, readers would slowly come to realize that even if Dante had been to the otherworld, his claims should not—indeed could not—be trusted. For what readers actually see in the course of Chaucer's comic *Legend* is exactly what Dante's *Commedia* attempted to achieve—the redemption of classical literature by means of a typological scheme, an ambitious synthesis of earthly love and *caritas*, and a vindication of the poet's previous works (a purpose alluded to in the *Legend* through Alceste's defense of Chaucer's own *Troilus* from the God of Love's attacks). These aims, as Chaucer wishes to show us, conflict with Dante's stated mission to "record the truth," just as the legends end up being grotesque parodies of what *verbum ex verbo* translations ("naked texts") would be.

I do not think that Chaucer wished merely to quarrel with Dante or to discredit his poetic achievements. Chaucer quite clearly admired Dante's works and felt that Dante was a poet against whom all future writers would be measured. But he saw in Dante's *Commedia* certain well-articulated principles that he found useful as contrasts to his own self-definition as a poet. The *Legend* shows us why Chaucer chose not to write in the Dantean mode, that is, why he did not attempt to write the kind of work that ambitiously purported to have the ultimate answers to divine and earthly mysteries.

Finally, then, like *The House of Fame* and the *Troilus,* the *Legend* calls into question all assertions of poetic truth, both historical and theological, for poetry is the product of a variety of rhetorical, sociological, and psychological forces, all of them in conflict with the claims to truth of even the most faithful of reality's scribes. No one's poems, Chaucer surely implies, should be seen as totally reliable, because poets—himself included—are always at the mercy of their own, and their audience's, desires. Chaucer never claims, of course, that his own poetry is any truer than Dante's, but he does suggest that his poetic strategy—to define himself as a scribe of what others believe to be true and to admit that his "lady" is a product of books and social attitudes more than of nature—at least allows him a chance to represent more freely than Dante the relationships between human life and art. He thereby achieves for his poetry a complex vision of poetic epistemology, one as intricate as what the ambitious *Commedia* could offer. And to readers wishing to learn from poetry about the complicated experience of love (the putative subject of the *Legend* and most of Chaucer's other works, too), Chaucer implies that they might learn more about it from his own inexperienced narrator than from Dante the lover, one who had claimed to live personally through the joys and pains it occasions. Somewhat paradoxically, then, by abandoning all authority as a lover, Chaucer actually gains it, a situation that his own narrator succinctly (and with typical Chaucerian impertinence) notes at the end of *The Legend of Phyllis*: "trusteth, as in love, no man but me" (2561).

CHAPTER SIX

Truth and Textuality in
The Canterbury Tales

I

✧ As we noted in Chapter Four, when Chaucer wrote his *Troilus and Criseyde,* he added to his source many scenes involving acts of interpretation, all of them somehow contributing to his general thesis that human beings (including artists, of course) are vulnerable, at all times, to the insinuations of their desires, the limitations of their knowledge, and the social agendas of their particular culture, when faced with interpretive decisions. Moreover, he showed that artists (represented by Pandarus and himself) inevitably manipulate their *matere* to suit the tastes and expectations of their audience, so that any hope of discovering the truth about reported events is thwarted by the sure fallibility of the human agents involved in any verbal transaction, whether they are the generators or the receivers of language. In making these additions and embellishing upon certain relevant passages that the *Filostrato* already contained, Chaucer was, in a sense, "Boccaccianizing" his *Troilus,* for the roles of the human will and the social institutions that shape it in bringing about interpretive confusion (not to mention the inadequacy of language itself) are common ideas not only in the *Filostrato,* but also in other works by Boccaccio, especially the *Decameron.*[1]

Although all of Boccaccio's works explore these ideas, the *Decameron* presents an astonishingly large number of reader figures, artist figures, and carefully developed scenes demonstrating how audiences of different kinds react to verbal constructs. Not only does the *brigata* of storytellers respond to each other's tales (often in inadequate ways), but also within the tales themselves there exist audiences reacting to both language and events in need of interpretation, allowing Boccaccio great freedom to explore the wide spectrum of possible (and often unpredictable) human response.[2]

Whether or not Chaucer's *Canterbury Tales* was influenced directly by Boccaccio's *Decameron*, it is instructive to see that the two works share some fundamental philosophical principles, which are worked out in generally similar artistic structures designed to allow for full disclosure of the skepticism both authors posit about the uncertain truth-value of human verbal constructs, either as they are made by artists, or as they are received by audiences. Indeed, when Chaucer adapted his sources to suit the fiction of *The Canterbury Tales*, he seems to have done so with an eye to making many of his adaptations function like Boccaccio's *novelle*.[3]

It is also true that both Boccaccio and Chaucer present in their collections of tales a forceful contrast to Dante's realist poetics, founded on the idea that *nomina sunt consequentia rerum*—"names are the consequences of things." Dante saw the poetic potential in the doctrine that words and things have a firm bond uniting them, something that is clear from the *Vita Nuova*, where Dante's narrator (a version of himself) learns through visionary prompting that Beatrice's essence and meaning are revealed in her name ("the bearer of beatitude") and that her life and his love for her could be "read" in the manner of Scripture, if one approached this analogical data in a properly selective way. Realizing this idea made possible the *Commedia*, a work that confidently imitated Scripture, liberating poets from their earthly chains by demonstrating that a sacred poem could be written. If read aright, all human activities (including love, politics, and poetry itself) were signs of God's own Truth. Throughout the *Vita Nuova* and the *Commedia* alike Dante provides his readers with examples of the kinds of interpretive strategies he thought necessary for them to adopt—both in life and in their encounter with his own poems. It was essential to the moral success of Dante's poetic experiment that they adopt the right ones.[4]

Boccaccio, however (like Chaucer after him), imagines a world in which reading strategies are unrestricted, because of the artist-narrator's failure to provide guidance, or unrestrictable, because of the tendency of signifiers to drift away from the signifieds when language is in actual use and because of the unpredictable social and personal agendas of individual readers, who will always do with texts whatever they wish. Boccaccio's poetic projects do not deny Dante's brilliance in achieving the seamless sacred verse of the *Commedia*, of course, but they certainly suggest that Boccaccio was not very optimistic about the survival rate of Dante's intentions once actual readers were brought into the picture and faced with the arduous task of following Dante through his elaborate poetic maze. This interest in the failure of readers to meet Dante's difficult requirements is visible in many of Boccaccio's works, and his frequent comic adaptations of the *Commedia* and the *Vita Nuova* often show some of Dante's concepts tried out in unideal circumstances before unideal readers.[5]

Dante's works raise other issues, too, for both Boccaccio and Chaucer. In what sense can Dante be said to have written the "truth"? As *The House of Fame,* the *Troilus,* and *The Legend of Good Women* show, Chaucer raises very real doubts about any poetic project that claims to have discovered, recorded, or in any way represented truth, especially truth that transcends the limited and contradictory data visible in everyday life. Yet Dante claimed (for his project demanded it) that he had witnessed, in corporeal form, the results of God's divine historical plan, and had later recorded them as accurately as his memory allowed. Though both Boccaccio and Chaucer certainly recognized that this was a necessary poetic lie, one that enabled Dante to represent what to him was a very great Truth indeed, both poets were fascinated enough by the implications of this claim for naive audiences to toy with them in their own narrative collections.[6]

Boccaccio, like Dante, claims outright that his narrative is true: his *brigata* of storytellers purportedly really existed, having set out together in the year of the plague, 1348, on Tuesday, March 25, after some of them had gathered by chance in a local church.[7] Boccaccio remarks that he has assigned his storytellers fictional names to protect their reputations—a strategy that underscores his interest in promoting the idea that his narrative is the record of an actual event. But he finally undercuts the authority of his collection by noting that he himself was not present on this occasion, having only heard about it from some unnamed "person worthy of credit" (1.16);[8] his narrative is thus mediated by someone else's version of what supposedly went on. At the end of the fourth day, Boccaccio's narrator intrudes to note, among other things, that some of his detractors do not believe he has been recording the truth, complaining that "the things recounted by me [were] otherwise than as I present them to you" (1.287). His comic defense—not really a defense at all— is that if these detractors can "produce the originals" (1.292) to prove that Boccaccio is deviating from a truthful copy of them, then he will confess to the charge of falsification. But until then, he will maintain his original position.

The ironies here fly in all directions, but the gist of Boccaccio's argument suggests a refusal to claim any authority for the *Decameron* at all, even though its narrator strenuously asserts its absolute truth. In the case of Chaucer's *Canterbury Tales,* however, the narrative frame contains claims closer to Dante's than Boccaccio's. Chaucer's narrator says that he was present himself at the pilgrimage and is accurately recording it (as Dante did, retrospectively, from memory).⁹ He also says he will be following the principle that "the word should be cousin to the deed"— a principle Dante too invokes, most clearly in *Inferno* 32.12, where he calls on his Muses to help him "*si che dal fatto il dir non sia diverso*" (so that the telling may not be diverse from the fact).¹⁰ Thus, Chaucer seems to be following Dante's strategies even more closely than Boccaccio did by claiming to offer an eyewitness report and by noting his narrator's confidence in the ability of words to convey the truth of events. Yet as the rest of this chapter will argue, *The Canterbury Tales* is actually constructed to demonstrate the weaknesses inherent in these claims of authority, with Chaucer often undercutting the truth of his work in a typically Boccaccian fashion.

One of the most important similarities between the *Decameron* and *The Canterbury Tales* is that both works are structured to call attention to their essential worldliness and fictionality. If either work is structurally indebted to Dante's *Commedia,* then it has severely restricted its frame of reference to exclude the confident otherworldliness so crucial to Dante's lofty purpose. The *Decameron's* many allusions to the entire *Commedia* notwithstanding, Boccaccio's work ends in a hilltop garden, a secular analogue to the earthly paradise of the *Purgatorio,* beyond which Boccaccio's storytellers cannot go.¹¹ And if *The Canterbury Tales* imitates Dante's pilgrimage in any way, we are provided with a version of it that is much more concerned with what might happen during a literal earthly manifestation than with what such a journey ultimately symbolizes: the pilgrimage of human life. Existing in a secularized *Commedia,* in a sense, Chaucer's pilgrims go from London to Canterbury— not from a state of sin to blessedness—and allegorical suggestions, though occasionally present, are definitely in the background. With an innkeeper as their guide instead of Vergilian reason, and with the final tale urging them to do penance for their sins (perhaps an earthly structural analogue to the *Purgatorio*), Chaucer's pilgrims—and his narrator—move in a very worldly environment, rarely attempting to adopt a transcendent view of what lies beyond their earthly lives. And if a Last Judgment is structurally present in *The Canterbury Tales,* it is there only in a secularized—even poeticized—sense through the storytelling contest, by whose rules the pilgrims' tales will be judged, not their souls.¹²

It is this emphasis on the primacy of fiction that the *Decameron* and *The Canterbury Tales* most decisively share. Both works, though making claims to be recording reality, persistently remind us that the world they are describing is at some remove from the realm of real life and that we must not mistake their fictional constructs for earnest attempts to represent the world as it is. This point is made most emphatically, of course, by having the storytellers' narrative fictions occupy center stage, with each fiction clearly encapsulated, attached to a speaker, and generated according to rules agreed upon in advance. In the case of Boccaccio's collection, the frame itself conveys this idea well, for the storytellers actually separate themselves from the real world of plague-torn society, retreating to a highly literary pastoral environment, a nonmimetic space, where their fiction-making occupies the better part of each day. Writing about a "world of words," as Guido Almansi has described it, Boccaccio has taken pains to structure his collection so that readers are aware of its highly mediated quality: each narrative is told within a narrated frame, so that whatever "reality" one might be tempted to discover in the tales is "at two removes from the lived universe."[13] (It is actually at three removes, since Boccaccio says that he received the whole *Decameron* through a report from someone else.) Moreover, in some of the individual tales themselves, Boccaccio thematizes his interest in the discontinuity between fiction and reality by telling of situations involving the clever fictionalization of the "objective" world by illusionists such as Ser Cepparello (Day 1.1) and Fra Cipolla (Day 6.10), to name only two of Boccaccio's consummate artist figures.[14]

The Canterbury Tales also shows "reality" doubly mediated, with the narrator-recorder standing between us and the pilgrims, who themselves stand between "reality" and the representation of it in their tales. The game aspects of Chaucer's collection (which it shares with Boccaccio's) further locates the work in a counterfeit world set apart from the real one by the rules of the storytelling contest, the focus on taking turns, and one of the purposes of the storytelling competition—to provide diversion for the pilgrims along the route.[15] Not only does Chaucer, like Boccaccio, call attention to the discontinuity between art and life in the frame of his collection, he also stresses this important concept in many of the tales themselves. Robert W. Hanning, in an excellent survey of this theme in Chaucer's works, rightly notes that "the pilgrims are forced, by their acquiescence in the Host's plan, into the role of artists," each of them ordering narrative material in a distinct way, and many of them disclosing Chaucer's own experimentation with the relationship between life and art through the narrative content of their tales.[16]

Throughout his poetic career, Chaucer was careful never to advance the claim that he was offering any unmediated visions of the world, being clearly hesitant to abandon the predictably subjective and openly untrue realm of the dream vision or of the untrustworthy textual tradition whose inconsistencies he could playfully explore as he did in the *Troilus*. Yet *The Canterbury Tales* presents us with a daring fictional experiment for the Chaucerian narrator: for the first time he is portrayed as writing from life rather than recording his dreams or the content of other people's texts. However, Chaucer preserves his evasive Boccaccian stance toward "reality" even though he attempts to do what Boccaccio did not, that is, to place his narrator in the actual presence of the events to be described. Exactly how Chaucer achieves his characteristic distance from this "reality" at the same time that he claims to be in its very presence is one of the major distinguishing marks of *The Canterbury Tales*.

II

That the narrator of *The Canterbury Tales* conceives of himself more as a scribe than as a shaper in his own right has long been noted; like the narrator of *Troilus and Criseyde*, and the translator-narrator in the prologue to the *Legend of Good Women*, his purpose seems to involve no more than merely reporting what is before him (texts, in the *Troilus* and the *Legend*, life and texts, in *The Canterbury Tales*). At the start of his project, he gives us no characterizing details about himself and mentions no idiosyncratic goals that he hopes to achieve with his reporting (contrast the *Troilus* here). He seems to begin his task with absolutely no preplanned sense of how it should be structured, beyond the notion that a generally chronological approach would effectively preserve the order of the events as they occurred.

In fact, his awkward movement from subject to subject creates the illusion that he is starting his project without the slightest bit of forethought, and that thus it can be trusted as a reliable record of "real" events. About the portraits of the pilgrims, for example, he says that he is placing them where they are only because he has "tyme and space" (35) at that point—not because there is a specific artistic purpose for such a placement (although for Chaucer the artist, of course, the move is strategic). After the portraits are complete, the narrator announces what he will do next—discuss the evening at the Tabard and then return to the pilgrimage itself—but he interrupts his chronological account to insist further on his role as a reporter: any "vileynye" (726) that readers will encounter is not the narrator's own, and although he sees that in some sense he is speaking others' words *in propria persona*—"thogh I speke hir wordes proprely" (729)[17]—he explains that this impersonation must not be misinterpreted. These tales are not his own; he is merely taking his role as objective transcriber very seriously.

> Whoso shal telle a tale after a man,
> He moot reherce as ny as evere he kan
> Everich a word, if it be in his charge,
> Al speke he never so rudeliche and large,
> Or ellis he moot telle his tale untrewe,
> Or feyne thyng, or fynde wordes newe. (731–35)[18]

Then, after noting that Scripture is not "villainous" even though it records Christ's "brode" words and that Plato too supports the project of exact reporting, the narrator apologizes for being artless in the structuring of his work: people are not placed in any "proper" order (that is, any artificial order) such as according to social rank. Rather, the implication is, this text is simply recording the order of appearances exactly as the facts demand. The narrator sees his text as one without artificial order; there has been no tampering with the way in which events actually occurred:

> Also I prey yow to foryeve it me,
> Al have I nat set folk in hir degree
> Heere in this tale, as that they sholde stonde.
> My wit is short, ye may wel understonde. (743–46)

Though the audience might expect (even desire) the kind of artificial artistic structuring that they saw in the opening lines of the poem and would have encountered in other sophisticated examples of courtly or allegorical verse, and though the narrator seems at times to wish that he had the ability to order things more skillfully, it is clear that he thinks of himself primarily as a servant of the truth, not as a purposeful arranger or selector of his material.

The narrator's stance as an artless transcriber is maintained whenever he appears during the dramatic links between the tales, most notably before *The Miller's Tale*, where he regrets having to "reherce" (3170) it at all. Yet in order not to "falsen som of my mateere" (3175), he notes, he will plunge ahead, though not without a warning to his audience. A more thorough exploration of the narrator's belief in his artlessness occurs when he is called upon by the Host to tell his own tale. In contrast to most of the other pilgrims—who are artist figures of great imagination, controllers and shapers of narratives to the extent that each of their tales serves its artist's purposes with astonishing closeness—the narrator offers up a "rym I lerned longe agoon" (709), something that is, he says, the only tale he knows, which underscores his lack of familiarity with (and possible distaste for) openly fictional discourse. Believing that he is merely reciting *The Tale of Sir Thopas*—transcribing it, if you will—the narrator tries to maintain the impression that he has introduced no changes of his own. His narrative is not tailored to suit his new audience (the "listeth, lordes" pose of the minstrel is quite out of place among the present company), and it does not contain much (if any) narratorial commentary that might serve to characterize its teller. Unlike the other performances on the Canterbury pilgrimage, this one seems largely uncontaminated by its performer's social or personal goals; the narrator claims that his tale consists of someone else's words remembered and then retrospectively recorded, making his performance here quite similar, at least in his view, to his function as transcriber of *The Canterbury Tales* themselves.[19]

When the Host interrupts this performance and asks for another tale, the narrator begins *Melibee* with a prologue that again contains information appropriate to the concerns of a transcriber. His greatest worry about *Melibee*'s reception is that his audience will not be familiar with the particular version of it that he is about to recite. Instead of being concerned with the genuinely serious rhetorical problems that he might encounter by rehearsing a long, "murtheless" treatise surely designed to be read silently rather than recited, he is more interested in defending the integrity and authenticity of his chosen version than in considering his audience or in shaping the tale to suit any particular artistic purpose. Noting that the Evangelists gave four different accounts of Christ's crucifixion, he reminds us that even though there exist discrepancies in these accounts (some said more and some said less), all four nonetheless basically agree—and "hir sentence is al sooth" (946). Each version, then, the narrator suggests, is trustworthy in and of itself, there being only negligible differences among the four.

This body of evidence—which moves suspiciously toward a nominalist position on language, one that supports the view that the words are *not* cousins of the deeds—is oddly applied by the narrator to establish a kind of *realist* basis for his *Melibee* project. What this argument should be teaching the narrator (and us) is that no one's recorded version of a historical event is the same as someone else's. Language cannot capture deeds, and all individual writers select and omit details depending on their own purposes and interests. Instead, however, he rather narrowly employs it here to reassure his audience that he is indeed basically a transcriber, not an artist,[20] and that anything not familiar to them in this particular version of the *Melibee* is absolutely not intended to alter in any way the original author's "sentence":

> If that yow thynke I varie as in my speche,
> As thus, though that I telle somwhat moore
> Of proverbes than ye han herd bifoore

> Comprehended in this litel tretys heere,
> To enforce with th'effect of my mateere;
> And though I nat the same wordes seye
> As ye han herd, yet to yow alle I preye
> Blameth me nat; for, as in my sentence,
> Shul ye nowher fynden difference
> Fro the sentence of this tretys lite
> After the which this murye tale I write.   (953–64)

Though the narrator notes that some of his words may differ from those in other versions of *Melibee* with which his audience may be familiar, he nonetheless insists that he has no purpose distinct from that which the original work pursues—and a perusal of Chaucer's main sources for this tale confirms the essential truth of the narrator's point. Both Chaucer and his narrator are acting as transcribers of the textual tradition here, not as independent shapers of it.

Do we have, then, a fictional representative of an objective narrator here, for the first time in Chaucer's works? Are we seeing an example of the artist so refined out of existence that he is faithfully recording others' words and "cheere" for posterity? We might be tempted to adopt this view if it were not for the narrator's scrupulosity about admitting to his own subjectivity at certain crucial points in the *General Prologue* and if we did not detect various subjective judgments that even the narrator does not see.

Before beginning his portraits of the pilgrims, the narrator notes that he will be telling "al the condicioun" (38) of each of them—but he hesitates to advertise any objectivity here, adding "so as it semed me" (39).[21] Yet his commitment to the role of transcriber is visible throughout the portraits, for he often employs a form of indirect discourse, reproducing what seem to be the pilgrims' own words about themselves—the portraits of the Friar, the Monk, and the Parson containing the best examples.[22] And even when he isn't using the pilgrims' actual words, he is certainly relying heavily on information about them that they have presumably provided for him, so that we are faced, not with "truth," but only with each pilgrim's self-projection, a "text" created out of their own selectively constructed autobiographies, perhaps put together with the social project of impressing others, or, more innocently, perhaps merely the result of the inevitable selectivity that characterizes human memory. The narrator, who often talks as if he believes in the truth of their fictions (thinking perhaps that all people are, like himself, scrupulous transcribers), records these "facts" as if they were true, often (but not always) arriving at judgments about the pilgrims that they hold about themselves or calculatedly want him to hold. Thus, Chaucer has in some sense recreated the circumstances of *The House of Fame*: even if a writer is himself a scrupulous recorder, his source material (whether written or spoken) is never to be trusted, making the certain discovery of any ultimate truth about the wellsprings of human behavior an impossible task—*pace* the literary claims of Dante and his visionary predecessors.

The ghostly presence of conventional medieval social stereotypes in the *General Prologue* portraits further serves to erode any confidence we might have in our ability to understand and judge the human characters represented there. As Jill Mann has convincingly argued, Chaucer drew from estates satire in creating some of his portraits, yet he systematically obscured the conventional moral clarity of the satiric material he used.[23] Although many of the portraits' descriptive details may ultimately derive from the writings of the moral reformers of the age, the narrator's final moral assessments of those details often run counter to those of medieval literary tradition or are left entirely unexpressed, creating morally neutral portraits that gain satiric import only if the reader supplies the original stereotypical judgments that Chaucer previously excised.[24] Even those portraits that confirm traditional satiric views are often shown to be inadequate once we meet the pilgrims they are purportedly describing: the "ideal" Parson, for example, turns out to have distinctly unideal prejudices about the value of literature. As Mann shows, the *General Prologue* is an epistemological minefield designed to threaten the security of our assumptions about what constitutes real knowledge.[25] Moreover, the very fact that so many of the portraits contain conventional literary stereotypes strongly suggests that Chaucer wanted us to note that his narrator is relying on literature to provide him with ways to describe life, making his account entirely suspect as a record of any "reality."

The individual consciousness of the narrator, however, as visible in the narrative choices he makes during his presentation, provides the *General Prologue* with its best examples of the subjective or socially determined nature of this ostensibly true record of life. As E. T. Donaldson first noted, the narrator's willingness to draw negative judgments about his fellow pilgrims is very often inversely proportional to their social class or level of traditional authority. The narrator begins his portraits with the Knight, presumably because the Knight represents a high-ranking member of the social order, and the narrator is respectful of him—as he is of the noble Prioress. But with the bourgeoisie and the pilgrims of lower social status, he is less hesitant about expressing a negative opinion.[26] Also at issue is the suggestion that some of the narrator's information about his companions comes not from imagined interviews with them or from any external physical observation but instead from the pilgrims' tales themselves. As a retrospective record of the narrator's experience, the *General Prologue* was supposedly written after the narrator had heard all of the tales, and there are several intriguing examples of what might be termed "seepage" of material from the tales into the narrator's seemingly objective view of the pilgrims.

Some of this seepage should perhaps be attributed to the narrator's personal opinions about the tales he had heard. He describes the Miller, for example, as a "janglere and a goliardeys, / And that was moost of synne and harlotries" (559–60)—but might not this assessment of the Miller's nature be derived primarily from a superficial judgment of the Miller's tale? Is the narrator's speculation about the Franklin, "Wo was his cook but if his sauce were / Poynaunt and sharp" (351–52), perhaps to be viewed as a recollection of one of the Franklin's alter-egos from his tale, the magician, who speaks sharply to his squire about the dinner preparations (1209–16)? Could some of the details from the Friar's and Summoner's portraits have come from the tales each tells about the other?[27] Is the Clerk's speech called "sownynge in moral vertu" (307) because the narrator remembers the Clerk's narrative about the Christian virtue of patience in adversity? The number of the Wife of Bath's husbands quite clearly comes from her own prologue, as perhaps does the narrator's information about her knowing "remedies of love" and the "olde daunce" (475–76). Certainly, too, some of what the narrator says about the Pardoner finds its source in the Pardoner's claims in his prologue, that he makes more money than the local parsons by duping ignorant congregations.[28] And to return to Chaucer's heavy reliance on the literature of social complaint for the construction of his portraits, is it not possible that he wanted his audience to recognize that the narrator has been deeply influenced in general by the stereotypes conveniently available in other works of art?[29]

The more one probes into the origins of the ostensible "facts" of the *General Prologue*, the more one discovers the profoundly textual nature, and thus the questionable truth-value, of the information the narrator provides about "life." Chaucer's point here is that even in the text of the most artless recorder, one with no conscious purpose whatsoever beyond that of accurately describing what is before him, all sorts of hidden acts of interpretation are carried out, not to mention the inevitable decisions that are made concerning what to report and what to omit in order to keep the record a reasonable length. No human recorders of the "truth" are to be trusted at their word; and Chaucer's self-styled objective narrator, who ends up not being objective at all, is a major piece of evidence for this proposition in *The Canterbury Tales*.[30]

Further evidence of the fictionalization of "truth" arises once we recognize the very dubious role of chance in the action of the *General Prologue*, for what the narrator often defines as accidental is interpretable as the result of art instead. To be sure, the narrator remarks that these particular pilgrims gathered together in fellowship "by aventure" (25), making the raw material of the narrator's project a result of unplanned accident. Moreover, even though there is a general tendency for the narrator to group together pilgrims who are, in fact, traveling as a unit, therefore showing him to be working with the general principle of following life rather than art as he records,[31] astute readers have noted that his failure to order the portraits strictly in a conventional artistic array (that is, by social degree or estate) does not mean that the *General Prologue* is free from the constraints of formal order altogether, even in the world of its fiction—for Harry Bailly very quickly assumes the role of "artist" of the pilgrimage when he organizes the contest and then chooses the Knight to draw lots first. (Social order is clearly honored here, and identified as a major force in the shaping of human art.)

And when, "by aventure, or sort, or cas" (844), as the all-too-trusting narrator says, the Knight lands first place again, we have the strong sense that Harry Bailly has become another Pandarus. While disguised as Fortune, he has manipulated the characters of his own little fiction into serving his personal, socially decorous, artistic ends. Because he wants the Knight to go first, he arranges for it to "happen."[32] This kind of studied interplay between chance and the artist's controlling hand is profoundly Boccaccian, appearing throughout the *Decameron*, where nature in the frame always looks oddly like art, and where artist figures exploit chance (or create it) to serve their own purposes.[33]

On a larger scale it is the same kind of interplay that allows Chaucer to sustain (however briefly) the illusion that his artful placement of *The Miller's Tale* next to *The Knight's Tale* was merely the result of life's chaotic disorder, or that the carefully considered choice of *The Parson's Tale* as the concluding narrative of *The Canterbury Tales* was attributable only to chance.[34] But "life" in *The Canterbury Tales* is always mediated by art—and Chaucer, like Boccaccio, never once wants us to mistake the one for the other, in spite of his narrators' beliefs to the contrary. Both writers call attention to the fictionalization of their recorded "truths," and both thus create illusions that contrast strongly with those of Dante.

III

The Host, Harry Bailly, very quickly establishes himself not only as the primary artist figure of *The Canterbury Tales* but also as its chief fictional audience, in a sense the patron, of the artists whose tales he commissions and judges. By arranging the storytelling contest and providing the pilgrims with some general narrative requirements to follow if they want their tales to compete favorably for the prize of a supper, Harry Bailly becomes not only the chief artistic director of the pilgrimage but also the creator of the standards by which the pilgrims' tales will ultimately be judged. As Alan Gaylord has noted, Harry's principle that the tales should have "sentence" and "solaas," which coincides with classical and medieval ideals, quickly proves to be applied in an erratic fashion, for Harry sees the two concepts as somehow incompatible, impossible to achieve in a single performance—and he defines these critical terms rather idiosyncratically in his actual responses to the tales.[35]

Walter Scheps adds that Harry also seems to call for stories set in a "whilom" sort of long-ago past, approving especially of those tales (mainly the Nun's Priest's) that project images of the kind of masculinity Harry himself tries to embody.[36] Cynthia Richardson and L. M. Leitch show that once the competition gets going, Harry frequently urges his flock of tellers to be brief, to "werken thriftily" (1.3131) as they tell their tales, and Leitch argues further that Harry in fact seems to prefer "solaas" in his art, even though he initially called for "sentence" as well.[37] These arguments have contributed much to our understanding of the dynamics of storytelling in *The Canterbury Tales* and perhaps in Chaucer's actual career as well, for they define (in Harry's negative example) some of the restrictions imposed on narrative artists by the tastes of powerful and unlearned audiences, those for whom an artist must write and those by whom his works will be judged.

In many respects, in his role as audience and commissioner of poetry and in the particular standards he adopts in determining a work's merit, Harry Bailly raises once again some of the same artistic issues that are present in Chaucer's earlier works. Like him, for example, the God of Love in *The Legend of Good Women* had asked Chaucer to be brief in telling the stories of faithful classical lovers: "For whoso shal so many a storye telle / Sey shortly, or he shal to longe dwelle" (F 576–77). Also like Harry, the fictional (and perhaps actual) audiences of *The Book of the Duchess, Troilus and Criseyde,* and *The Legend of Good Women* desire stories that promote a particular, well-defined ideology. In

Harry's case, he likes stories and narrators that reflect male virility and machismo; in the *Troilus* and the *Legend,* the audience wanted to see erotic love uncomplicatedly supported; and, if *The Book of the Duchess* is indeed a commissioned poem, its listeners expected Blanche to be artfully—yet "truthfully"—praised. Harry Bailly, then, takes his place at the end of a series of Chaucerian portrayals of the artist's demanding audience, those who want their own desires or prejudices confirmed—not questioned or undermined—in art.

Also, like some of Chaucer's previous audience figures (the implied audience of *The Book of the Duchess,* for example, and the God of Love in the *Legend*), Harry Bailly has certain expectations about art's relationship to life, believing that the two are uncomplicatedly and closely (often too closely) allied. As Alan Gaylord has suggested, Harry tends to apply the pilgrims' fictions rather narrowly to actual life, most notably to his own.[38] The tales are especially appealing to him if they remind him of his wife (as we see in his response to *The Clerk's Tale, The Merchant's Tale,* and *Melibee*) or can be viewed as the source of good business sense for innkeepers (as in his moralization of *The Shipman's Tale*). Nearly every tale is some kind of exemplum to Harry Bailly—art to him is a close representation of life that exists primarily to recall (and perhaps directly affect) the reader's own life; it is a mirror with a motto, if you will. Indeed, one of the tales that does not fit these specific requirements, at least in Harry Bailly's reading of it, he openly criticizes: he says that he dislikes *The Monk's Tale* because it fails to provide its audience with a practical "remedie" (7.2784–85) for Fortune's havoc. And when the Canon's Yeoman arrives on the scene, as soon as Harry discovers that this newcomer might have some practical (even potentially profitable) knowledge to convey, he forgets his original request for a "myrie" tale (8.597–98) and asks instead to hear straight information: "Syn of the konnyng of thy lord thow woost / Telle how he dooth, I pray thee hertely" (8.653–54). In this case, Harry betrays his real priorities: he'd much rather hear some immediately useful news than listen to a merry tale—and art loses out to potentially profitable gossip.

Chaucer further knows that those same audiences who want art both to mirror their own beliefs and to provide them with some useful *matere* also want stories to be demonstrably true, to reflect events or characters that really existed. *The Book of the Duchess,* for instance, was surely expected to give its audience a picture of the Blanche they actually knew; and the God of Love in *The Legend of Good Women* is angry at "Chaucer" partly because he thinks that the *Troilus* paints an inaccurate picture of real-life classical lovers. In the latter work, this charge results in the narrator's very funny insistence that his lying legends are "storyal sooth"—not "fable" (702), and he hopes that his truth-claim will be sufficient to allay the ire of his literal-minded reader.[39]

Again, Harry Bailly has features in common with these earlier Chaucerian fictional audiences, as well as with what we know of Chaucer's actual audience (who wanted history and *exempla* together), for one of his requirements for the Canterbury storytellers is that they narrate "true tales," of "aventures that whilom han bifalle" (795), to use his own words. Thus, in addition to wanting his stories to have a lesson or a punch line ("sentence" or "solaas"), he also wants them to be drawn directly from life, making for a set of requirements quite difficult for a storyteller to meet. Real life is seldom organized into preformed storylike units that artfully and pleasantly yield up their "sentence" and "solaas," and though memory herself is an artist of sorts since she inevitably shapes our vision of the past, the artistry of memory is usually insufficient to please an audience. Watching the pilgrims strain to meet Harry's real-life requirement, then, is in itself a marvelously rich illustration of the nature of poetic lying, for most of the pilgrims—with a few exceptions—either assert or imply that their stories, even the least credible ones, actually occurred.

By making Harry Bailly the primary audience figure of *The Canterbury Tales,* and by assigning to him the specific tastes we have just described, Chaucer is able to introduce and sustain a complex series of meditations on the conflicts between art and life, for as the pilgrims advance their truth-claims to meet Harry's requirements, we are asked to measure these claims against the various kinds of distortion (both obvious and subtle) that the pilgrims engage in as they offer up their tales. In the pilgrims, then, we have a group of recorders who are not asked to create their own fictions (in which case distortion, personal bias, and subjectivity would not be crucial issues), but who are assigned the job of narrating something true, however mediated it will have to be by the version or versions that lie between their immediate sources and the events themselves. In this respect, we have a fictional situation very much like the one we saw in the *Troilus,* where the narrator takes on the responsibility of transcribing another's "true" text. By the time he has finished his task, however, his transcription, like those of the Canterbury pilgrims, distinctly shows the marks of motivated tampering, especially in those sections where the "truth" conflicts with the narrator's own personal goals. In *The Canterbury Tales* this process, repeated each time a pilgrim claims that an obviously manipulated narrative is true (either to life or to someone else's text), is worked out in all its instructive permutations, each of them constituting yet more evidence for Chaucer's lack of faith in the ultimate moral or historical utility of human discourse.

IV

The first fragment of *The Canterbury Tales* raises the issue of narrative truth in some conspicuous ways.[40] The Knight, who begins the storytelling, chooses a tale distinctly historical in its subject matter (actually, of course, Chaucer is working closely with Boccaccio's *Teseida*). Though the Knight does not overtly claim that the events of his story really happened (as many of the other pilgrims do), he definitely implies throughout his narration that his Theban characters were actual people and that his source is a long and intricately detailed historical text. Because of the sheer amount of information in the source he is trying to transmit, the Knight struggles to shorten his *matere,* knowing that he cannot possibly report everything his *auctor* tells about these peoples' lives, for it would simply take too long.

Hence, he relies heavily on *occupatio*—a device very useful to a recorder who has time limitations to observe. On occasion, his awkward digressions show him to be somewhat frustrated by the need to edit his material on the spot, as when he begins at one point to elaborate on a subplot before cutting it short with "But of that storie list me nat to write" (1201). Also, he frequently lets us know that there is a lot of detail in his source he wishes he had time to rehearse, "But it were al to longe for to devyse" (994). In one instance, he openly admits he has forgotten to add some detail bearing on Theseus's decorative lists, a remark that suggests he is sincerely attempting to reproduce his source as accurately as time and memory will allow: "But yet hadde I foryeten to devyse / The noble kervyng" (1914–15). And when he realizes the length of his descriptive passages, he notes that his memory contains even more information that he'll have to abridge: "Ther saugh I many another wonder storie, / The whiche me list nat drawen to memorie" (2073–74). Indeed, his long catalogues near the end of the tale (2920–66) demonstrate that the Knight's memory is truly capacious and that it is a matter of principle to him to relate as much of what it holds as possible, even though the result may be passages that seem awkwardly intrusive. Yet in many of his self-conscious asides, he himself notices what Charles Muscatine says of this tale, that "a great deal of [its] descriptive material has a richness of detail far in excess of the demands of the story."[41]

What we encounter in the Knight, then, is a narrator whose legitimation devices point toward the illusion of narrative truth in his discourse, suggesting that he is trying as hard as he can to "tell it all," exactly as his historical source served it up. But even this transcriber, who is represented as being generally reliable, cannot or will not reproduce his source exactly; Harry Bailly has asked for "sentence" or "solaas" in addition to "history," and the Knight is aware that if he gives his audience an unabbreviated version of his "truthful" source it would bore them. So, in an attempt to keep his narrative artful enough to hold his listeners' attention, he opts for the principle of selectivity, which results in a "history" that is highly ordered, indeed, pervasively artificial in its narrative symmetries and in its balance.[42] In this case, then, history is openly sacrificed at the altar of art, and the Knight, in a narrative power play that places him in an exalted position, has very nearly adopted the godlike role of Supreme Artificer that his pagan characters so desperately seem to seek. Yet the personal reliability of the Knight is never in question, since he is candid about admitting why and exactly where his selectivity is at work. Like Theseus, the artist figure in his tale, who is his narrative double, the Knight has striven for order in his realm, and he has found it by a tyrannical shaping of the [implied] chaos of his source text.

In the Miller's performance, we also have truth-claims in conflict with artistic purposes, but the Miller is less open than the Knight about calling attention to his manipulation of his *matere*. Though he makes no overt claim to be telling the truth in his tale, the Miller nonetheless addresses the inherent conflict between history and narrative pleasure or instruction by coopting for his story a generic label that implicitly grants him the freedom to ignore the conflict altogether. In calling his tale a "legende and a lyf" (3141), the Miller argues that it is generically related to saints' lives, moral biographies that are "true," but only in a general sense, for they depend on selectivity and distortion for their classic shape. The veracity of hagiographic narrative is of a special kind, for in serving the didactic interests of higher Christian truth, hagiographers violate the plainer truth of biographical record. They are thus artists whose ideology requires that they be unfaithful recorders, for they draw only on those events from an individual's life that contribute to a Christian message.[43]

The Miller, of course, has none of the religious purposes sanctioned by the dominant ideology of high Christian culture; his narrative is chosen and shaped solely in order to serve his socially motivated interest in "quiting" *The Knight's Tale*. His appropriation of the genre of hagiography, however, allows him to meet Harry's requirement for truth and at the same time carry on with his class-based narrative vendetta against the Knight. Indeed, the skill with which he pursues this artistic goal is visible in the tale's plot, characterizations, and setting, all of which prove the Miller to be a talented manipulator of narrative material. But unlike the Knight, he is obviously not interested in recording anything accurately; we never know where he is altering his inherited story (if it is inherited at all), for we have no self-conscious narrative voice to call attention to possible additions or deletions. The narrator duly notes the Miller's unreliability as a conveyor of the truth, warning us before the Miller's performance begins that if we want "storial thyng" (3174), we should find another tale. Thus, in contrast to the Knight, we have in the Miller a more covert narrator—and one who offers a tale more tightly in his own control.

But the Reeve, who clearly thinks—even before the Miller, Robyn, begins—that he intends to defame a real person in his tale (probably the Reeve himself), chides the Miller for preparing to tell a narrative he fears will be too close to life. And, still with reality on his mind, he follows the Miller's tale with a story that he strenuously insists is absolutely true: "this is verray sooth that I yow telle" (3924). Yet the Reeve has so effectively manipulated his *matere* into serving as a weapon of revenge on the Miller that there is scarcely a line in it that has not been shown to reflect either the Reeve's own personal assessment of Robyn or his own barely concealed regret that his verbal action against the Miller and his female family members cannot be more physical than it is. Here, in a perversely interesting way, even his claim to be telling the truth itself works to support the Reeve's personal artistic purposes, for the more he can prove that Robyn is actually like the miller he portrays (or even perhaps that they are one and the same person), the more quickly he will be able to persuade the other pilgrims to accept a negative view of their fellow pilgrim. Ironically, then, his claim of truthfulness is employed mainly to lend support to the Reeve's uncharitable artistic intent.

Truth and fiction come into play once more at the beginning of the Cook's performance. Openly declaring that his tale is true—it is a "litel jape that fil in oure citee" (4343)—Roger the Cook looks as if he is about to continue the Reeve's method of using art (but calling it truth) to slander someone. Harry Bailly, surely worried that the upcoming story will feature him, coyly lets Roger know that the game of personal attack is one that he too can play, and he gives the Cook a sample of what might be said, if this game were to continue, about Roger's less than conscientious food preparation.

But Harry implies that he is only kidding—"be nat wroth for game" (4354) he tells Roger—for Harry, now that his own character is in line for some personal abuse, suddenly realizes that he would much prefer a work of fiction from the Cook than any tale that approaches the reality of which he himself is a part. He thus commissions a different kind of truth from the Cook, not the kind that reflects what actually befell (his earlier requirement), but rather the kind of generalized truth that only fiction is able to propound: "A man may seye ful sooth in game and play" (4355).[44] Personal involvement, then, has influenced Harry enough so that he actually changes the original rules of the storytelling contest in order to prevent any damage being done to his professional image; he now selfishly prefers fiction to anything that might resemble fact. The Cook, who gets the point, does not tell his tale about a "hostileer" (4360)—although he claims he will do it later to "quit" Harry—and he quotes a proverb that bears very directly on the nature of art and reality. "Sooth play, quaad play" (4357), he says, "a true jest is a bad jest." That is, Roger knows quite well that the best jokes are not those that record what really happened (Dame Kind is rarely a good creator of funny stories) but those that have been shaped by the controlling hand of the artist.

In the opening fragment of *The Canterbury Tales*, then, we have a rough progression in narrative methodology that supplements the other progressions critics have commonly noted in the first four tales of the collection. If the Knight tries (but fails) to record faithfully as much as possible from his narrative source, the Miller, Reeve, and Cook "quite" him by demonstrating a greater degree of individual control over their tales and less interest in fidelity to their inherited stories (although in the Cook's fragment we cannot be sure, since the narrative is cut short). Even though their claims of truthfulness are stated more vociferously than the Knight's, these pilgrims actually demonstrate—and to some extent celebrate—the artist's ability to lie, to transform others' raw material into a vehicle for personal or social artistic goals. And those goals—especially in the case of the three fabliau tellers—definitely do not result in what one would want to judge as an accurate portrayal of "reality"; rather, what we see are only intensely personal versions of it, sponsored by individual (and sometimes inexplicable) biases. As a comment on the textual tradition, then, the first fragment of Chaucer's poem discloses its author's profound distrust of textual claims to truth.

V

Other tales in Chaucer's collection further elaborate, although in very different ways, on the untrustworthy testimony of the Canterbury recorders. *The Friar's Tale* and *The Summoner's Tale* operate much like the early fabliaux, for example, by employing dueling narrators who try to convince their audience that their real-life opponent is the main character in their tales, and both employ their fictions (strongly implied to be true) as rhetorical weapons in a personal and occupational war.[45] The canny Nun's Priest, who satirizes authorial truth-claims in general as well as the naiveté of those who believe them, presents his fable as part of the ancient history of wildlife, set in the long ago past when "Beestes and briddes koude speke and synge" (2881). His tale, he ironically asserts, is "also trewe . . . / As is the book of Lancelot de Lake" (3211–12). The Clerk, though he makes no overt claim for the veracity of his material, definitely places his fiction in the real world of historical time, both by identifying Walter as a former marquis of a specific, real Italian locale and by complaining that women "now-a-dayes" (1164) simply cannot match the deceased Griselda in virtue: "Grisilde is deed, and eek hire pacience, / And both atones buryed in Ytaille" (1177–78). The Man of Law and the Physician, however, attempt—in a much more elaborate fashion—to impress their listeners with the historical reliability of their stories, and it is in these two tales that we find some of Chaucer's most interesting analyses of the limits of narrative truth.

With the Man of Law, we encounter a narrator whose authenticating devices are more subtle than those of the fabliau-tellers before him, but no different in the effect they are meant to produce: he wants his audience to believe that his tale is unimpeachable as a record of history. Indeed, he himself seems to believe naively that the narrative he learned from the traveling merchants is truthful in every respect. In his prologue, we learn that the Man of Law admires merchants both for their prudence in attaining wealth and for their being good suppliers of "tydings and tales" (123–30). By the second line of his narrative, his admiration for merchants shows itself to be nothing less than idolatry, for he actually asserts that the "chapmen" in his tale were rich and *therefore* absolutely trustworthy—"thereto sadde and trewe" (135), in his words. Already, then, we have a narrator who sees truth in his source simply because he likes the kind of people who have transmitted it. A few stanzas later, his credulity is further demonstrated when he claims that the spreading rumor about Custance's virtue and beauty contained nothing but the facts: "al this voys was sooth, as God is trewe" (169). One certainly wonders how the Man of Law, removed from the events by some thousand years and acquainted with this obviously hagiographic story only through a version of it passed on through merchants' gossip, could possibly make a sound judgment about Custance—but he nonetheless thinks he is able to do so, blindly trusting that the report about her is an accurate one.[46]

Ironically, situations involving reporting weave throughout the Man of Law's tale, and most of them prove that one cannot trust even the simplest of messages to be carried ungarbled from one person to another. The very merchants whom the Man of Law has such faith in at the tale's beginning, for example, go to Rome on business precisely because, it is suggested, they know enough not to entrust their business to messengers:

> Now fil it that the maistres of that sort
> Han shapen hem to Rome for to wende;
> Were it for chapmanhod or for disport,
> Noon oother message wolde they thider sende,
> But comen hemself to Rome; this is the ende.   (141–45)

Moreover, the plot of the Man of Law's tale is heavily dependent on false reporting of one sort or another, and on situations that show how difficult it can be to ascertain the truth. Custance is accused of murdering Hermengyld—a "wrong suspecioun" (681) whose falsity only God, through a miracle, is able to prove; the truthful message sent to Alla announcing the birth of his healthy son is intercepted and falsified by Donegild to say that the child is a "feendly creature" and his mother an "elf"; Alla's charitable answer to this lying report is also rewritten so that it orders Custance and the child to be sent into exile; and the people in general who come in contact with the secretive Custance have a very difficult time figuring out who she is and why she is floating about on the sea.

Even people who are as close to an event as it is possible to get end up construing it erroneously, as when Alla, late in the tale, notes that perhaps he may be confused in thinking that the child Mauricius might be his lost son:

> "Parfay," thoghte he, "fantome is in myn heed.
> I oghte deme, of skilful juggement,
> That in the salte see my wyf is deed."   (1037–39)

But the truth is often quite other than our rational faculties predict, and the Man of Law's inherited narrative repeatedly underscores the fact that humans tend to interpret things wrongly just as often as they stumble upon the truth.

Ironically, at the end of his tale, the Man of Law himself suggests that there exist alternative versions of the conclusion to his story, noting that exactly how Custance arranged to see her father again is not agreed upon by all redactors:

> Som men wolde seyn how that the child Maurice
> Dooth this message unto this Emperour;
> But, as I gesse, Alla was not so nyce
> To hym that was of so sovereyn honour
> As he that is of Cristen folk the flour,
> Sente any child, but it is bet to deeme
> He wente hymself, and so it may wel seeme.   (1086–92)

This stanza (again, by the way, raising doubts about the ability of messengers and go-betweens to carry out their roles properly) very clearly shows how individual transcribers end up falsifying their *matere*. The Man of Law willfully rejects those versions of the story that do not accord with his own sense of social decorum—his sense that Alla would surely have behaved honorably when dealing with a man as important as the Emperor. For this reason, says the Man of Law, "it is bet to deeme" that Alla observed social proprieties by going in person to arrange the meeting. Yet in saying this, the Man of Law is unreflectively assuming that the truth is whatever conforms to his own ideologically satisfying code of manners. Thus, whatever authority the Man of Law was originally able to project is here called into question, and if we were inclined at first to believe in his reliability as a transcriber of the merchant's reports, we are now suitably warned to think twice before trusting him.[47]

In *The Physician's Tale*, we encounter another extreme example of a narrator's falsification of his *matere*. Opening his narrative by identifying its source in Livy, the Physician thus implies that his story will recount an episode of Roman history. Later, when he introduces the evil judge Appius, he strengthens his claim to be telling the truth by reminding his audience of the story's historicity:

> This false juge, that highte Apius—
> So was his name, for this is no fable,
> But knowen for historial thyng notable;
> The sentence of it sooth is out of doute—   (154–57)

In spite of these assertions, however, it quickly becomes clear that the Physician has tampered with his classical source, for his idiosyncratic version of the story of Virginius and his daughter imposes, often very awkwardly, a variety of Christian concepts on its pagan material. Before her father puts her to death, for example, Virginia asks him to let her lament in the manner of Jephthah's daughter (how could a character from Livy's history have read the Old Testament?), and the Physician himself derives a Christian message about sin—"Forsaketh synne er synne yow forsake" (286)—from this classical story, whose original purpose was to document the political corruption of the Roman patriciate, represented by Appius in his capacity as a judge.[48]

The Physician has performed other Christianizing tricks on his source as well. Excising from it all signs of its original political and historical content, he downplays Appius's role and elevates Virginia's, turning his narrative into a Christian story that generically resembles the Man of Law's in its hagiographical and romantic aspects and in its elevation of a woman of beauty and virtue into something like a Christian martyr.[49] (In fact, the Physician may be attempting to compete with the Man of Law in this respect, especially given the traditional medieval rivalry between the two professions.)[50] Yet in making Virginia the focus of the tale, with a detailed characterization of her beauty and virtue consuming a large portion of this brief narrative, the Physician inadvertently confuses the story by making her father's murder of her seem even more inexplicably evil than it is in the original sources. In fact, the new emphasis of the story as it is told in *The Physician's Tale* is on the subject of innocence betrayed, not only by Appius and his co-conspirators but by Virginius as well. The Physician himself seems to think that this sort of treason is the worst kind of sin, saying:

> Of alle tresons sovereyn pestilence
> Is whan a wight bitrayseth innocence.   (91–92)

And he spends an inordinate amount of time warning parents and guardians of innocent children not to assent to their involvement in vice. But Virginius, the father of the pious Virginia, obviously takes this principle to an extreme when he decides that his daughter deserves death rather than the shame that would accompany her if she submitted to Appius's will. Far from preserving Livy's purposes, the Physician's story is definitely marked by the manipulations of a narrator with his own, perhaps somewhat confused, goals.

The contents of *The Physician's Tale* may, in fact, be a suggestive comment on the Physician's betrayal of Livy even as he claims to be keeping Livy's history inviolate, for the story contains several allusions to "counterfeiting," "betrayal," and "false witnessing." At the opening of the narrative, the Physician introduces the personified Nature, imagining

her taking pride in having created the fair and virtuous Virginia. Nature
notes that her creative abilities far exceed those of human artists, who
consistently fail to imitate her exactly:

> "Who kan me countrefete?
> Pigmalion noght, though he ay forge and bete,
> Or grave or peynte, for I dar wel seyn
> Apelles, Zanzis, sholde werche in veyn
> Outher to grave or peynte or forge or bete,
> If they presumed me to countrefete."   (13–18)

With this boast, Nature rightly suggests that no one can record, transcribe, or in any way embody an exact replica of life and human history.
Human artists will always fall short in their attempts to reproduce her
creations, for she alone has the skill to fashion the natural world in all
its variety and richness. Yet she herself is really not an "artist" here; God
is the "formere principal" (19), and he has merely made her his deputy,
instructing her to carry out his will and give form to his purposes. Having no purposes of her own, she is in charge of seeing to it that God's
will is done; as she herself notes, "My lord and I been ful of oon accord"
(25).

When we compare Nature's role as an accurate transcriber of God's
purposes to the role of human artists attempting to transcribe history,
we can see that even Livy is being called into question as a successful
counterfeiter of earthly events. And the Physician by adding to Livy his
own purposes and special interests, locates himself even farther from
whatever truth lay behind Livy's account of the putatively historical
events involving Appius, Virginia, and Virginius. Thus, we simply cannot believe him when he confidently claims that his narrative is "historial
thyng" (155), whose "sentence . . . sooth is out of doute" (157), for his
betrayal of history is clearly visible—and in many ways comparable to
the betrayal of Virginia herself by Appius and her father.

In *The Legend of Good Women* and *The House of Fame*, Chaucer employed, in the voice of his female characters, the language of male betrayal and lust to signify the artist's manipulation of narrative sources to
serve his own selfish artistic goals.[51] Virginia in *The Physician's Tale*,
who shares some of the traits of the classical women in Chaucer's earlier
works, may be functioning (as they are) as a symbol of the victimized
source, the innocent pagan individual whose life story is altered or selectively mined by later writers for details conforming to some new purpose. In a section of this tale original to Chaucer, Virginia's father is
characterized as troubled by his decision to kill her, even though he
would "from his purpos nat converte" (212). Yet his sacrifice of his

daughter to avoid the shame she might incur makes him a poor steward indeed of this young woman who "needed no maistresse" (106). Moreover, Virginia herself is falsely provided with action and speech that show her to be in agreement with her father's cold ultimatum, a position that none of Chaucer's sources even implies:

> "Blissed be God that I shal dye a mayde.
> Yif me my deeth er that I have a shame.
> Dooth with youre childe youre wyl, a Goddes name!"
>
> (248–49)

Although Virginia is not actually said to be a martyr here, her proto-Christian rhetorical stance makes her eerily resemble the victimized women in Chaucer's *Legend,* whose biographies are rewritten to fulfill the requirements of the God of Love. Virginia is thus thrice a victim of false witnessing, first by Claudius's testimony in the courtroom, second by her father's decision to create an unnecessary ultimatum, and finally by the manipulations of the Physician who tells her story.

One of the ways in which Chaucer undermines the truth-claims of the Man of Law and the Physician is to give them putatively historical narratives that are set in the distant past and survive in more than one version. In having these narrators piece together their own accounts of "historical" events, Chaucer is able to demonstrate the principles of selectivity and distortion that inevitably come into play when a narrative report passes through the hands of several redactors, none of whom was present as an actual witness to the events in question, and each of whom has his own idiosyncratic views to promote through his tale. But Chaucer sets for himself a much different task when he includes among the pilgrims a group of autobiographers, tellers who recount the events of history as eyewitnesses and participants. These pilgrims—the Wife of Bath, the Pardoner, and the Canon's Yeoman—might seem to offer hope for the reader desiring to escape the lies and uncertainties of the textual tradition, for through them we are provided with the illusion of immediacy, of being only at one remove from life itself. But with these three recorders of life, Chaucer experiments even further, this time examining the unavoidable creativity and revisionistic shaping that structures the raw material of autobiographical record.

In their prologues, the Wife of Bath and the Pardoner supply highly self-conscious versions of their lives designed primarily to appeal in specific ways to the audience they address. This allows Chaucer to explore the social effect of audience awareness on a narrator's representation of personal history. With the Canon's Yeoman, who has had no time to shape his material to suit the unanalyzed audience that suddenly mate-

rializes before him, we witness a confession less constrained by its narrator's desire to produce certain preplanned effects. Yet for a variety of
reasons, which I will discuss below, we get no closer to the "real life" of
the Canon's Yeoman than we do to the lives of the others, whose candor
is certainly less manifest than his. With these three autobiographers
(and, to a lesser extent, with the Merchant), Chaucer strengthens and
deepens his case for the elusiveness of true "auctoritee" by representing
his personal historians as either narrative strategists of the highest order
who employ the techniques of the artist to aid them in creating socially
and personally satisfying self-portraits or—like the Canon's Yeoman—
as sincere but unskillful communicators whose attempts to record the
events of life fail in complex ways.[52]

VI

It has become something of a truism among modern critics that the
Wife of Bath's performance demonstrates the close relationship between
narrative and personal desire. As many have noticed, the Wife's prologue
at times seems to represent a life narrative that has been fictionalized by
certain strong yearnings for the power and happiness denied medieval
women in actual life, while her tale continues to express the same desires
by promoting them in a thinly disguised but more succinct version of the
issues raised in the "life" of the prologue. If her prologue is "fictionalized autobiography," then her tale is "autobiographical fiction," as Robert Burlin has noted,[53] and the lines between normally distinct kinds of
narration—factual and fictional—become intriguingly blurred in the
pairing of her prologue and tale.

Indeed, Chaucer's text encourages us to ponder these complexities by
having the Wife repeatedly call her autobiographical narrative a "tale"
(169, 172, 193, 586) and by having her actually intrude into the world
of her fiction, becoming absorbed in the issues raised by its plot; though
she usually talks about women in the third person ("their") in her tale,
she suddenly begins to include herself among the narrative's women, in
the passage starting, "somme seyde that oure hertes been moost
esed . . ." (929–60). These moments, coupled with others such as the
Wife's construction of the "happy ending" of her last marriage,

> After that day we hadden never debaat.
> God helpe me so, I was to hym as kynde
> As any wyf from Denmark unto Ynde,
> And also trewe, and so was he to me   (822–25),[54]

and the strongly personal dimensions of her story, persuasively suggest that the Wife's prologue and tale are not to be separated into factual or fictional categories, since both have been fashioned by this skillful cloth-maker from identical thread.

Unfortunately for the Wife of Bath, however, many critics who have noticed the fictionalization of her autobiography and the autobiographicizing of her fiction have used their observations as evidence against her, arguing that she is represented as being unaware of the commerce between fact and fiction in her prologue and tale. They argue that the real truth of her life has escaped her, and that although she often presents us with a record of the "truth," she herself cannot skillfully read it, misconstruing it as extensively and as often as she misconstrues Scripture. Her tale too has been seen as continuing this pattern. The Wife's personal desires and aversions are seen as being mirrored in the tale, which derives largely from hidden psychological elements that control her narrative's content and form.[55]

Although this kind of explanation may be encouraged by many Chaucerian texts (even at certain points in the Wife's own narration), Chaucer often portrays the Wife as knowing more about how to exploit the uncertain boundary between truth and fiction than she is usually credited with. Perhaps more than any other pilgrim in *The Canterbury Tales,* she raises the issue that "truth" is positional, that all narratives, whether drawn from life or openly regarded as fictional, are purposeful rhetorical acts created to advance the ideological positions of their speakers. And she realizes this, of course, primarily because she herself has been a victim of such posturing from the antifeminist tradition advanced by Jankyn's clerks.

To be sure, the Wife makes truth-claims of her own in her prologue, both implicitly and explicitly. The opening lines of her prologue, for example, imply that her story, because it is drawn from "experience," should be received as the truth about her life. And later, as the Wife begins her narration about her five marriages, she directly claims her report is true: "I shal seye sooth" (195).

But both of these claims are negated by their contexts and are overwhelmingly contradicted by other evidence in the Wife's prologue that shows her to be well aware of her own fictionalization, or at the very least, her own rhetorical shaping—indeed, textualization—of the life-record she provides.[56] First of all, the Wife sees her own experience as containing raw material for an exemplary narrative, one that proves a point—the "wo that is in mariage" (3)—announced unambiguously before she begins. In this respect, she is making the shape and the purpose of her life story conform to those governing the collections of exempla read to her by Jankyn, exempla which she well knows were selected and fashioned primarily to support a single restricted perspective, not to demonstrate, dutifully and disinterestedly, the truth.

Casting herself in the role of preacher, which the Pardoner (himself a rhetorician par excellence) immediately recognizes—"Ye been a noble prechour in this cas" (165)—the Wife announces that the purpose of her autobiographical speech will be to persuade her audience of her proposition by the use of selective examples:

> For I shal telle ensamples mo than ten.
> "Whoso that nyl be war by othere men,
> By hym shul othere men corrected be."   (179–81)

And she is careful (unlike many preachers and the collectors of antifeminist exempla) to remind her audience that what she tells them about her life is not necessarily going to provide them with any authoritative perspective; rather, it is to be received as a rhetorical act, a narrative informed at every turn with the particular biases of its shaper:[57]

> But yet I preye to al this compaignye,
> If that I speke after my fantasye,
> As taketh not agrief of that I seye,
> For myn entente nys but for to pleye.   (189–92)

By openly announcing that her story follows her "fantasye" and that it is "pleye" rather than an earnest attempt to reproduce reality fairly or accurately, the Wife also concurs here with a basic Chaucerian principle—that narratives in general, even (perhaps especially) those drawn from life, are everywhere suffused with the marks of their author's controlling hand; the painters of lions are always engaged in some aspect of the art of self-portraiture.

By studying some of the Wife's narrative habits in her prologue, we can further detect her wisdom about the essentially relational nature of human discourse. Throughout her prologue, she spends an inordinate amount of time setting forth other people's opinions about the world; in fact, an astonishingly large part of her speech is either quotation or some form of indirect discourse whereby a clearly articulated position is introduced into the debate. What is perhaps most noticeable about the Wife's anthology of arguments is that she is remarkably careful to attribute each view to a well-defined speaker or writer. These ideas are not general truths, she implies by this strategy, but pieces of so-and-so's arguments about such-and-such an issue. We don't have true propositions; we have Paul's argument or Mark's argument or Ptolemy's argument or Valerius's argument or Theophrastes's argument or her husband's argument or the various arguments of the personally identified authors of the book of wicked wives, such as Tertullian, Crisippus, Trotula, Heloise, Solomon, and Ovid.

Just as important as the content of these remarks is the identity of the person who sponsored them, for the Wife knows that what matters about the statements of human beings is "who dide hem wirche?"—a question put by *The House of Fame*'s narrator and, at another point, by Criseyde.[58] Even when she is discussing her own heterodox views on Scriptural teaching, she usually makes it clear (unlike most biblical commentators) that her readings are her own, having absolutely no claim to authority beyond that of personal opinion. The tags accompanying her explication of Scripture almost always show hedging, or she may give a clear attribution of the reading to no one but herself: "What that he mente therby, *I* kan nat seyn" (20), "but that *I* axe" (21), "But wel *I* woot" (27, 30, passim), "*I* trowe" (36), "as to *my* wit" (41), "as ferforth as *I* kan" (56), "clepe *I*" (93), "*I* seye this" (126), "But *I* seye noght" (135), "this sentence *me* liketh" (162), and so on (emphasis mine). Never pretending to offer definitive readings of Scripture, the Wife plays the game of "glosyng up and doun" as well as any exegete, but, unlike the exegetes, she is willing to expose the fact that her discourse is interested.

In reporting the facts of her married life, the Wife again proves herself to be a quoter of others' speech. Much of the narration involving her five husbands consists of her reproducing, in the form of direct or indirect quotation, the actual words she claims they uttered to her—most of them accusatory and painful to hear (248–378).[59] Interestingly, though, the Wife does not refer to these husbands in the third person (*he* said), but instead resurrects them, speaking to them in the second person as if they were once again present before her (*you* said), which in some sense they are, since they have shaped the very "self" she projects. By employing direct address with these former husbands, quoting back at them their own discourse along with her angry responses to it, the Wife momentarily seems to lose sight of her new audience, returning to a previous reality to confront it once again (this time perhaps more effectively). Even if we are somewhat inclined to trust her reports of their speech, we are less likely to believe in the accuracy of her accounts of her own valiant responses, for we get the distinct sense that the Wife is replaying the script partly in order to improve the effectiveness of the heroine's role, to convince them and others that she has actually "quitte hem word for word" (422).

This kind of fictionalizing in the Wife's report of her life is also coupled with fictionalizing of another sort, which derives its shape from purposes external to her own project. The Wife's capacious memory, or the subtle analytical skill usually visible in the transcription of her life, fails at several crucial points to separate opinion from truth, and the Wife is represented as having internalized some of the antifeminist constructions of reality served up to her by Jankyn and others. Usually an active critical reader of others' texts, the Wife has uncritically accepted some of their fictions (perhaps occasionally selecting which to believe in for selfish purposes). That women swear and lie more boldly than men (227–28), are given deceit by God (400), or are less reasonable than their male disputants (441)—these generalizations advanced by the Wife herself show that her understanding of a "self" has indeed been fashioned by the antifeminist constructions of it created by "clerkes . . . Withinne hire oratories" (694), as the Wife might say.⁶⁰ But the Wife neglects to attach these statements to their ideologically driven and self-interested speakers, and they therefore float by unsponsored, uncriticized, and masquerading as the truth. Even though they are someone else's fictional analyses of the Wife's (or other women's) life narratives, she herself has come to believe that some of the events of her life are merely exempla of these theses. Others' texts have come to influence her life so profoundly that, as Robert Hanning has noted, at times she even speaks about her physical body in textual terms: sex, for example, is the activity of being "glossed" by men (508–10).⁶¹ The Wife sees herself as inevitably there to be read, misread, and commented upon.

Yet in spite of her willingness to accept some of men's generalizations as the truth, the Wife never abandons her position that people say and do things not because they are true or right but because they help people to achieve certain personal or ideological goals. Her tale continues to display this view of the world, focusing on the variety of human opinion and the basically rhetorical nature of human discourse. Even before the tale's action gets under way, we can detect the Wife's unwillingness to claim her narrative is true. Her tale's setting and characters are identified as constituents of someone else's opinion and report:

> In th'olde dayes of Kyng Arthour,
> Of which that Britons speken greet honour,
> Al was this land fulfild of fayerye.
> The elf-queene, with hir joly compaignye,
> Daunced ful ofte in many a grene mede.
> This was the olde opinion, as I rede;
> I speke of manye hundred yeres ago.   (857–63)

Unlike most of the pilgrims before her, the Wife refuses to grant her source any authority by advancing claims about its veracity or historicity. Nor does she claim that she is following her source exactly (as did the Knight and the Man of Law). Instead she remains acutely aware of her performance (and that of her source, presumably) as a form of opinion, a vehicle for promoting certain views—of which some of her own immediately intrude when she digresses on the replacement of fairies by friars.

The diversity of human opinion is also demonstrated for the knight of her tale, who learns a lesson that the Wife wants all men to absorb: there can be genuine disagreement even among those who are experts on the issues at hand—in this case, women on the subject of their own desires. The Wife is careful to stress this initial disagreement in her long cataloguing of women's various responses to the single question put to them, "What thyng is it that wommen moost desiren?" (905). Piling up the "somme seyde" clauses in a dazzling display of contradictory information (925–48), the Wife demonstrates that without supernatural arbitration, in the form of the hag's "right" answer, humans will endlessly debate:

> he koude arryven in no coost
> Wher as he myghte fynde in this mateere
> Two creatures accordynge in-feere.   (922–24)

Disagreement is indeed the hallmark of the world in which the Wife's tale is set, to the dismay of the knight whose life depends on finding a single "correct" response.[62]

That the Wife of Bath is aware of how certain rhetorical purposes require the taking of positions neither true nor even personally maintained is clear from the hag's utterly convincing defense of old age, poverty, and low birth. At least two of these states (age and poverty) have clearly been resisted by the Wife herself in her life narrative—but here, in her tale, she is able to collect authorities who resoundingly argue against her own personal fears. Again, as in her prologue, these positions are clearly attached to specific speakers, underscoring our sense of the Wife's canny awareness of the interested, rhetorical nature of human discourse; the opinions cited by the hag have a variety of sources, each carefully labeled: "Wel kan . . . Dant speken in this sentence" (1125–26), "as seith Valerius" (1165), "Reedeth Senek, and redeth eek Boece" (1168), "This wole Senec and othere clerkes seyn" (1184), "Juvenal seith" (1192). And even when she chooses not to name a particular person as her source on old age, she slyly notes that all "ye gentils of honour" (1209) talk about respecting the aged and that she could easily turn up a specific authority if she bothered to look: "And auctours shal I fynden, as I gesse" (1212). One never gets the feeling that the Wife herself believes in these arguments, which are fully and persuasively set forth primarily as a form of advertising directed toward potential husbands in her audience, nor is one necessarily asked to believe that the hag puts much stock in them either—after all, she, too, is merely using them to convince an audience to accept her as a desirable spouse. Both speakers here, in other words, are engaged in a form of hard-sell marketing designed to overcome the fears of nervous consumers, and both clearly enjoy the game. In the hag's case, it is played largely for its own sake, since she is performing well after the man is already caught in her trap and just before she magically becomes young and beautiful again.

The Wife of Bath's prologue and tale, then, show her to be a skillful adopter of voices, a first-rate practitioner of rhetorical posturing who understands that others, too, take positions that run counter to the truth of experience or help to further their personal goals in self-serving ways. To the Wife of Bath, no human discourse (including biography and exegesis) is to be trusted as a repository or record of the truth; rather, it always turns out to be a kind of fiction with its own informing purposes and interests that function very much like those one might identify as the bases of narrative art. Indeed, through the Wife's performance, one can detect Chaucer's own awareness (perhaps portrayed in the extreme) of the human urge to organize and politicize knowledge—and thus to select, distort, and misrepresent it. Along with the Pardoner, whose autobiographical narrative is also carefully organized to reveal to his audience a governing purpose that conflicts with the facts discernible behind it, the Wife of Bath raises issues that are central to Chaucer's entire poetic corpus.

Turning to the Pardoner's autobiography, we can see that it too ostensibly provides the pilgrim audience with a factual account, this time of the typical context in which the Pardoner delivers his exemplary narratives. It too raises several intriguing problems, however, for it asks us to believe in the power and success of the Pardoner's deceptions, a belief that is sometimes difficult to sustain. Can this freakish character, who has failed to deceive even the credulous narrator of the *General Prologue,* actually have duped as many audiences as he suggests? Is it possible that this poorly-dressed man can be as rich as he claims he is, or that the poverty-stricken rural communities he claims to have bilked could have the gold and silver he says that he wins from them? The lies of the Pardoner may, in fact, be operating on more than one level, for he may be lying to us even about the success of his lies before others. Like the allegorical character from whom he partially derives, Faux Semblant in *The Romance of the Rose,* the Pardoner may be fundamentally "irreferent," a character constitutionally unable to flee the mendacity that is so central to his professed livelihood.[63]

Indeed, the falsity of the Pardoner's claims becomes openly visible at one point in his narration. Concluding his speech to the pilgrims about his evil intentions as a preacher and his desire for a large income, he says, "I wol drynke licour of the vyne / And have a joly wenche in every toun" (452–53), two boasts whose truth is definitely undermined by other textual evidence: the Pardoner is drinking cheap ale as he utters this remark, and his obvious sexual deficiencies mitigate against the likelihood that he enjoys (or even wants to enjoy) the company of women. That is, the image that the Pardoner hopes to project to the pilgrims may not be an image he has ever successfully matched in the real life he is ostensibly recording. The self-fictionalization that his autobiography allows is perhaps a representation of the Pardoner's attempt to be, at least momentarily, something that in actual life he is not—a socially potent and persuasive figure whose words cause audiences to act. But his pilgrim audience surely sees through this illusion; even the benign narrator is careful to record the lack of correlation between what the Pardoner thinks about himself and what his actual audience is concluding: "*Hym thoughte* he rood al of the newe jet" (682; emphasis mine).

The Pardoner's tale, traditionally praised by critics, also shows problems if one imagines it delivered orally before an audience. Performed in a voice "smal as hath a goot" (General Prologue, 688), the narrative's effectiveness for an audience would surely be hindered by the Pardoner's early and digressive moralizing, which interrupts the story line, wandering from sin to sin and from exemplum to exemplum with the kind of agitated awkwardness that one might expect from the Squire, not from such an experienced preacher as the Pardoner claims to be. Indeed, it is not until the story of the three rioters finally gets underway (at line 661) that the Pardoner gains full control of his material, telling "by rote" (332) the narrative that has earned him such praise from modern critics. It is by no means certain, however, that the Pardoner's success before his rural congregations is any greater than that which he achieves with his pilgrim audience. Surely this effeminate man, who makes the serious rhetorical mistake of approaching the manly Harry Bailly with a request that he unbuckle his purse, cannot be viewed as a skillful deviser of marketing strategies of the kind a substantial income would depend upon. Compared to that of the Wife of Bath, the Pardoner's sense of audience is both superficial and inflexible.

The Pardoner, then, may be much more of a deceiver than critics have suggested, for he may be lying about the success of his lies. He is attempting to create an image of himself as a powerfully manipulative man, one who deserves admiration for the courage and skill it takes to victimize his listeners. However, though "hym thoughte" he appeared to be a disturbingly potent figure of evil, in fact he looks pathetic—both to us and to the pilgrims in the company. His self-fictionalizing creates a lie that no one really believes, except perhaps himself—for his foolish attempt to sell relics on the pilgrimage suggests that he has come to have faith in the illusion he has spun just minutes before. Carried away by the constituted self he projects to his audience, he acts upon it as though it were real.

Both the Wife of Bath and the Pardoner thus demonstrate, perhaps more than the other pilgrim narrators, that the contours of their discourses are socially determined and that the contours of their lives—though never truly visible—are also likely to be the results of social forces working upon them. Autobiographers have a stake in how their audiences perceive them, and the record of their lives will always be radically selective and rhetorically organized in order to reveal an imagined identity. And hiding (or creating) details about one's life in order to alter its shape and its effect is—at least in the case of the Pardoner—a way of deceiving oneself as much as it is a way of deceiving one's audience, for the Pardoner is tragically attempting to hide from even himself the sad implied reality of his defective physical and spiritual states.

To contrast with the Wife's and the Pardoner's autobiographical manipulations, Chaucer created *The Canon's Yeoman's Tale*, a "life story" narrated by a character ready to face the failures in his past, one eager (perhaps overly eager) to tell the truth, to confess to the self-deceptions he had formerly labored under, and to arrive at a soberly critical view of the role played by illusion in his previous life. In all of medieval literature, there is nothing quite like the experience of reading the Canon's Yeoman's prologue and tale. Abruptly violating the integrity of the "closed system" of the tale-telling game, the Canon and his Yeoman arrive on the scene as outsiders who have no stake in the contest, no preplanned agenda, no previously developed sense of audience, and no shared sense of storytelling history with which to contend. This fact alone makes *The Canon's Yeoman's Tale* something of a medieval literary anomaly, for the reader is encouraged to be mildly disturbed by the sudden change in the narrative situation: the storytelling rules and conventions formerly set up do not apply to these new arrivals, who stand just beyond the reach of the artist's controlling hand. To be sure, Harry

Bailly tries to include them in the ad hoc community of game-players he has organized, asking the Yeoman for a "myrie tale or tweye" (597), but it quickly becomes clear that the Yeoman is not interested in meddling with fictions; rather, he very urgently feels the need to "seye the sothe" (662).[64]

Yet as his prologue makes clear, the particular circumstances surrounding the Yeoman's represented past life make him distrust his own abilities as a knowledgeable or reliable witness to its truth. Because he has come to realize the ease with which people can be led to believe in illusion as if it were truth (indeed, his experience with alchemy drove home this lesson's applicability to himself), he is quick to disclaim any sure or real knowledge about his master or the "elvysshe craft" (751) that consumed them both, even though he has personally experienced the events he narrates. When the Canon is present, the Yeoman is especially hesitant to disclose information, probably out of fear of reprisal from his paranoid master:

> He hath take on hym many a great emprise,
> Which were ful hard for any that is heere
> To brynge about, but they of hym it leere.   (605–607)

> I seye, my lord kan swich subtilitee—
> But al his craft ye may nat wite at me.   (620–21)

> (But I wol nat avowe that I seye,
> And therfore keepe it secree, I yow preye.)   (642–43)

Even after the Canon leaves and the Yeoman feels free to speak, he still refuses to pose as a deeply learned informant or as a reliable authority on the subject of alchemy. Before beginning his "tale," he notes that his wit is insufficient to the task of disclosing "al that longeth to that art" (716), so he must restrict himself to the little that he knows. In addition, his tale proper begins with a disclaimer of knowledge: "With this Chanoun I dwelt have seven yeer, / And of his science am I never the neer" (720–21).[65]

In spite of (or perhaps partly because of) this narrator's insistence on his own shortcomings as a reporter, however, he manages to project the illusion of being a speaker deserving trust and confidence. We feel that we are in the presence of a speaker who, though intensely committed to achieving a specific moral purpose in his autobiographical narrative, is nonetheless sincere about his responsibility to tell some kind of truth, to expose and undermine the illusion that he and his acquaintances have so blindly followed. Indeed, many of the narrative strategies that Chaucer employs in the Yeoman's tale are clearly designed to suggest the artlessness of this presentation and thus its speaker's reliability as a recorder of fact.[66]

For example, in structuring the narrative, the Yeoman openly admits his inability to classify the alchemists' arcane supplies:

> Though I by ordre hem nat reherce kan
> By cause that I am a lewed man,
> Yet wol I telle hem as they come to mynde,
> Thogh I ne kan nat sette hem in hir kynde.   (786–89)

What follows, of course, is one of the Yeoman's several disorderly lists, the significance of which eludes the uninitiated audience unfamiliar with the real-world referents of the items named. Breathlessly delivered, this list (like the others) threatens never to end as the yeoman continues to remember things he neglected to mention:

> Yet forgat I to maken rehersaille
> Of watres corosif, and of lymaille,
> And of bodies mollificacioun,
> And also of hire induracioun;
> Oilles, ablucions, and metal fusible—
> To tellen al wolde passen any bible
> That owher is . . .   (852–57)

Not user-friendly, this cryptic information spills out as if it were intended to satisfy only the referential memory of the Yeoman himself rather than his audience of baffled listeners.

The essential artlessness of the Yeoman's discourse continues even when he is telling his story about the canon who deceived a priest, a narrative that shows a definite beginning, middle, and end. As he is furnishing his audience with the background to this story, he begins to wander a bit into inessential narrative territory, suggesting that he does not wish to leave anything out even if it means introducing digressions that threaten to ruin the tale. Catching himself providing more historical detail than is necessary to his plot, he says at one point, "Therof no fors; I wol procede as now, / And telle forth my tale of the chanoun" (1019–20). He is also careful to identify those details in the story that he doesn't understand, for example, "A poudre, noot I wherof that it was / Ymaad" (1148–49), and to make sure that his listeners are not confused about the real-life identities of the characters in his story:

> This chanon was my lord, ye wolden weene?
> Sire hoost, in feith, and by the hevenes queene
> It was another chanoun, and nat hee.   (1088–90)

Moreover, the sincerity represented by this narrator is never in doubt; though the secrets of his subject matter may remain veiled, his emotions are always in full view:

> Evere whan that I speke of his falshede,
> For shame of hym my chekes wexen rede.
> Algates they bigynnen for to glowe.   (1094–96)

In the Canon's Yeoman's performance, then, we are faced with something approaching a paradox, for although we are given the illusion that this shapeless autobiographical narrative comes closer to representing the truth of an actual experience than any of the other life stories we have heard, we must admit that the experience purportedly recorded there remains mysteriously vague, its real-life referents shrouded by the occult terminology and the emotional disturbance that cloud this narrator's relationship to reality. Indeed, *The Canterbury Tales'* most trustworthy portrayer of historical truth ends up being incapable of conveying it, and Chaucer thematizes this idea in the tale itself when he has the Yeoman argue against the futile search for hidden truth: "Philosophres speken so mystily / In this craft that men kan nat come therby" (1394–95). Just as it had eluded the Black Knight in *The Book of the Duchess,* the real eludes the Yeoman; the limitations of human knowledge and the language meant to convey it are nowhere more complexly or definitively expressed than in these speakers' unsuccessful attempts to refer us to a world we will never quite understand.

VII

The Canterbury Tales, Chaucer's narrative experiment in escaping the limits of the book and the dream by replacing their testimony with a record of life instead, is designed to lay to rest the notion that human discourse can represent the world. If some imaginary audience were to be momentarily seduced by Chaucer's Canterbury narrators into believing that they were hearing true stories duplicated verbatim by trustworthy reporters who themselves had recorded everything they saw or heard, it would not take long before this initial view would have to yield to its opposite. In spite of the tellers' claims to tell the truth, these are fictions, fashioned by a variety of shapers, some of whom want to tell the truth, but can't, others who are there primarily to market their lies. The only truth that emerges from Chaucer's work, then, is that truth is impossible to ascertain—even in the best of circumstances, when both its purveyors and its receivers are sincere in their desire to capture it.

The final fiction of *The Canterbury Tales, The Manciple's Tale,* concludes Chaucer's meditations on the recording of truth by providing one last communicative act involving an event, a reporter of that event, and an audience with a deep-seated personal investment in what occurred. In some ways, *The Manciple's Tale* presents us with an ideal situation for the reporting function of this paradigm, since the event in question (the adultery of Phebus's wife) is seen and reported by a witness whose only motive is to tell the truth. Adopting the Manciple's (and our narrator's) realist precept that "the word moot nede accorde with the dede" (207), the crow faithfully (if tactlessly) tells Phebus of his wife's adultery. But there are problems with respect to the audience function of the paradigm: Phebus, in spite of the "sadde tokenes" (258) that confirm the truth of the crow's report, ultimately decides not to believe it—but only after killing his wife in a fit of anger. The truth-telling crow, now accused of treacherous lying, is blackened, banished, and finally held culpable for the woman's death.

This tale raises a variety of questions about truth-telling and about any audience's ability to accept truths once they are reported. If the fate of truth-tellers hinges so completely on the self-serving whims of a powerful audience, what point is there in reporting anything at all? Phebus was not ready to be confronted with the news about his wife's adultery, nor was the crow politically astute enough to predict the horrible result of his unvarnished report of "Cokkow, Cokkow, Cokkow . . . on thy bed thy wife I saugh hym swyve" (243–55). One might want to argue that it would have been better for all concerned if, in this case, history had been left unreported by the kept crow—who was hired, after all, only to entertain his master. Censorship, or at the very least, politically motivated tampering with the historical record, might have saved the crow, the wife, and Phebus's minstrelsy. Only reports that are carefully targeted political acts are sure to protect the interests of the reporters, who must always take into account the specific illusions and desires of their audiences. Otherwise, their function as truth-tellers may become a useless, even dangerous, role instead of a laudable duty. It is no wonder, then, that history is absent from even those documents that claim to record it, for even if it were possible to capture the past, reporters, learning to "thenk upon the crowe" (363), end up depending on various forms of lying for their own survival.[67]

With *The Manciple's Tale,* we are once again entangled in a system reflecting politicized narrators who address self-deluding readers, much as we saw in the *Troilus* and *The Legend of Good Women.* And with *The Canon's Yeoman's Tale,* we are revisiting the dream world represented in *The Book of the Duchess,* in which the Black Knight's sincere but unsuccessful attempts at "true" referentiality fail to evoke his White. The Wife of Bath recalls for us the subversive attack in *The House of Fame* on the illegitimacy and contradictory nature of the textual tradition. And the pronounced subjectivity of the bookish narrator of *The Canterbury Tales,* who does not see how his transcript of life is profoundly shaped by the books and the social norms he has internalized, calls to mind both the Wife of Bath and the reading dreamer who records the intensely textualized *Parliament of Fowls.* Indeed, Chaucer's poetic corpus is remarkably consistent in its approach to truth and textuality, showing that even when we think we have escaped from the world of words into the surer realm of things, we discover that this realm is itself part of a mysterious code, one whose secrets reach beyond our consciousness. The world (to borrow a well-known medieval metaphor) is a book—and we readers are doomed to interpret its signs through the glosses of our own and our society's constructions. Chaucer's decision to approach the text that is the world by representing only a labyrinthine variety of possible glosses upon it is visible at every stage of his career as a writer. An authority on deauthorization, he seized for himself the power to doubt.

Notes

All quotations from Chaucer's works are from *The Riverside Chaucer,* 3d ed., ed. Larry D. Benson (Boston: Houghton Mifflin, 1987). Quotations from *The Canterbury Tales* give fragment and line numbers where necessary, and line numbers only when it is clear which story is referred to.

Introduction (pages 1–10)

1. This position has been articulated by, among others, Stewart Justman, "Medieval Monism and Abuse of Authority in Chaucer," *Chaucer Review* 11 (1976): 95–111.

2. For a convenient summary of the evidence concerning courtly taste, see Richard Firth Green, *Poets and Princepleasers: Literature and the English Court in the Late Middle Ages* (Toronto: University of Toronto Press, 1980), 133–38. For the wider popularity of the *Polychronicon* and the prose *Brut,* see John Taylor, *English Historical Writing in the Fourteenth Century* (Oxford: Clarendon Press, 1987), 14, 44, 56, and 97; and A. S. G. Edwards, "The Influence and Audience of the *Polychronicon,*" *Proceedings of the Leeds Philosophical and Literary Society* 17 (1980): 100–119.

3. Green, *Poets and Princepleasers,* 136–37. See also Joseph M. Levine, *Humanism and History: Origins of Modern English Historiography* (Ithaca: Cornell University Press, 1987), 19–53. Hayden White discusses and critiques the survival of these beliefs in our own age through his exploration of the hidden ideological content of historical narrative. See especially "Interpretation in History," "The Historical Text as Literary Artifact," and "Fictions of Factual Representation" in *Tropics of Discourse: Essays in Cultural Criticism* (Baltimore: Johns Hopkins University Press, 1978), 51–80, 81–100, and 121–34. His arguments have stimulated my thinking throughout this study. I have also benefited from the research of modern investigators of medieval historiographic theory, who have assembled many of the remarks made by medieval historians that show their own adherence to a fact/fiction model in spite of their rhetorically based practice. See especially Levine, *Humanism and History,* 19–53; Nancy F. Partner, *Serious Entertainments: The Writing of History in Twelfth-Century England* (Chicago: University of Chicago Press, 1977), 183–230; and Suzanne

Fleischman, "On the Representation of History and Fiction in the Middle Ages," *History and Theory* 22 (1983): 278–310. For some of the classical views that had an influence on later periods, see Nancy S. Struever, *The Language of History in the Renaissance: Rhetorical and Historical Consciousness in Florentine Humanism* (Princeton: Princeton University Press, 1970), 17–32. For some specific studies of the rhetorical bases of medieval history, see Ernst Breisach, ed., *Classical Rhetoric and Medieval Historiography*, Studies in Medieval Culture 19 (Kalamazoo: The Medieval Institute, 1985).

4. Isidore of Seville, *Etymologiae sive Originum*, trans. Roy M. Liuzza from the edition of W. M. Lindsay (Oxford: Oxford University Press, 1911), 1:1.41.

5. Macrobius, *Macrobius' Commentary on the Dream of Scipio*, trans. William Harris Stahl (New York: Columbia University Press, 1952), 1.2.7–11, p. 85. For two of Cicero's most important claims about truth in historical discourse, see *De Oratore* 2.9.36 and 15.62.

6. *Boccaccio on Poetry*, trans. Charles G. Osgood (1930; rpt. Indianapolis: Bobbs-Merrill, 1956), esp. chaps. 9–13, pp. 47–69.

7. See David A. Lawton, *Chaucer's Narrators*, Chaucer Studies 13 (Cambridge: D. S. Brewer, 1985), 62–75, for a useful discussion of how Chaucer's narrator is indebted to the narrator of the *Roman de la Rose*.

8. John M. Fyler, *Chaucer and Ovid* (New Haven: Yale University Press, 1979), 2.

9. Teodolinda Barolini, *Dante's Poets, Textuality and Truth in the Comedy* (Princeton: Princeton University Press, 1984), 285, 275. For the title of my own study I have played a variation on the subtitle of Barolini's remarkable book on the *Commedia*.

10. Robert M. Jordan, *Chaucer's Poetics and the Modern Reader* (Berkeley: University of California Press, 1987). His thesis is an extension of that advanced in his earlier book, *Chaucer and the Shape of Creation: The Aesthetic Possibilities of Inorganic Structure* (Cambridge, Mass.: Harvard University Press, 1967).

11. This argument, essentially opposing E. T. Donaldson's position on the narrator in his influential essay, "Chaucer the Pilgrim," *PMLA* 69 (1954): 928–36, and George Lyman Kittredge's dramatic criticism in *Chaucer and His Poetry* (Cambridge, Mass.: Harvard University Press, 1915), is articulated not only by Jordan, *Chaucer's Poetics*, 18–19, 120–23, 148, but also in various ways by H. Marshall Leicester, Jr., "The Art of Impersonation: A General Prologue to the *Canterbury Tales*," *PMLA* 95 (1980): 213–24; Lawton, *Chaucer's Narrators*, esp. 1–8; and C. David Benson, *Chaucer's Drama of Style: Poetic Variety and Contrast in the "Canterbury Tales"* (Chapel Hill: University of North Carolina Press, 1986), 3–22, 26–43.

12. Judith Ferster, *Chaucer on Interpretation* (Cambridge: Cambridge University Press, 1985), 12 and 13. Ferster is working here with a Gadamerian model of hermeneutics. See also Robert B. Burlin's work on the Canterbury narrators in the section entitled "Psychological Fictions" of his book, *Chaucerian Fiction* (Princeton: Princeton University Press, 1977), esp. 149–52, 155–61; and David R. Aers, *Chaucer, Langland and the Creative Imagination* (London: Routledge and Kegan Paul, 1980), 50–116. For strong evidence of the late medieval interest in how texts, both secular and sacred, betray signs of individual authorship, see A. J. Minnis, *Medieval Theory of Authorship: Scholastic Liter-*

ary Attitudes in the Later Middle Ages (London: Scolar Press, 1984), esp. 73–117.

13. Robert O. Payne, "Chaucer's Realization of Himself as Rhetor," in *Medieval Eloquence: Studies in the Theory and Practice of Medieval Rhetoric,* ed. James J. Murphy (Berkeley and Los Angeles: University of California Press, 1978), 282–87. Also still pertinent to the examination of Chaucer's rhetorical poetics is Payne's "book/dream/experience" model as set forth in *The Key of Remembrance: A Study of Chaucer's Poetics* (New Haven: Yale University Press, 1963), although this model is too simple. In analyzing audience-related issues, I have benefited from Paul Strohm's "Chaucer's Audience(s): Fictional, Implied, Intended, Actual," *Chaucer Review* 18 (1983): 137–45. Also useful has been the work of Peter J. Rabinowitz, "Truth in Fiction: A Reexamination of Audiences," *Critical Inquiry* 4 (1977): 121–41, and "Assertion and Assumption: Fictional Patterns and the External World," *PMLA* 96 (1981): 408–19; and the work of the modern reader-response critics.

14. An argument along these same lines has been advanced by Lee Patterson in *Negotiating the Past: The Historical Understanding of Medieval Literature* (Madison: University of Wisconsin Press, 1987), 70–74, and in greater detail in Gabrielle M. Spiegal's "History, Historicism, and the Social Logic of the Text in the Middle Ages," *Speculum* 65 (1990): 59–86. For a discussion of models depending on the practical bases of social behavior, see Harold Garfinkel, "Studies of the Routine Grounds of Everyday Activities," in *Studies in Ethnomethodology* (Cambridge: Polity Press, 1984), 35–75. Paul Strohm's *Social Chaucer* (Cambridge, Mass.: Harvard University Press, 1989), 47–83, begins to outline some of the sociohistorical dimensions of Chaucer's verse, but I will more thoroughly deploy the concept of audience in my treatment of Chaucer's works.

1. True and False "Portrayture" in *The Book of the Duchess* (pages 11–24)

1. See Green, *Poets and Princepleasers,* esp. 112–14. Two essays specifically about English courtly culture of the Renaissance have influenced my thinking about the social codes embedded in Chaucer's art: Heinrich F. Plett, "Aesthetic Constituents in the Courtly Culture of Renaissance England," *New Literary History* 14 (1983): 597–621; and Frank Whigham, "Interpretation at Court: Courtesy and the Performer-Audience Dialectic," *New Literary History* 14 (1983): 623–39. Strohm, in *Social Chaucer,* 51–55, briefly addresses the social relations visible between the narrator of *The Book of the Duchess* and John of Gaunt, but I wish to take this inquiry further.

2. For some recent observations about the elaborate and self-conscious experimentation with the interplay of fact and fiction in the poetry of Machaut and Froissart, see William Calin, *A Poet at the Fountain: Essays on the Narrative Verse of Guillaume de Machaut* (Lexington: University of Kentucky Press, 1974), 48, 67, 70, 158–59, 169–78, 196–98, 202; Kevin Brownlee, *Poetic Identity in Guillaume de Machaut* (Madison: University of Wisconsin Press, 1984), esp. 35, 94–156, 161–62, 203–205; and Michelle A. Freeman, "Froissart's *Le Joli Buisson de Jonece*: A Farewell to Poetry?" in *Machaut's World: Science and Art in the Fourteenth Century,* ed. Madeleine Pelner Cosman and Bruce Chandler, Annals of the New York Academy of Sciences 314 (1978): 235–

47. For some suggestive comments on Chaucer's acknowledgment of the fiction-ality of *The Book of the Duchess,* see Robert W. Hanning, "The Theme of Art and Life in Chaucer's Poetry," in *Geoffrey Chaucer,* ed. George D. Economou (New York: McGraw-Hill, 1975), 16–17, and Gale C. Schricker, "On the Re-lation of Fact and Fiction in Chaucer's Poetic Endings," *Philological Quarterly* 60 (1981): 15–16.

3. Although many critics have noted this strategy, it was first observed by Wolfgang Clemen. See his *Chaucer's Early Poetry,* trans. C. A. M. Sym (New York: Barnes and Noble, 1963), 43. It is worth noting that this device is also used by Machaut in *La Fonteinne amoureuse*; the poet-narrator responds to his patron's command for a *complainte* by providing the "actual" words of the pa-tron, recorded the night before.

4. The rhetorical set-pieces used to describe Blanche are nearly all taken (though reshuffled) from Chaucer's French models. For a listing of these pas-sages, see Colin Wilcockson's note in *The Riverside Chaucer* to lines 817–1040. See also James I. Wimsatt, "The Apotheosis of Blanche in *The Book of the Duchess,*" *Journal of English and Germanic Philology* 46 (1967): 26–44 and his *Chaucer and the French Love Poets: The Literary Background of the Book of the Duchess,* University of North Carolina Studies in Comparative Literature 43 (Chapel Hill: University of North Carolina Press, 1968), 92–93, 155–62; Marc M. Pelen, "Machaut's Court of Love Narratives and Chaucer's *Book of the Duchess,*" *Chaucer Review* 11 (1976): 144–45; and B. A. Windeatt, *Chau-cer's Dream Poetry: Sources and Analogues,* Chaucer Studies 7 (Cambridge: D. S. Brewer, 1982), 3–70. On the general conventionality of the Black Knight's demeanor, see W. H. French, "The Man in Black's Lyric," *Journal of English and Germanic Philology* 56 (1957): 235–39. On his artificial diction, see Martin Stevens, "Narrative Focus in *The Book of the Duchess*: A Critical Revaluation," *Annuale Mediaevale* 7 (1966): 30. On the Black Knight's frustration with con-ventional language, see John Lawlor, "The Pattern of Consolation in *The Book of the Duchess,*" 1956; rpt. in *Chaucer Criticism,* ed. Richard J. Schoeck and Jerome Taylor (South Bend: University of Notre Dame Press, 1961), 2:255; and Philip C. Boardman, "Courtly Language and the Strategy of Consolation in *The Book of the Duchess,*" *English Literary History* 44 (1977): 570–74, some of whose views on the Black Knight section are similar to my own. See also David R. Aers, "Chaucer's *Book of the Duchess*: An Art to Consume Art," *Dur-ham University Journal* 69 (1977): 201–205. Finally, Barbara Nolan's fascinat-ing essay on conventional language in this poem, "The Art of Expropriation: Chaucer's Narrator in *The Book of the Duchess,*" in *New Perspectives in Chau-cer Criticism,* ed. Donald M. Rose (Norman, Okla.: Pilgrim Books, 1981), 203–22, is at times relevant to the concerns of my essay, but it underestimates the sophistication of the medieval French verse that Nolan believes Chaucer con-sciously subverts.

5. Julia G. Ebel, in "Chaucer's *The Book of the Duchess*: A Study in Medieval Iconography and Literary Structure," *College English* 29 (1967): 202–205, dis-cusses the dreamer's consistent misunderstanding of the Knight's conventional discourse.

6. Bertrand H. Bronson, in *"The Book of the Duchess* Reopened," *PMLA* 67 (1952): 870–71, also argues that the Black Knight is a projection of the dreamer, but he does so on the basis of their both being "love-sick," a view with

which I do not concur. D. W. Robertson, Jr., in *A Preface to Chaucer: Studies in Medieval Perspectives* (Princeton: Princeton University Press, 1962), 465, also thinks that both dreamer and Knight are products of the narrator's mind, but he argues that the former is Reason and the latter Will, making *The Book of the Duchess* a Christian allegory. Since then, others have worked with the idea of projection, but none in the way presented in this book. See A. C. Spearing, *Medieval Dream-Poetry* (Cambridge: Cambridge University Press, 1976), 59–60; and Ferster, *Chaucer on Interpretation*, 74. William Calin, in *A Poet at the Fountain*, 47–48, 157, shows how Machaut had also used doubling between the narrator and the lover-protagonists in *Le Jugement dou Roy de Behainge* and *La Fonteinne amoureuse*. See also Calin's "The Poet at the Fountain: Machaut as Narrative Poet" in *Machaut's World: Science and Art in the Fourteenth Century*, ed. Madeleine Pelner Cosner and Bruce Chandler, New York Academy of Sciences 314 (1978): 183.

7. The tradition that writing is a way to combat idleness is alluded to in Chaucer's *Second Nun's Prologue* in *The Canterbury Tales* (22–28). Russell Peck, in "The Ideas of 'Entente' and Translation in Chaucer's *Second Nun's Tale*," *Annuale Mediaevale* 8 (1967): 17–18, neatly compares the sense of this prologue to its companion idea in *The Book of the Duchess*.

8. Spearing, *Medieval Dream-Poetry*, 4–5, 62, notes some of the features connecting dreams and poetry in medieval (and modern) thought. One of the clearest expressions of this idea in medieval French poetry occurs at the end of Froissart's *Paradys d'Amour* (1696 ff.), where the poet thanks Morpheus and Orpheus for his poem! It is worth noting in passing that the usual cause for sleeplessness in medieval French poetry is the lover-narrator's anxiety about his lady. By the time Chaucer wrote *The Book of the Duchess* and adopted the French convention of sleeplessness, he was already taking the pose of the nonlover, one whose major obsession is his art, not his lady.

9. See Ovid, *Metamorphoses* 11.603 ff.

10. This pagan version of "resurrection" might also be meant as a comic foreshadowing of the Christian resurrection gently implied for Blanche in the poem's cryptic lines alluding to St. John, the white castle, and the bell that strikes twelve (1316–23). For the possible Christian suggestions here, see especially Bernard F. Huppé and D. W. Robertson, Jr., *Fruyt and Chaf: Studies in Chaucer's Allegories* (Princeton: Princeton University Press, 1963), 91–92.

11. Chaucer leaves out the Ovidian metamorphosis (in which both husband and wife are turned into birds) precisely because he wishes the story to end unhappily, with no sense of Christian resurrection, thus allowing its tragedy to stand in marked contrast to his own treatment of Blanche's implied resurrection at the end of the poem.

12. See Marcelle Thiébaux, *The Stag of Love: The Chase in Medieval Literature* (Ithaca: Cornell University Press, 1974), for medieval hunt-narratives. See also Pelen, "Machaut's Court of Love Narratives," 141, 153, 153n., for some of the French poems which Chaucer may be imitating. Treatments of the "hart/heart" correspondence include Donald C. Baker's "Imagery and Structure in Chaucer's *Book of the Duchess*," *Studia Neophilologica* 30 (1958): 23; Joseph Grennen's "Hert-Huntyng in the *Book of the Duchess*," *Modern Language Quarterly* 25 (1964): 131–39; and M. Angela Carson's "Easing of the 'Hert' in the *Book of the Duchess*," *Chaucer Review* 1 (1966): 157–60.

13. Thiébaux, *The Stag of Love*, 120, notes the metaphor of the writer's "chase" of his story in the work of Gottfried von Strassburg, Wolfram von Eschenbach, Cervantes, and Chaucer (*Clerk's Tale*, 341).

14. Cited in ibid., 79. See also Gaston Phebus's *Livre de chasse*, ed. Gunnar Tilander (Stockholm: Almqvist and Wiksell, 1971), 52–55, and the other French hunting manuals describing hunting as an antidote for idleness, listed in John Fox's *A Literary History of France: The Middle Ages* (New York: Barnes and Noble, 1974), 334–36. See also Thiébaux, *The Stag of Love*, 77–80.

2. Eschatological Poetics in *The House of Fame* (pages 25–41)

1. For the uniqueness of Dante's historical claims, see Nancy F. Partner, "The New Cornificius: Medieval History and the Artifice of Words," in Breisach, *Classical Rhetoric and Medieval Historiography*, 21.

2. For the visionary elements in *The House of Fame*, see especially Alfred David, "Literary Satire in *The House of Fame*," *PMLA* 75 (1960): 333–39; Joseph E. Grennen, "Chaucer and Chalcidius: The Platonic Origins of *The Hous of Fame*," *Viator* 15 (1984): 260–61; and David Lyle Jeffrey, "Sacred and Secular Scripture: Authority and Interpretation in *The House of Fame*," in *Chaucer and Scriptural Tradition*, ed. David Lyle Jeffrey (Ottawa: University of Ottawa Press, 1984), 207–28. For *The House of Fame*'s indebtedness to Dante, see the summary of criticism in Howard H. Schless, *Chaucer and Dante: A Revaluation* (Norman, Okla.: Pilgrim Books, 1984), 29–76. See also B. G. Koonce, *Chaucer and the Tradition of Fame: Symbolism in "The House of Fame"* (Princeton: Princeton University Press, 1966), esp. 81, 84–88; and Piero Boitani, "What Dante Meant to Chaucer," in *Chaucer and the Italian Trecento*, ed. Piero Boitani (Cambridge: Cambridge University Press, 1983), 118–25. For a recent scholarly description of the genre of the apocalypse within which Chaucer and Dante are working, see John J. Collins, "Towards the Morphology of a Genre," in *Apocalypse: The Morphology of a Genre, Semeia* 14 (1979): 9: Apocalypse is "a genre of revelatory literature with a narrative framework, in which a revelation is mediated by an otherworldly being to a human recipient, disclosing a transcendent reality which is both temporal, insofar as it envisages eschatological salvation, and spatial, insofar as it involves another supernatural world." For some of the common features of medieval apocalypses, see Barbara Nolan, *The Gothic Visionary Perspective* (Princeton: Princeton University Press, 1977), 128–55.

3. Sheila Delany, *Chaucer's House of Fame: The Poetics of Skeptical Fideism* (Chicago: University of Chicago Press, 1972), 41.

4. Burlin, *Chaucerian Fiction*, 47. See also Fyler, *Chaucer and Ovid*, 26–27, 29; Clemen, *Chaucer's Early Poetry*, 75; Francis X. Newman, "*House of Fame*, 7–12," *English Language Notes* 6 (1968): 5–12; and Jacqueline T. Miller, "The Writing on the Wall: Authority and Authorship in Chaucer's *House of Fame*," *Chaucer Review* 17 (1982): 100. For a different view, see Koonce, *Tradition of Fame*, 54.

5. For Morpheus as a source of fantasy in *The House of Fame*, see Koonce, *Tradition of Fame*, 55 and Jeffrey, "Sacred and Secular Scripture," 214–15. For forgetfulness as a problem, see Delany, *Chaucer's House of Fame*, 45. Dante, of course, repeatedly invokes (and distrusts) his powers of memory, which are cru-

cial to his literary project of recording his vision accurately; see, for example, *Inferno* 2.8, *Paradiso* 23.53–54, 33.55–66 and 73–75. Chaucer's suggestion that Morpheus, god of forgetfulness, is involved in his poem is thus quite possibly a comic allusion to Dante.

6. The pose of the nonlover, already visible in *The Book of the Duchess*, is also adopted in *The Parliament of Fowls*, 8–9, 157–68; the *Troilus*, 1.15–21, 2.13–21, 3.40–42, and 3.1331–36; and *Envoy to Scogan*, 25–42.

7. See lines 132, 151, 193, 198, 209, 212, 219, 221, 253, 433, 439, 451, 482, 499. For the "I saw" formula in general as a generic marker of the apocalypse, see Adela Yarbro Collins, "The Early Christian Apocalypses," in *Apocalypse: The Morphology of a Genre*, 85 and 93; and Jacques Le Goff, *The Birth of Purgatory*, trans. Arthur Goldhammer (Chicago: University of Chicago Press, 1984), 36. Dante himself employs this formula repeatedly in the *Commedia*; of the over one hundred examples of it that I counted, see especially *Inferno* 4.121–40 and *Purgatorio* 12.22–34. The device is also conspicuously present in *The Book of Revelation*; see, for example, 5:1, 5:6, 5:11, 6:1. Chaucer's use of this device is, then, surely functional as a generic marker, rather than merely as a strategy to "purposely impair the narrative flow," as William Joyner argues in "Parallel Journeys in Chaucer's *House of Fame*," *Papers on Language and Literature* 12 (1976): 6, or as a tic he acquired from translating the *Roman de la Rose*, as John A. Norton-Smith suggests in *Geoffrey Chaucer*, Medieval Authors Series (London: Routledge and Kegan Paul, 1974), 49.

8. On the bookishness of the dream, see Fyler, *Chaucer and Ovid*, 28, 36–37, and 51–52; Piero Boitani, *Chaucer and the Imaginary World of Fame*, Chaucer Studies 10 (Cambridge: D. S. Brewer, 1984), 216; Payne, *The Key of Remembrance*, 87–88; and Jeffrey, "Sacred and Secular Scripture," 209. On the mix of Vergilian and Ovidian elements, see especially Delany, *Chaucer's House of Fame*, 50–57 and Miller, "The Writing on the Wall," 105–107. On the narrator's subjectivity, see Fyler, *Chaucer and Ovid*, 36–37.

9. Schless, *Chaucer and Dante*, 46–50, reviews the scholarship on this point. The resemblances occur mainly in wording here, but many have argued that Chaucer's eagle imitates the function of Dante's Vergil in his role as teacher of certain scientific principles. See Schless, 32–33; Boitani, "What Dante Meant to Chaucer," 118; Burlin, *Chaucerian Fiction*, 521–53; and Koonce, *The Tradition of Fame*, 154.

10. See Schless, *Chaucer and Dante*, 50–51; Boitani, "What Dante Meant to Chaucer," 123; and Robert J. Allen, "A Recurring Motif in Chaucer's *House of Fame*," *Journal of English and Germanic Philology* 55 (1956): 398.

11. See Schless, *Chaucer and Dante*, 55, and Boitani, "What Dante Meant to Chaucer," 119.

12. Quoted from Charles S. Singleton, *Dante's "Commedia": Elements of Structure* (1954; rpt. Baltimore: Johns Hopkins University Press, 1977), 87.

13. Developed by Augustine and Aquinas, this classical doctrine appears in *Purgatorio* 17.91–96; 18.19–33; *Paradiso* 1.103–41; and *Convivio* 3.3. Schless, *Chaucer and Dante*, 55–58, however, argues against Dante's works as a source for this section of *The House of Fame*. For more information on this doctrine in Chaucer's poem, see Koonce, *The Tradition of Fame*, 154–55 and 161.

14. See J. A. W. Bennett, *Chaucer's Book of Fame: An Exposition of "The*

House of Fame" (Oxford: Clarendon Press, 1968), 98. See also Koonce, *The Tradition of Fame,* 171 and Paul G. Ruggiers, "Words Into Images in Chaucer's *Hous of Fame*: A Third Suggestion," *Modern Language Notes* 69 (1954): 34–37. Again, Schless, *Chaucer and Dante,* 66–67, disagrees.

15. For a discussion of Dante's innovation here, see Patrick Boyde, *Dante Philomythes and Philosopher: Man in the Cosmos* (Cambridge: Cambridge University Press, 1981), 279–81. More traditional, of course, is the doctrine of the condition of bodies after the general resurrection on doomsday, about which it is agreed that all people will be uniquely themselves both physically and spiritually. See Augustine, for example, on the subject of the blessed, *City of God,* 22.19–20.

16. The Apocalypse of Mary contains a scene like this one, where Mary sees the names of the just and the names of sinners inscribed on separate columns. See Martha Himmelfarb, *Tours of Hell: An Apocalyptic Form in Jewish and Christian Literature* (Philadelphia: University of Pennsylvania Press, 1983), 20–21. Moreover, in the medieval vision of the woman of Laon, when nearing the Earthly Paradise the visionary sees the names of the blessed engraved, some of them beginning to fade. See Arnold Barel Van Os, *Religious Visions: The Development of the Eschatological Elements in Mediaeval English Religious Literature* (Amsterdam: H. J. Paris, 1932), 23. Certain purgatorial visions also show souls being subjected to extremes of heat and cold on a mountain, as Chaucer's "names" are. Le Goff, *The Birth of Purgatory,* 190, notes this in the *Vision of Tundale,* for example. Alternating heat and cold are also forms of punishment in *The Pricke of Conscience,* the *Poema Morale,* the *Vision of Dryhthelm,* the *Speculum Historiale* (cap. 84), and so on. See Barel Van Os for details.

17. Koonce, *The Tradition of Fame,* 181–279. See also John Gardner, *The Poetry of Chaucer* (Carbondale: Southern Illinois University Press, 1977), 176–77, for a description of Lady Fame's court as a "factitious New Jerusalem." On Lady Fame's judgments as a perverse version of God's justice, see Paul G. Ruggiers, "The Unity of Chaucer's *House of Fame,*" *Studies in Philology* 50 (1953): 25, and Fyler, *Chaucer and Ovid,* 57. On this scene as an ironic Last Judgment, see Sheila Delany, "Chaucer's *House of Fame* and the *Ovide moralisé,*" *Comparative Literature* 20 (1968): 260, and Norton-Smith, *Geoffrey Chaucer,* 43–44.

18. On cathedrals as anagogical images of the Celestial City, see Otto von Simson, *The Gothic Cathedral: Origins of Gothic Architecture and the Medieval Concept of Order,* Bollingen Library (New York: Harper and Row, 1962), 8–10, 134; George Henderson, *Gothic* (Baltimore: Penguin Books, 1972), 70–73; and Nolan, *The Gothic Visionary Perspective,* 45–54. Koonce, *The Tradition of Fame,* 197–98, suggests this idea for *The House of Fame* but comes to different conclusions. See also Mary Flowers Braswell, "Architectural Portraiture in Chaucer's *House of Fame,*" *Journal of Medieval and Renaissance Studies* 11 (1981): 105–109, for actual churches that may have inspired Chaucer's description of Fame's House.

19. Koonce, *The Tradition of Fame,* 198.

20. In *On Celestial Hierarchy,* Dionysius the Pseudo-Areopagite writes that "within each Hierarchy there are first, middle, and last ranks and powers, and the higher are initiators and guides of the lower; . . . each order is the interpreter

and herald of those above it" and those who are highest are "thought worthy to become first workers . . . of the imitation of the Divine Power and Energy, and beneficently uplift those below them . . . to the same imitation." See *The Mystical Theology and the Celestial Hierarchies*, trans. the editors of The Shrine of Wisdom (Godalming: Shrine of Wisdom, 1965), 34, 50, and 56. Dante, too, rehearses the doctrine of the hierarchies, in *Paradiso* 28.103ff.

21. See Sheila Delany, " '*Ars Simia Naturae*' and Chaucer's *House of Fame*," *English Language Notes* 11 (1973): 1–5, for other interesting implications of the metaphor of "craft" counterfeiting "kynde."

22. St. Augustine, *The City of God*, 20.14, trans. Marcus Dods (New York: Modern Library, 1950), 733. See also, for example, St. Bonaventure, *The Breviloquium*, 7.1.

23. 2 Corinthians 12:4. See Fyler, *Chaucer and Ovid*, 47.

24. For cathedral statuary of the patriarchs and prophets, see Emile Mâle, *The Gothic Image: Religious Art in France of the Thirteenth Century*, trans. Dora Nussey (New York: Harper and Row, 1958), 152, 158–63, 173–74. See also Nolan, *The Gothic Visionary Perspective*, 52, and Wilbur Owen Sypherd, *Studies in Chaucer's "House of Fame"* (1907; rpt. New York: Haskell House, 1965), 64–66.

25. Koonce, *The Tradition of Fame*, discusses the typology of the temple of Solomon, 97–105. For the temple as a type of the Church and the Heavenly Jerusalem, see, for example, St. Augustine, *The City of God*, 17.3, 17.8; Prudentius's *Psychomachia*, esp. 11.804–915; Bede, *De templo Salomonis*, cap. 1; Rabanus Maurus, *Comment. in Libros IV Regum, Patrologiae Latinae*, ed. J. P. Migne, 109, col. 186; Isidore, *Allegoriae Quaedam Scripturae Sacrae, PL* 83, col. 113; and Adam of St. Victor, *In dedicatione templi, PL* 196, cols. 1460–64. See also Henderson, *Gothic*, 70–73. Jeffrey, "Sacred and Secular Scripture," 220–24, however, in an interesting argument, sees the Temple of Venus as an image of the temple seen by Ezekiel.

26. For Dante's desire that his poem be read in the manner of Scripture, see the Letter to Can Grande, translated and discussed in Singleton, *Elements*, 89–92. On Dante's originality in creating a poetic salvation history, see Giuseppe Mazzotta, *Dante, Poet of the Desert: History and Allegory in "The Divine Comedy"* (Princeton: Princeton University Press, 1979), 221–26. For an example of Dante's "private typology," see Joseph Anthony Mazzeo, *Structure and Thought in the Paradiso* (Ithaca: Cornell University Press, 1958), 102.

27. Ruggiers, "Unity," 25.

28. Indeed, Bennett, *Chaucer's Book of Fame*, 159–60, 162, notes that some of Fame's petitioners appear in scenes resembling those in Dante's *Inferno* and *Paradiso*. See also Boitani, *Chaucer and the Imaginary World of Fame*, 77–80, 170.

29. Delany, *Chaucer's House of Fame*, 110. See also Boitani, *Chaucer and the Imaginary World of Fame*, 183, 191, 209–10.

30. Koonce, *The Tradition of Fame*, 250–51. To this notion one can add that *mundus* is often provided with the etymology *undique motus* to suggest the world's constant motion, a feature of Chaucer's unstable and whirling structure. See, for example, Honorius of Autun, *De imagine mundi*, 3, *PL* 172, col. 121. See also John Lydgate, *Reson and Sensuallyte*, 1901 ff.; "Thy lyf . . . ys lyk a cercle that goth aboute, round and swyfft as any thouht, wych in hys course ne

cesset nouht," cited in Koonce, 250n. St. Augustine may also be helpful here, for, following Scripture, he compares attachment to earthly things to placing confidence in a building of wood, hay, or stubble rather than in a building of gold, silver, and stones, such as "living in Christ" provides. See the *Enchiridion,* chap. 68.

31. See, for example, Alexander of Hales's *Gloss on the Sententiae of Peter Lombard,* cited in Le Goff, 248.

32. Boitani, in *Chaucer and the Imaginary World of Fame,* 76, toys with the idea of Dante as a dispenser of Fame, but he is arguing at this point merely that poets confer a kind of immortality on their human subjects. See Schless, 21, for the contrast between Chaucer and Dante as judges of their characters.

3. "Making" in *The Parliament of Fowls* (pages 42–55)

1. John P. McCall, "The Harmony of Chaucer's *Parliament,*" *Chaucer Review* 5 (1970): 23.

2. H. Marshall Leicester, Jr., "The Harmony of Chaucer's *Parlement*: A Dissonant Voice," *Chaucer Review* 9 (1974): 21.

3. David R. Aers, "*The Parliament of Fowls*: Authority, the Knower and the Known," *Chaucer Review* 16 (1981): 14.

4. Jordan, *Chaucer's Poetics and the Modern Reader,* 98. Jordan's reading of the *Parliament* derives from his thesis that Chaucer's poetry in general reflects a medieval tradition of "inorganic structure."

5. Leicester, "Harmony," 21; Aers, "*The Parliament of Fowls,*" 14. See also Ferster, *Chaucer on Interpretation,* 50–55.

6. On the reference to poetry writing in this opening stanza, see especially Charles O. McDonald, "An Interpretation of Chaucer's *Parlement of Foules,*" *Speculum* 30 (1955): 444–45; Payne, *The Key of Remembrance,* 138; James J. Wilhelm, "The Narrator and His Narrative in Chaucer's *Parlement,*" *Chaucer Review* 1 (1967): 202; Marion L. Polzella, " 'The Craft So Longe to Lerne': Poet and Lover in Chaucer's 'Envoy to Scogan' and *Parliament of Fowls,*" *Chaucer Review* 10 (1976): 282–83; Kathleen Dubs and Stoddard Malarkey, "The Frame of Chaucer's *Parlement,*" *Chaucer Review* 13 (1978): 17–19; and Lawton, *Chaucer's Narrators,* 38–39.

7. The only critics who have seen this analogy clearly are Dubs and Malarkey, "The Frame of Chaucer's *Parlement,*" 19, and Lawton, *Chaucer's Narrators,* 39ff. But Charles A. Owen, Jr., has noticed the dominant theme of failure in the poem in his article, "The Role of the Narrator in *The Parlement of Foules,*" *College English* 14 (1953): 265, and Robert W. Uphaus has discussed the narrator's frustrations about writing in "Chaucer's *Parlament of Foules*: Aesthetic Order and Individual Experience," *Texas Studies in Literature and Language* 10 (1968): 349–58. None of these critics extends this idea to involve the dream's love imagery, however.

8. Chaucer's use of the language of love to refer to his writing in other works is explored by Paula Neuss in "Images of Writing and the Book in Chaucer's Poetry," *Review of English Studies* 32 (1981): 385–97, and by Polzella, " 'The Craft So Longe to Lerne,' " 279–86. Also, see *The Book of the Duchess,* where the love hunt is a metaphor for the narrator's pursuit of his subject; *The House of Fame,* where the amatory/theological visit relates to art; and *The Legend of*

Good Women, where Chaucer's lady (Alceste) turns out to be his creative work as a poet. Chaucer would have noticed, of course, that sex is compared to writing in several authoritative medieval books, including the *Roman de la Rose,* 19543–635. Moreover, medieval French love poetry traditionally represented a fusion of the narrator's experience of loving and his act of writing the poem about it. See, especially, Brownlee, *Poetic Identity,* 13, 97, 100; and R. Howard Bloch, *Etymologies and Genealogies: A Literary Anthropology of the French Middle Ages* (Chicago: University of Chicago Press, 1983), 131–40, and "New Philology and Old French," *Speculum* 65 (1990): 54. For the relationship between loving and reading, see Ferster, *Chaucer on Interpretation,* 65–68.

9. See Claudian's *Panegyricus de sexto consulatu Honorii Augusti,* preface, 1–20, especially where the poet writes, "I am a lover of the Muses and in the silent night I too am haunted by that my accustomed task" (11–12), in *Claudian,* trans. Maurice Platnauer, Loeb Classical Library edition (New York: G. P. Putnam's, 1922), 2:70–71. Robert A. Pratt, in "Chaucer's Claudian," *Speculum* 22 (1947): 419–29, points out that this preface was included in a standard medieval school text and would have been very familiar to Chaucer's audience. We can thus assume that at least some readers would have known immediately what Chaucer had omitted.

10. These quotations are from *Macrobius' Commentary on the Dream of Scipio,* trans. William Harris Stahl (New York: Columbia University Press, 1952), 88, 89. See also the *Roman de la Rose,* which amplifies Macrobius's description of the *insomnium*'s worthlessness (18343–425), and which may have been one of Chaucer's sources (in addition to the Claudian passage) for lines 99–105; John of Salisbury, *Policraticus* 2.15; and Cato, *Distichs* 2.31, quoted by Chaucer himself in the *Nun's Priest's Tale.* In addition, Francis X. Newman, "Hous of Fame," 11, argues that the word *sweven,* used in lines 115 and 118 to refer to the narrator's dream, was the Middle English term for *insomnium.* Ferster, *Chaucer on Interpretation,* 62, too, categorizes the dream as an *insomnium.*

11. J. A. W. Bennett notices these "crossweavings of phrase," but he does not interpret them. See *The Parlement of Foules: An Interpretation* (Oxford: Clarendon Press, 1957), 65. See also George D. Economou, *The Goddess Natura in Medieval Literature* (Cambridge, Mass.: Harvard University Press, 1972), 128–30; and Fyler, *Chaucer and Ovid,* 84 and 88.

12. See Lawton, *Chaucer's Narrators,* 40–41, for a similar interpretation of this garden.

13. Leicester, "Harmony," 22, also sees this as an "archetypel [sic] *poet's list.*"

14. For this property of jasper and its use by Chaucer here, see Howard Schless, "Transformations: Chaucer's Use of Italian," in *Geoffrey Chaucer,* ed. Derek Brewer, *Writers and Their Background* (Athens: Ohio University Press, 1975): 198–99.

15. Chaucer has omitted the character Idleness from this group because he wants to suggest that preparation for writing involves much labor and "busyness." For Idleness in Boccaccio's original scene, see the *Teseida* 7.54.

16. Chaucer has altered Boccaccio's Priapus scene to suit his own purposes here. Boccaccio's garlands are on the walls of the temple, where they stand as symbols of success in love. By having Priapus's companions attempt (but fail) to crown the deity himself, Chaucer underscores Priapus's lack of success in completing the physical act of love.

17. In Boccaccio's original, the narrator notes that Venus's flimsy lower garment conceals almost nothing (*Teseida* 7.65). Again, Chaucer has de-eroticized the goddess somewhat to imply a lack of sexual activity in her temple.

18. Alain de Lille, *The Complaint of Nature*, trans. Douglas M. Moffat (Hamden, Conn.: Archon, 1972), 55.

19. For Nature as artifex and craftsman, see Macrobius's *Commentary on the Dream of Scipio* 1.6.63.112, Alain de Lille's *Complaint of Nature* (e.g. prosa 4, lines 350–57), the *Roman de la Rose*, lines 16005–82, and John of Salisbury's *Policraticus*, 2.16. We must not forget that Chaucer himself imagines Nature talking of her enviable artistic powers in *The Physician's Tale* (lines 11–28). Economou notes, too, that this idea is present in Chalcidius's *Commentary on the Timaeus*, 23–24 and in Bernard Silvestris's *De mundi universitate* 64. See also Bennett, *The Parlement of Foules*, 121, and Uphaus, "Chaucer's *Parlement of Foules*," 353–54.

20. For other medieval uses of birds as poet figures, see Chaucer's own *Book of the Duchess* and *The Manciple's Tale*. Note also that several of the birds in Chaucer's list (337–64) are characterized as singers of certain kinds of songs. In the troubadour tradition, birds were often identified as the inspiration and carriers of love-verse, and in French *dits amoureux* and *balades*, birds often symbolize the poet's own role as a singer. See, for example, Eustace Deschamps's *"Fiction d'oisseaulx,"* and *Balades* 33 and 68; William Dunbar's "All Erdly Joy Returnis in Pane," and "The Thrissill and the Rois"; and John Skelton's "Speke, Parott." The reader should refer to Leicester, "Harmony," 32, for a different view of the narrator's identification with the tercels and the formel.

21. Medieval bestiaries routinely describe the turtledove not only as a faithful mate but also as a symbol of chastity. Thus, in identifying with the turtledove, Chaucer's narrator is again emphasizing his lack of sexual/literary activity. For the turtledove's chastity, see, for example, Bartholomaeus Anglicus's *De Proprietatibus Rerum*, ed. M. C. Seymour, trans. John Trevisa (Oxford: Clarendon Press, 1975), 641: "The turtur . . . is a symple bridde . . . [and] is a chast bridde and haþ þat name of þewes for he[o] foleweþ chastite." See also Alexander Neckam, *De Naturis Rerum*, ed. Thomas Wright, in *Rerum Britannicarum Medii Aevi Scriptores* (London: Longmans, 1983) 34:108.

22. For the ways in which Chaucer has made his formel eagle an emblem of chastity, see Bennett, *The Parlament of Foules*, 153 and 176.

23. Ibid., 174. Bennett's argument, however, differs significantly from mine.

24. It is useful to compare this irony with that of Machaut's *Voir-Dit*: the painstaking construction of the *Voir-Dit* is a major subject of the *Voir-Dit*, and the work is only completed when the narrator is finished with his task of describing its construction. See Brownlee, *Poetic Identity*, 116.

4. The Rhetoric of Reading in
Troilus and Criseyde (notes to pages 56–94)

1. On the narrator as a historian, see Morton W. Bloomfield, "Distance and Predestination in *Troilus and Criseyde*," rpt. *Chaucer Criticism II*, ed. Richard J. Schoeck and Jerome Taylor (South Bend: University of Notre Dame Press, 1961), 197; A. J. Minnis, *Chaucer and Pagan Antiquity*, Chaucer Studies 8 (Cambridge: D. S. Brewer, 1982), 67–68; and Lawton, *Chaucer's Narrators*,

77–79. For a useful study of the narrator's role, see especially R. A. Shoaf, *Dante, Chaucer and the Currency of the Word: Money, Images, and Reference in Late Medieval Poetry* (Norman, Okla.: Pilgrim Books, 1983), 124–28; Shoaf, however, sees the narrator as arriving at an awareness of his own role in telling this story as early as Book 2, whereas I will argue that this does not occur until the poem's epilogue, if at all. See also Sherron E. Knopp, "Narrator and Audience in Chaucer's *Troilus and Criseyde*," *Studies in Philology* 78 (1981): 323–40; Varda Fish, "The Origin and Original Object of *Troilus and Criseyde*," *Chaucer Review* 18 (1984): 304–15; Bernard F. Huppé, "The Unlikely Narrator: The Narrative Strategy of the *Troilus*," in *Signs and Symbols in Chaucer's Poetry*, ed. John P. Hermann and John J. Burke, Jr. (University: University of Alabama Press, 1981), 186–94; and Murray F. Markland, "*Troilus and Criseyde*: The Inviolability of the Ending," *Modern Language Quarterly* 31 (1970): 147–59. Fish's, Huppé's, and Markland's views on a few of the narrator's character traits are similar to my own, but we do not agree on how the narrator is deployed throughout the poem.

2. For the role of the audience as supplier of meaning, see Dieter Mehl, "The Audience of Chaucer's *Troilus and Criseyde*," in *Chaucer and Middle English Studies in Honour of Rossell Hope Robbins*, ed. Beryl Rowland (London: Allen and Unwin, 1974), 176–79. See also Piero Boitani, *English Medieval Narrative in the 13th and 14th Centuries*, trans. Joan Krakover Hall (Cambridge: Cambridge University Press, 1982), 202–23; and Knopp, "Narrator and Audience," 329–30.

3. The narrator's various similarities to Pandarus the "artist" have been treated extensively. Some of the best arguments are by Adrienne Lockhart, "Semantic, Moral, and Aesthetic Degeneration in *Troilus and Criseyde*," *Chaucer Review* 8 (1973): 117–18; E. Talbot Donaldson, "Chaucer's Three 'P's': Pandarus, Pardoner, and Poet," *Michigan Quarterly Review* 14 (1975): 289–90; Donald W. Rowe, *O Love O Charite!: Contraries Harmonized in Chaucer's "Troilus"* (Carbondale: Southern Illinois University Press, 1976), 153, 154; Rose A. Zimbardo, "Creator and Created: The Generic Perspective of Chaucer's *Troilus and Criseyde*," *Chaucer Review* 11 (1977): 287–88; Fyler, *Chaucer and Ovid*, 129–30, 133; Boitani, *English Medieval Narrative*, 203, 204; Karla Taylor, "A Text and Its Afterlife: Dante and Chaucer," *Comparative Literature* 35 (1983): 11; Richard Waswo, "The Narrator of *Troilus and Criseyde*," *English Literary History* 50 (1983): 10–11; and Winthrop Wetherbee, *Chaucer and the Poets: An Essay on "Troilus and Criseyde"* (Ithaca: Cornell University Press, 1984), 195–96. For the narrator's identification with Troilus, see especially Bloomfield, "Distance and Predestination," 208; Rowe, *O Love*, 155–56, 163–66; Waswo, "The Narrator," 16; Wetherbee, *Chaucer and the Poets*, 35–36; and Fish, "Origin and Original Object," 311–12.

4. Donaldson, "Chaucer's Three 'P's,'" 283.

5. Shoaf, *Dante, Chaucer*, 118, notes that Pandarus uses the lovers as if they were "characters" and tries to "experience in language what he cannot experience in fact." See also Fyler, *Chaucer and Ovid*, 132 and Boitani, *Medieval English Narrative*, 216.

6. See Rowe, *O Love*, 88–89, for an excellent discussion of Pandarus as artistic intermediary. See also Taylor, "A Text," 11, 12.

7. On Pandarus as a rhetorician, see especially Thomas A. Van, "Chaucer's

Pandarus as an Earthly Maker," *Southern Humanities Review* 12 (1978): 89–
97. Rowe, *O Love*, 87–88, too, argues for Pandarus's basic "for the nones"
qualities, as does Zimbardo, "Creator and Created," 292–93.

8. See Taylor, "A Text and Its Afterlife," 11.

9. Fyler, *Chaucer and Ovid*, 131, notes that Pandarus, too, compares himself
to a blind man. But Pandarus is arguing a position the opposite of the narrator's;
he says that the blind are often better leaders than the sighted (1.628–29), a view
that proves to be true in Pandarus's case: the unsuccessful lover brings success
to others.

10. Wolfgang Iser's conception of the process of reading has been helpful in
my analysis of the *Troilus*. Noting how texts are realized in the process of reading
them, Iser provides a useful model by which to understand this poem's fictional
strategy: at times, we are watching how the narrator is interpreting Lollius's
text—and appropriating it as his own—while he reads it. The same process is
at work with the characters in the story proper. See *The Implied Reader: Patterns
of Communication in Prose Fiction from Bunyan to Beckett* (Baltimore: Johns
Hopkins University Press, 1974), 274–94. The idea of self-interested readers appears again in *The Legend of Good Women*, written after the *Troilus*. See Lisa
J. Kiser, *Telling Classical Tales: Chaucer and the Legend of Good Women* (Ithaca: Cornell University Press, 1983), 71–94.

11. Were Criseyde not so ready to accept love at this point, she might have
remembered that the nightingale's song could just as easily have been Philomela's tragic song of rape—related earlier to Pandarus by Philomela's sister, the
swallow Procne (2.64–70). For more on these birds in the *Troilus*, see Marvin
Mudrick, "Chaucer's Nightingales," rpt. *Chaucer's Troilus: Essays in Criticism*,
ed. Stephen A. Barney (Hamden: Archon Books, 1980), 91–99. For a useful
discussion of characters as interpreters in fictional works, see Naomi Schor, "Fiction as Interpretation/Interpretation as Fiction," in *The Reader in the Text: Essays on Audience and Interpretation*, ed. Susan R. Suleiman and Inge Crosman
(Princeton: Princeton University Press, 1980), 165–82; see also Steven Mailloux's "Learning to Read: Interpretations and Reader-Response Criticism,"
Studies in the Literary Imagination 12 (1979): 93–108.

12. See also 4.1422–28, where Troilus, against his better judgment, chooses
to believe in the unlikely success of Criseyde's plots to return: "Fynaly, he gan
his herte wreste / To trusten hire, and took it for the beste."

13. "Experience, Language, and Consciousness: 'Troilus and Criseyde,' II,
596–931," in Barney, 174–75. See also Aers, *Chaucer, Langland and the Creative Imagination*, 125–26.

14. But see Elizabeth R. Hatcher, "Chaucer and the Psychology of Fear: Troilus in Book V," *English Literary History* 40 (1973): 319–20, who is perhaps
right in arguing that the boar dream, too, is deeply colored by Troilus's psychological state.

15. On this scene and Pandarus as a bad friend indeed, see Alan T. Gaylord,
"Friendship in Chaucer's *Troilus*," *Chaucer Review* 3 (1969): 239–64, and
Leah R. Freiwald, " 'Swych Love of Frendes': Pandarus and Troilus," *Chaucer
Review* 6 (1971): 120–29.

16. On the narrator's emotional response to his love story, see especially
Thomas H. Bestul, "Chaucer's *Troilus and Criseyde*: The Passionate Epic and
Its Narrator," *Chaucer Review* 14 (1980): 366–78; but see also Bloomfield,

"Distance and Predestination," 208; Rowe, *O Love,* 155–61; Burlin, *Chaucerian Fiction,* 131; Evan Carton, "Complicity and Responsibility in Pandarus' Bed and Chaucer's Art," *PMLA* 94 (1979): 47–61; Shoaf, *Dante, Chaucer,* 128; Wetherbee, "Chaucer and the Poets," 35–36; and Fish, "Origin and Original Object," 311.

17. For other sites, see 3.531, 1058, 1223–25, 1246, 1310–23, 1373–1400, 1688–94, 1804.

18. Rowe, *O Love,* 92, has expertly noted the harmonizing impulse here. But I agree with Wetherbee, "Chaucer and the Poets," 47–49, who more clearly sees this as a problem in the narrator rather than as a possible belief of Chaucer himself. For more on the ambiguity here, see Ida Gordon, *The Double Sorrow of Troilus: A Study of Ambiguities in "Troilus and Criseyde"* (Oxford: Clarendon Press, 1970), 30–33, and the remarks on this proem by Chauncey Wood, *The Elements of Chaucer's Troilus* (Durham: Duke University Press, 1984), 102–14. Troilus, too, harmonizes these two kinds of love, as is seen in his speech "O Love O Charite" and his *Canticus Troili* in Book 3. However, he has a good excuse for being confused on this matter: he's a pagan, without the benefit of Christian truth.

19. Earlier, too, in Book 1, Criseyde blames "the world" instead of the real culprit Pandarus (409–20). Also, Troilus and Pandarus ("for the nones") both blame Fortune or other forces in Book 4 for things that people, including Criseyde, have brought about, since both are unwilling to admit that their friends, relatives, or lovers are culpable, having wills of their own. See 4.260, 323, 385–92, and 5.207–10.

20. See C. S. Lewis, *The Allegory of Love: A Study in Medieval Tradition* (Oxford: Oxford University Press, 1936), esp. 184–87. See also Minnis, *Chaucer and Pagan Antiquity,* 83–84 and Rowe, *O Love,* 50. The most thorough arguments on behalf of Criseyde have been advanced by feminists and new historicists, who see Criseyde's threatened position in a hostile society. See Aers, *Chaucer, Langland, and the Creative Imagination,* 117–42 and Maureen Fries, "'Slydynge of Corage': Chaucer's Criseyde as Feminist and Victim," in *The Authority of Experience: Essays in Feminist Criticism,* ed. Arlyn Diamond and Lee R. Edwards (Amherst: University of Massachusetts Press, 1977), 45–59.

21. See also 2.297, 367–71, 461–62, 468, 470–72.

22. See also 2.701–705, 736–39, 1290–95.

23. See also Pandarus's remark to Criseyde about Troilus's possible (actually real) presence in his house; he assures Criseyde that even if Troilus were there, no one would ever know (3.568–95).

24. Other critics have noted the similarities between the first and second wooing of Criseyde. See, for example, Dieter Mehl, *Geoffrey Chaucer: An Introduction to His Narrative Poetry* (Cambridge: Cambridge University Press, 1986), 90. Mehl sees the Diomede section as "a parody of the first two books of the poem." See also Alfred David, *The Strumpet Muse: Art and Morals in Chaucer's Poetry* (Bloomington: Indiana University Press, 1976), 35; Gordon, *Double Sorrow,* 123–24 and Rowe, *O Love,* 75.

25. See especially her seemingly sincere promises to Troilus in 4.1534–54 and the narrator's assessment of her "good entente" in 4.1415–21. For a harsher view of Criseyde, especially in Books 4 and 5, see E. Talbot Donaldson, "Criseide and Her Narrator," in *Speaking of Chaucer* (New York: Norton, 1970), 73–

83; and Sister Francis Dolores Covella, "Audience as Determinant of Meaning in the *Troilus*," *Chaucer Review* 2 (1968): 236–41.

26. On the medieval view of the pagans' need for the concepts of fame and reputation, see Minnis, *Chaucer and Pagan Antiquity*, 128–31, who applies it to *The Knight's Tale*. See also Boitani, *Chaucer and the Imaginary World of Fame*, 31–39, 80, 88, 124, 132.

27. The narrator here is, of course, no different from Troilus in the face of Cassandra's truth about Criseyde. Not wanting to believe her, he calls Cassandra a liar.

28. It is worth noting that like the narrator, Criseyde too begins needlessly to doubt Troilus's honesty once she is settled in the Greek camp and unwilling to confront the fact of her betrayal. See her last letter (5.1606–16).

29. Nearly all the criticism on the epilogue finds it somehow problematic, although critics do not agree on exactly how we are to define the problems. Of those who believe that the narrator (rather than Chaucer himself) is speaking throughout the epilogue, a position with which I agree, there are several who offer readings generally related to but not the same as my own. See especially Robert M. Jordan, "The Narrator in Chaucer's *Troilus*," *English Literary History* 25 (1958): 254–57; T. P. Dunning, "God and Man in *Troilus and Criseyde*," in *English and Medieval Studies Presented to J. R. R. Tolkien*, ed. Norman Davis and C. H. Wrenn (London: Allen and Unwin, 1963), 181–82; Wetherbee, *Chaucer and the Poets*, 232, 235, who, like Jordan, in "The Narrator," sees that the narrator's emotional response to his story is challenged by "the moral and spiritual questions his poem raises"; John M. Ganim, *Style and Consciousness in Middle English Narrative* (Princeton: Princeton University Press, 1983), 100–102, who offers a fine description of the epilogue's complexities; Rowe, *O Love*, 166–67, who closely and effectively attends to the narrator's troubles here; and Mehl, *An Introduction*, 95.

30. E. Talbot Donaldson's reading of these stanzas addressed to the women shows that visible here is the panic of a court poet who has accidentally stumbled into the awkward position of potentially offending the socially superior women in his audience. This is surely true, but there is also a deeper realization being represented as well, relating to the concept of entrapment that threads throughout the poem. See E. T. Donaldson, "The Ending of *Troilus*," in *Speaking of Chaucer*, 94–95. For other interesting questions raised here about the politics of court poetry, see Waswo, "The Narrator," passim.

31. For various articulations of these problems and their possible solutions, see those critics mentioned in note 29, and also Markland, "*Troilus and Criseyde*," 147–59; Bestul, "Chaucer's *Troilus and Criseyde*," 374–76; Donaldson, "Ending," 91–97; and Gerald Morgan, "The Ending of *Troilus and Criseyde*," *Modern Language Review* 77 (1982): 257–71. Waswo, however, believes that in the epilogue there is no real resolution to the poem's contradictions, either by Chaucer or by the narrator (who are close, in his view).

32. I read the stanzas on Troilus's death in light of John M. Steadman's arguments about their medieval contexts in *Disembodied Laughter: Troilus and the Apotheosis Tradition: A Reexamination of Narrative and Thematic Contexts* (Berkeley: University of California Press, 1972).

33. Variations on the "double vision" reading of the end of the poem are, of course, common. For some well-argued examples of this reading, see Anthony E.

Farnham, "Chaucerian Irony and the Ending of the *Troilus*," *Chaucer Review* 1 (1967): 207–16; Knopp, "Narrator and Audience," 338; and Peter Elbow, *Oppositions in Chaucer* (Middletown, Conn.: Wesleyan University Press, 1975), 66–70; Rowe, *O Love*, 166–69; and Fyler, *Chaucer and Ovid*, 137.

34. Of interest here are the remarks of Dominick LaCapra in *History and Criticism* (Ithaca: Cornell University Press, 1985), 36: "Historians generally recognize that they begin not with a 'virgin' historical record but with a record processed by the accounts of other historians. But they often tend to reduce their role to the 'revision' of standard accounts on the basis of new facts. . . . This restricted view obscures the strangeness of a dialogue with the dead who are reconstructed through their 'textualized' remainders."

35. Bloomfield, "Distance and Predestination," 204–205, noticed this a long time ago, and it has been worked with since then by others. See, for example, Minnis, *Chaucer and Pagan Antiquity*, 71; Martin Stevens, "The Winds of Fortune in the *Troilus*," *Chaucer Review* 13 (1979): 285–307 (Stevens sees the narrator as much more fated than I do); Richard Osberg, "Between the Intention and the Act: Intentions and Ends in Chaucer's *Troilus*," *English Literary History* 48 (1981): 263–64; Mehl, *An Introduction*, 93–94; and Carton, "Complicity and Responsibility," 58.

36. My reading of the *Filostrato* is indebted to the work of Janet Levarie Smarr, *Boccaccio and Fiammetta: The Narrator as Lover* (Urbana: University of Illinois Press, 1986), 15–33; Robert Hollander, *Boccaccio's Two Venuses* (New York: Columbia University Press, 1977), 31–65; Chauncey Wood, *The Elements*, 3–37; and Huppé, "The Unlikely Narrator," 192. This interpretation of Boccaccio's narrator is by no means common; see, for example, recent straight readings by James Dean, "Chaucer's *Troilus*, Boccaccio's *Filostrato*, and the Poetics of Closure, *Philological Quarterly* 64 (1985): 175–84; and Fish, "The Origin," 304–15.

37. For Dante's truth-claims as a scribe of God, see especially Barolini, *Dante's Poets*, 60 and Singleton, *Commedia: Elements of Structure*, 62. I discuss this idea in greater detail in the next chapter.

38. For Dante's independent influence on the *Troilus*, see especially Boitani, "What Dante Meant to Chaucer," 127–28; Schless, *Chaucer and Dante*, 101–47; Wetherbee, *Chaucer and the Poets*, 43–44, 56, and 145–78; Elizabeth Kirk, " 'Paradis Stood Formed in Hire Yën': Courtly Love and Chaucer's Revision of Dante," in *Acts of Interpretation: The Text in its Contexts, 700–1600, Essays in Medieval and Renaissance Literature in Honor of E. Talbot Donaldson*, ed. Mary J. Carruthers and Elizabeth Kirk (Norman, Okla.: Pilgrim Books, 1982), 257–77; Jeffrey Helterman, "The Masks of Love in *Troilus and Criseyde*," *Comparative Literature* 26 (1974): 14–31; Bonnie Wheeler, "Dante, Chaucer, and the Ending of *Troilus and Criseyde*," *Philological Quarterly* 61 (1982): 105–23; and Taylor, "A Text and Its Afterlife," 1–20. In my text I cite those with whom I agree or whom I overlap.

39. Kirk, " 'Paradis,' " 264–65.

40. Wetherbee, *Chaucer and the Poets*, 43–44.

41. Ibid., 56, 145, 156. See also Rowe, *O Love*, 71–72, 99, 108, 147; and the allusions to Dante mentioned in the work of the other comparativists in note 37.

42. Kirk, " 'Paradis,' " 273–76.

43. Taylor, "A Text and Its Afterlife," 9, 18–19. Bestul, 373–76, "Chaucer's *Troilus*," also begins to get at this idea by suggesting that the emotional response of the narrator to the love affair blinds him to the morally right view. See also Fish, "Origin," 311, and Alan T. Gaylord, "Chaucer's Tender Trap: The *Troilus* and the 'Yonge, Fresshe Folkes," *English Miscellany* 15 (1964): 24–25 and "The Lesson of the *Troilus*: Chastisement and Correction," in *Essays on Troilus and Criseyde*, ed. Mary Salu, Chaucer Studies 3 (Cambridge: D. S. Brewer, 1979), 23–42.

44. Others besides Taylor have seen Pandarus as a figure who raises questions about the responsibilities of artists. See especially Carton, "Complicity," 50–59 and Shoaf, *Dante, Chaucer*, 117–18 and 124–26.

45. See John M. Fyler, "The Fabrications of Pandarus," *Modern Language Quarterly* 41 (1980): 118–20, for the other ironies here.

46. Taylor, "A Text," 7–14, fully and effectively incorporates the Paolo and Francesca episode into her argument about readers. Wetherbee, *Chaucer and the Poets*, 37, and Rowe, *O Love*, 153, also rightly see its relevance here. Dante, of course, implies that the book is not entirely to blame and that Francesca is conveniently using it to exculpate the role of her own will in the sin. For the general point of artistic pimping (especially in the Pandarus/Chaucer connection), see also Donaldson, "Chaucer's Three 'P's,'" 288–91.

5. *The Legend of Good Women*: Chaucer's *Purgatorio* (pages 95–110)

1. I quote from the F Prologue in all cases, but where there is a corresponding version in the G Prologue, I refer the reader to those lines too. Though the two prologues differ in many details, I believe that in substance they agree.

2. For three representative readers who see an allusion to Dante in the opening lines of the *Legend*, see Mario Praz, "Chaucer and the Great Italian Writers of the Trecento," in *The Flaming Heart: Essays on Crashaw, Machiavelli, and Other Studies in the Relations Between Italian and English Literature from Chaucer to T. S. Eliot* (New York: Doubleday, 1958), 53; David, *The Strumpet Muse*, 42; and Boitani, "What Dante Meant to Chaucer," 125.

3. Kiser, *Telling Classical Tales*, esp. 95–131.

4. See Schless, *Chaucer and Dante*, 149–68. But see also Praz, *The Flaming Heart*, 31–34.

5. See Wetherbee, *Chaucer and the Poets*, 21–22, 145–47, 165–78, and Shoaf, *Dante, Chaucer*, 15, 139, 143, 145, 235–38. For the *Purgatorio*'s possible influence on Chaucer's structuring of *The Canterbury Tales*, see Glending Olson, "Chaucer, Dante, and the Structure of Fragment VIII (G) of the *Canterbury Tales*," *Chaucer Review* 16 (1982): 222–36.

6. Dante describes the plan of his Purgatory in Canto 17.91–139. Love may err "either through an evil object, or through too much or too little vigor" (95–96).

7. Many of these elements, of course, are drawn from the same stock of conventional amatory verse that Dante himself drew from in his construction of the *Commedia*. Thus, Chaucer and Dante might be seen as independently mining the same traditions for their imagery and action. Moreover, Chaucer is certainly deeply indebted to Machaut, Deschamps, and Froissart for his daisy imagery and for some of the *Legend*'s scenes. See James I. Wimsatt, *The Marguerite Poetry*

of Guillaume de Machaut (Chapel Hill: University of North Carolina Press, 1970), and Robert M. Estrich, "Chaucer's Prologue to *The Legend of Good Women* and Machaut's *Le Jugement dou Roy de Navarre,*" *Studies in Philology* 26 (1939): 20–39. Machaut's *Dit dou Vergier* probably helped Chaucer with his creation of the all-powerful God of Love, and the *Remede de Fortune* contains a lady mediator who is compared to a flower and the sun. Froissart's *Paradys d'Amours: La Prison amoureuse,* and *Joli Buisson de Jonece* raise issues concerning textual truth-value, as does Machaut's *Voir-Dit*—so Chaucer was almost certainly inspired to address these issues by a careful reading of the poetry of his French models. But the pronounced theological slant in the *Legend*'s action and language, which I will describe below, and the poem's interest in the Dantean issue of the relationship between pagan and Christian, amatory and religious verse, point to the *Commedia* as Chaucer's major subtext here.

8. For recent statements about the *Purgatorio*'s emphasis on art, see John Freccero, "An Introduction to the *Paradiso,*" in *Dante: The Poetics of Conversion,* ed. Rachel Jacoff (Cambridge, Mass.: Harvard University Press, 1986), 210; Barolini, *Dante's Poets,* esp. 13, 40–44, 274–75; Mazzotta, *Dante, Poet of the Desert,* 190–226; Robert L. Montgomery, *The Reader's Eye: Studies in Didactic Literary Theory from Dante to Tasso* (Berkeley: University of California Press, 1979), 64–65, 70–74, 92; and Kenneth John Atchity, "Dante's *Purgatorio*: The Poem Reveals Itself," in *Italian Literature, Roots and Branches: Essays in Honor of Thomas Goddard Bergin,* ed. Giose Rimanelli and Kenneth John Atchity (New Haven: Yale University Press, 1976), 85–115. On Dante's remarkable poetic synthesis of the love of a woman with the love of God as early as the *Vita Nuova,* see Charles S. Singleton, *An Essay on the Vita Nuova* (Cambridge, Mass.: Harvard University Press, 1949), 64–74, and "Dante: Within Courtly Love and Beyond," in *The Meaning of Courtly Love,* ed. F. X. Newman (Albany: SUNY Press, 1968), 43–54.

9. On the critical debate surrounding the supposed existence of a school of *stilnovisti,* see Mario Marti, *Storio della Stil nuovo,* vol. 1 (Lecce: Milella, 1973).

10. Singleton, *An Essay on the Vita Nuova,* 77.

11. On the meaning of Beatrice's death, see Singleton, ibid., 20, 113–14, who rightly sees the likeness between Beatrice and Christ as a typical medieval "analogy of proportion." See also J. A. Scott, "Dante's 'Sweet New Style' and the *Vita Nuova,*" *Italica* 42 (1965): 98–107.

12. See Barolini, *Dante's Poets,* 15 and 22, and Jerome Mazzaro, *The Figure of Dante: An Essay on the "Vita Nuova"* (Princeton: Princeton University Press, 1981), xii, 92–94, 123.

13. In Statius's speech, he discusses the "lantern" that Vergil held behind him (*Purgatorio* 22.67–69), a metaphor for the idea that Vergil saved others but not himself. These lines are quite probably the source for Chaucer's lines about Vergil's lantern in *The Legend of Dido* (925–26).

14. See Mazzotta, *Dante, Poet of the Desert,* 185–91, 218–26. See also Barolini, *Dante's Poets,* 251–52, and R. A. Shoaf, *Dante, Chaucer,* 54–57.

15. For an extended discussion of the sun in Chaucer's *Legend,* see Kiser, *Telling Classical Tales,* 36–48.

16. See also Cantos 2.37–40; 15.7–33; 24.142; 27.59–60; 32.10–12.

17. In the F Prologue, the God of Love actually wears a sun on his head (230–31). Praz believes that the God of Love and the lines introducing him are mod-

eled on Canto 2 of the *Purgatorio* (37–39), which describes the appearance of an angel of God. See Praz, *The Flaming Heart*, 32.

18. For the source of Dante's conception of his lady as mediator, see Singleton's discussion of Guinizelli's verse in *Essay*, 69.

19. Perhaps this fact accounts (in part) for Alceste's mediation being symbolized by a *literary* device; her predream name, "day's-eye," is a metaphor for "sun."

20. Compare Beatrice's "the high decree of God would be broken . . . without some scot of penitence that may pour forth tears" (30.142–45) with Alceste's "Love ne wol nat countrepleted be. . . . Now wol I seyn what penance thou shalt do" (F 476–79, G 466–69).

21. Mazzotta notes that Dante viewed his verse as an analogue of the Incarnation (*Dante, Poet of the Desert*, 202–10). Beatrice's role here would seem to confirm this idea, showing that Dante hoped to "make literary history into a history of faith-producing messages in which each text . . . becomes the prophecy of an event which in turn may lead to that history which is at one with the Revelation of the Word" (218). See also James Thomas Chiampi, *Shadowy Prefaces: Conversion and Writing in the "Divine Comedy,"* L'interprete 24 (Ravenna: Longo Editore, 1981), esp. 40–45, 106–108, 137, 150–52.

22. See Kiser, *Telling Classical Tales*, 101–111.

23. Boccaccio, too, even though his reverence for Dante was undeniable, clearly avoided repeating Dante's daring claims about the synthesis of earthly and heavenly love. Like Chaucer, in fact, Boccaccio seems to parody Dante's attempts to redeem the poetry of erotic love, often secularizing material borrowed from Dante's works. In the occasionally pornographic *Ameto*, for example, there is a Beatrice figure, and he makes many allusions to the *Purgatorio* and *Paradiso*. The *Amorosa Visione* contains strained Dantean images of synthesis (i.e., an eagle/lion/God of Love figure, an Angel/Venus conflation) and an angelic woman to imitate Beatrice. In its prologue, too, Boccaccio says that his lady resembles Amore (sonn. 3.23); his female dream-guide is decorated with a sun-like crown (1.37–38) and uses Beatrice's words from the *Purgatorio* to rebuke her charge when he opts for earthly rather than heavenly love (30.13–21). Finally, Boccaccio's poem rejects any easy synthesis of the two. See Sylvia Huot, "Poetic Ambiguity and Reader Response in Boccaccio's *Amorosa Visione*," *Modern Philology* 83 (1985): 121–22. See also Boccaccio's *Filocolo* and *Filostrato*, which contain ironic and untenable Dantean syntheses of the two loves. The *Filocolo*, for instance, has a Cupid with eyes (cf. *Legend of Good Women* F 237–38, G 169–70) to stand for an artificial union of pagan and Christian marital love. Both of these poems also have Beatrice figures (Fiammetta), as does the *Teseida*. See David Wallace, *Chaucer and the Early Writings of Boccaccio*, Chaucer Studies 12 (Cambridge: D. S. Brewer, 1985), 65–70; and Hollander, *Boccaccio's Two Venuses*, where the author argues that Boccaccio's shorter poems in Italian are designed to mock the "religion of love" by parodying its literary manifestations (3–4), a purpose very close to Chaucer's in the *Legend*. In short, Boccaccio's works may well have influenced Chaucer's response to Dantean thought.

24. On Dante's typologizing of biography and autobiography in his works and how this technique serves his Christian purpose, see A. C. Charity, *Events and Their Afterlife: The Dialectics of Christian Typology in the Bible and in Dante* (Cambridge: Cambridge University Press, 1966), 252–55.

25. Chaucer's collection of legends makes this point repeatedly; just as the men in the legends use the women for their own advancement (and salvation, in the case of Theseus), so Chaucer the narrator uses the life stories of these women to secure his own "salvation" from the God of Love. In a sense, then, Chaucer's parallelism suggests that such a use of these women's lives is a form of exploitation.

26. On the daisy and Alceste as symbols of Chaucer's poetic principles, see Kiser, *Telling Classical Tales*, 43–48, 92, 134–35. There are scholars who see Beatrice, too, as a symbol for the poet's craft. See, for example, the most extended treatment of this idea in Michele d'Andria, *Beatrice simbolo della poesia con Dante dalla terra a Dio*, Collana di Cultura 29 (Rome: Edizioni Dell'ateneo and Bizzarri, 1979). But most agree that Beatrice's significance to Dante goes beyond this into theological realms.

27. See chapter 25 of the *Vita Nuova* for Dante's famous discussion of the God of Love as a literary creature with no substance or reality. For this deity's imitation of the Christian God, see especially chapter 12 of the *Vita Nuova*, where he defines himself in the same transcendent terms applied to the Christian God.

28. See the *Vita Nuova*, chapter 24. On the God of Love's superfluity, see Singleton, *Essay*, 57, 76, 91. See also Marianne Shapiro, "Figurality in the *Vita Nuova*: Dante's New Rhetoric," *Dante Studies* 97 (1979): 118–19, 122; James T. S. Wheelock, "A Function of the *Amore* figure in the *Vita Nuova*," *Romanic Review* 68 (1977): 284–85; and Margherita de Bonfils Templer, "Amore e le visioni nella *Vita Nuova*," *Dante Studies* 92 (1974): 21.

29. For a longer discussion of the significance of the God of Love in Chaucer's poem, especially as a figure for Chaucer's audience, see Kiser, *Telling Classical Tales*, 62–69 and 81–85.

30. Chaucer's deity, however, is described as having certain governmental powers; he is "a god, and eke a kyng" (F 431, G 421). Thus, he seems to rule in both a religious and a secular sphere, a situation that Dante would have found intolerable. Throughout his later career as a poet, he repeatedly railed against the notion that the secular and religious spheres could be mingled in the same governmental structure (see *Purgatorio* 16.106–108, for example: "Rome, which made the world good, was wont to have two Suns . . . that of the world and that of God"). Chaucer's sunlike God of Love rules—and ineptly at that— two worlds at once, and needs to be advised by Alceste about the role of a god (F 345–47, G 321–23) and about just kingship (F 373–411, G 353–97), the latter advice being drawn from that section of Dante's *Convivio* where the poet defines his views on the separation of church and state. See Schless, *Chaucer and Dante*, 154–57. Thus, Chaucer's deity offends Dante's principles on the governmental level but complies with them on the level of poetics. It is not hard to imagine how Dante would have felt about this travesty.

31. The twenty-four elders ultimately derive, of course, from *Apocalypse* 4:4.

32. See Charles S. Singleton, *Journey to Beatrice* (1958; rpt., Baltimore: Johns Hopkins University Press, 1977), 92–94, for commentary on this aspect of Dante's *Purgatorio*.

33. The number of ladies who escort Alceste is, in both the F and G Prologues, nineteen—a number that does not correspond to the number of Dante's

elders (twenty-four). However, in Chaucer's *Retraction,* he refers to the *Legend of Good Women* as "the book of the XXV. Ladies," suggesting that one possible plan was to have twenty-four ladies represented (not including Alceste). This number, then, would have equaled the number of Dante's elders (not including, of course, Beatrice).

34. Praz believes that the passage about the "tras of wemen" is closely dependent upon the *Inferno* 3.55–57. If this is true, then perhaps we are faced with a further Chaucerian irony: these women only seem to be worthy of salvation, when in reality, if judged by Dante's own Christian standards, they would not make it at all. See *The Flaming Heart,* 31–32, for Praz's argument.

35. Piero Boitani notes this same basic difference between Chaucer's *House of Fame* and Dante's *Commedia.* See "What Dante Meant to Chaucer," 120–28.

36. *Dante's Poets,* 90.

37. *Commedia: Elements of Structure* (1954; rpt., Baltimore: Johns Hopkins University Press, 1977), 62. Barolini extends this phrase, noting that the *Commedia*'s "strategy is that there is no strategy," *Dante's Poets,* 90.

6. Truth and Textuality in *The Canterbury Tales* (pages 111–149)

1. It is by no means certain that Chaucer knew the *Decameron* firsthand. But traditional arguments that he did not have been challenged by recent scholars and critics; see especially Donald McGrady, "Chaucer and the *Decameron* Reconsidered," *Chaucer Review* 12 (1977): 1–26. For some of the artistic goals shared by both poets in their collections of tales, see Robin Kirkpatrick, "The Wake of the *Commedia*: Chaucer's *Canterbury Tales* and Boccaccio's *Decameron,*" in *Chaucer and the Italian Trecento,* ed. Piero Boitani (Cambridge: Cambridge University Press, 1983), 201–230.

2. For Boccaccio's dramatization of the variousness of interpretation, see especially Millicent Joy Marcus, *An Allegory of Form: Literary Self-Consciousness in the Decameron,* Stanford French and Italian Studies 18 (Saratoga, Cal.: Anma Libri, 1979), esp. 102–109; Robert M. Durling, "Boccaccio on Interpretation: Guido's Escape (*Decameron* VI.9)," in *Dante, Petrarch, Boccaccio: Studies in the Italian Trecento in Honor of Charles Singleton,* ed. Aldo Bernardo and Anthony Pellegrini, Medieval and Renaissance Texts and Studies 22 (Binghamton, N.Y.: MARTS, 1983), 273–304; and Smarr, *Boccaccio and Fiammetta,* 192–93 and 201–204.

3. I do not mean to deny the important influence of Ovid's *Metamorphoses* on the frame of *The Canterbury Tales.* See the discussion by Richard L. Hoffman, *Ovid and the Canterbury Tales* (Philadelphia: University of Pennsylvania Press, 1966), 3–11. The richly self-reflexive French poets also experimented with frames and individualized narrators; they too surely had a deep influence on Chaucer's conception of *The Canterbury Tales.* But Chaucer's collection shows at least four Boccaccian narratives (*The Reeve's Tale, The Clerk's Tale, The Franklin's Tale,* and *The Shipman's Tale*); *The Pardoner's Tale,* too, has been argued to be profoundly Boccaccian in its stance. See Paul Beckman Taylor, "*Peynted Confessiouns*: Boccaccio and Chaucer," *Comparative Literature* 34 (1982): 116–29.

4. Dante was well aware of the variousness of human interpretive strategies,

and he attempts to guide his readers toward responsible interpretation at several points in the *Commedia*. He does this by addressing the reader directly, by raising the issue of interpretation in the action of his poem (see *Inferno* 10, for example), by showing some of the consequences of misreading (as in the Paolo and Francesca episode), and by showing the virtues of the Augustinian precept to "despoil the Egyptians" by reading pagan texts in a Christian manner (as in Statius's reading of Vergil's *Aeneid* in *Purgatorio* 22).

5. For some of the ways in which Boccaccio handles interpretive issues differently from Dante, see Franco Fido, "Boccaccio's *Ars Narrandi* in the Sixth Day of the *Decameron*," in *Italian Literature, Roots and Branches: Essays in Honor of Thomas Goddard Bergin*, ed. Giose Rimanelli and Kenneth John Atchity (New Haven: Yale University Press, 1976), 236–40; Marcus, *An Allegory*, 110–12; and Durling, "Boccaccio on Translation," 281–90.

6. The history of classical and medieval truth-claims was, however, a long one and Dante was not the first to exploit it for his artistic purposes. For some general discussions of truth-claims in medieval narrative, see M. L. Levy, "'As myn auctour seyth,'" *Medium Aevum* 12 (1943): 25–39; William Nelson, *Fact or Fiction: The Dilemma of the Renaissance Storyteller* (Cambridge, Mass.: Harvard University Press, 1973), 1–37; Wesley Trimpi, "The Quality of Fiction: The Rhetorical Transmission of Literary Theory," *Traditio* 30 (1974): 47–51, 98, 103–104; and Jeanette M. A. Beer, *Narrative Conventions of Truth in the Middle Ages* (Geneva: Librairie Droz, 1981). On the recording of history in medieval Britain, see Robert W. Hanning, *The Vision of History in Early Britain* (New York: Columbia University Press, 1966) and Charles W. Jones, *Saints' Lives and Chronicles in Early England* (Ithaca: Cornell University Press, 1947). See also the scholarly treatments of medieval historiography listed in note 3 of my introduction.

7. Giuseppe Mazzotta, however, in "The *Decameron*: The Marginality of Literature," *University of Toronto Quarterly* 42 (1972): 66, rightly notes that Boccaccio's artful choice of this particular date—the Feast of the Annunciation—undercuts the work's truth-claim, since it suggests a symbolic structure for the frame of the *Decameron*. See also Mazzotta's *The World at Play in Boccaccio's "Decameron"* (Princeton: Princeton University Press, 1986), 18–20 and 51–54.

8. All quotations from the *Decameron* are from the John Payne translation as revised by Charles S. Singleton, 2 vols. (Berkeley: University of California Press, 1982). Volume and page numbers will be noted in the text.

9. On the retrospective nature of Dante's frame and the role of memory and forgetting in his record of a past experience, see Mazzotta, *Dante, Poet of the Desert*, 260–69. Donald Howard, in *The Idea of the Canterbury Tales* (Berkeley: University of California Press, 1976), 140, notes that "this fictional premise [is] probably Chaucer's greatest debt to Dante"—although he does not discuss the implications of the debt. Morton W. Bloomfield, in "Chaucerian Realism" in *The Cambridge Chaucer Companion*, ed. Piero Boitani and Jill Mann (Cambridge: Cambridge University Press, 1986), 179–93, discusses the "authentication" provided by Chaucer's frame.

10. On the ways in which Boccaccio and Chaucer are confronting Dante's principle, see G. D. Josipovici, "Fiction and Game in *The Canterbury Tales*," *Critical Quarterly* 7 (1965): 185–97; and P. B. Taylor, "Chaucer's *Cosyn to the Dede*," *Speculum* 57 (1982): esp. 317–20.

11. See Smarr, *Boccaccio and Fiammetta,* 167–68. Ever since Francesco DeSanctis called the *Decameron* a "commedia umana" in his *Storia della letteratura italiana,* ed. Benedetto Croce (Bari: Laterza, 1912), critics have actively pursued the idea that Boccaccio is secularizing the *Commedia* by adapting its structure to decidedly earthly locales.

12. There have been several studies of Chaucer's possible structural borrowings from the *Commedia* for the frame of his *Canterbury Tales.* In addition to Howard, *The Idea of the Canterbury Tales,* see the more detailed studies of A. L. Kellogg, "Chaucer's Self-Portrait and Dante's," *Medium Aevum* 29 (1960): 119–20; Glending Olson, "Chaucer, Dante, and the Structure of Fragment VIII," 222–36; and Bruce Kent Cowgill, " 'By *corpus dominus*': Harry Bailly as False Spiritual Guide," *Journal of Medieval and Renaissance Studies* 15 (1985): 157–81.

13. Guido Almansi, *The Writer as Liar: Narrative Technique in the "Decameron"* (London: Routledge and Kegan Paul, 1975), 6–7. See also Mazzotta, "Marginality," 64–81, and *The World at Play,* passim.

14. See Almansi, *Writer as Liar,* 28–30; Mazzotta, *The World at Play,* 58–67; and Marcus, *An Allegory of Form,* 9, 65–77. For the theme of the interplay between illusion and the objective record of reality in Boccaccio's work, see Giovanni Getto, *Vita di forme e forme di vita* (Torino: G. B. Petrini, 1958), 164ff.

15. On the importance of the game aspects of the *Canterbury Tales,* see Josipovici, "Fiction and Game," 189–96; Richard A. Lanham, "Game, Play, and High Seriousness in Chaucer's Poetry," *English Studies* 48 (1967): 1–24; Stephen Manning, "Rhetoric, Game, Morality, and Geoffrey Chaucer," *Studies in the Age of Chaucer* 1 (1979): 105–18; and Glending Olson, *Literature as Recreation in the Later Middle Ages* (Ithaca: Cornell University Press, 1982), esp. 155–63. See also Jordan, *Chaucer and the Shape of Creation,* 123–29, for other ways in which Chaucer calls attention to his work's fictionality.

16. Hanning, "The Theme of Art and Life in Chaucer's Poetry," 28.

17. The word "proprely" here is usually interpreted as meaning "according to literary propriety." See, for example, Jesse M. Gellrich, *The Idea of the Book in the Middle Ages: Language Theory, Mythology, and Fiction* (Ithaca: Cornell University Press, 1985), 231–34, who uses this definition to support a reading of the *General Prologue.* However, the definition *in propria persona* works much better, for it reflects the impersonated artistry that the narrator so worries about in his role as objective recorder.

18. The most common reading of these lines suggests that they are present largely to allow Chaucer the freedom to write anything he pleases. Although this is true, they also, more importantly, introduce the issue of objectivity by announcing the narrator's belief in his role as accurate historical reporter. Two important published arguments briefly raise this point: Ferster, *Chaucer on Interpretation,* 150–54 and Barbara Nolan, " 'A Poet Ther Was': Chaucer's Voices in the General Prologue to *The Canterbury Tales,*" *PMLA* 101 (1986): 162–63. I disagree, however, with Nolan's suggestion that the pilgrim-narrator recognizes the complications involved in the impossible task of recording truth; I think, rather, that the narrator optimistically begins his poem believing he can be successful at it, much like the *Troilus* narrator. On the traditional medieval role of "lewd compilator" that Chaucer is exploiting here, see Minnis, *Medieval Theory of Authorship,* esp. 190–210.

19. Some readings of *Sir Thopas* ascribe its brilliant parody to the narrator's intention. I am arguing against this reading, locating the success of the parody outside of the narrator's grasp. For the first view, see especially Alan T. Gaylord, "Chaucer's Dainty 'Dogerel': The 'Elvyssh' Prosody of *Sir Thopas*," *Studies in the Age of Chaucer* 1 (1979): 98–104.

20. In this reading, I agree with John W. Clark, "'This Litel Tretys' Again," *Chaucer Review* 6 (1971): 152; and Glending Olson, "A Reading of the *Thopas-Melibee* Link," *Chaucer Review* 10 (1975): 150–51. I do not agree with Ferster, *Chaucer on Interpretation*, 155, that this passage is in any way a "reversal of [the narrator's] promise in the *General Prologue* to copy reality exactly"; rather, it underscores his commitment to the role of transcriber since it manifests the worries of someone who is scrupulous about preserving the integrity of individual versions of texts. I also disagree with Benson, *Chaucer's Drama of Style*, 29–30, in that I see no inconsistency here in the narrator's "character." On the ways in which the *Thopas-Melibee* section calls attention to the fictionality of *The Canterbury Tales*, see David, *The Strumpet Muse*, 220–21.

21. Ferster, *Chaucer on Interpretation*, 152, also makes this point.

22. See Edgar Hill Duncan, "Narrator's Points of View in the Portrait-Sketches, Prologue to the *Canterbury Tales*," in *Essays in Honor of Walter Clyde Curry* (Nashville: Vanderbilt University Press, 1955), 94–97; Howard, *The Idea of the Canterbury Tales*, 82; Jerome Mandel, "Other Voices in *The Canterbury Tales*," *Criticism* 19 (1977): 338–49; and Roger Ellis, *Patterns of Religious Narrative in the Canterbury Tales* (Totowa, N.J.: Barnes and Noble, 1986), 23.

23. Jill Mann, *Chaucer and Medieval Estates Satire: The Literature of Social Classes and the General Prologue to the Canterbury Tales* (Cambridge: Cambridge University Press, 1973), 190–91.

24. This approach is encouraged by those who argue for a conventional satiric purpose in *The Canterbury Tales*. See, for example, Rosemary Woolf, "Chaucer as a Satirist in the General Prologue to the *Canterbury Tales*," *Critical Quarterly* 1 (1959): 150–57.

25. See especially the last chapter of Mann, *Chaucer and Medieval Estates Satire*, 187–202.

26. Donaldson, "Chaucer the Pilgrim," 4–7.

27. Robert Burlin, in *Chaucerian Fiction*, 163–64, points out some of the verbal echoes in the portraits and tales of the Friar and Summoner.

28. To this list one might add, as H. Marshall Leicester, Jr., suggests, the line about the Physician, "His studie was but litel on the Bible" (438), which might find its source in the unconventional use of an Old Testament narrative in *The Physician's Tale*. See Leicester's "The Art of Impersonation," 218.

29. Perhaps the audience is also being asked to notice the narrator's bookish reliance on the portraits from *The Romance of the Rose* as models for his own real-life reporting, even though he is not in a dream vision and is therefore employing the conventions of art in an idiosyncratic and—on the fictional level of the "real" pilgrimage—inappropriate fashion. For *The Romance of the Rose* as a source for the portraits, see J. V. Cunningham, "The Literary Form of the Prologue to the *Canterbury Tales*," *Modern Philology* 49 (1952): 172–81; and Duncan, "Narrator's Points of View," 82–91.

30. Those critics, such as Leicester, Gellrich, Jordan, and Lawton, who wish to argue for the textuality of the *General Prologue* by jettisoning the concept of

a narrator and replacing it with a voice of uncertain origins and sponsorship might note here that the argument for textuality, the way the work breaks "the illusion of the frame to call attention to itself as a written thing" (Leicester, *Art of Impersonation,* 216), is actually supported by retaining the concept of a narrator. Like Ferster, in *Chaucer on Interpretation,* 151, I believe that the hermeneutical problems raised by Chaucer in *The Canterbury Tales* require a narrator figure who definitely leaves the mark of a shaping consciousness on the material he claims is free of any such personal or political bias. The narrator need not be a character, of course, or show psychological or mimetic essences of any sort, but it is important that he be seen as an interpreter whose discourse is responsible for the creation of the reality he thinks he is recording.

31. See Hanning, "The Themes of Art and Life," 25–26.

32. See Ferster, *Chaucer on Interpretation,* 144.

33. See Smarr, *Boccaccio and Fiammetta,* 178, and B. J. Layman, "Boccaccio's Paradigm of the Artist and His Art," *Italian Quarterly* 13 (1970): 19–36, for examples.

34. If Harry Bailly (the artist figure) had been able to assert his control successfully over the ordering of the tales, the Parson would have spoken after the Man of Law (that is, in a less artistically satisfying place than at the end); and who knows where the Miller would have been placed—last, perhaps?

35. Alan T. Gaylord, "*Sentence* and *Solaas* in Fragment VII of the *Canterbury Tales*: Harry Bailly as Horseback Editor," *PMLA* 82 (1967): 226–35.

36. Walter Scheps, " 'Up Roos Oure Hoost, and Was Oure Aller Cok': Harry Bailly's Tale-Telling Competition," *Chaucer Review* 10 (1975): 113–28.

37. Cynthia C. Richardson, "The Function of the Host in *The Canterbury Tales*," *Texas Studies in Literature and Language* 12 (1970–71): 333–34; L. M. Leitch, "*Sentence* and *Solaas*: The Function of the Host in the *Canterbury Tales*," *Chaucer Review* 17 (1982): 8–12.

38. Gaylord, "*Sentence* and *Solaas*," 231. For this principle as it operates in *The Legend of Good Women,* see Kiser, *Telling Classical Tales,* 98–99.

39. Kiser, *Telling Classical Tales,* 102.

40. The approach I take to the pilgrim storytellers does not require that they be seen as consistently mimetic characters or that their tales participate in some kind of realistic project. However, I do argue that the pilgrims have consistent and individualized narrative personae in that they have narrative stances toward their material that distinguish them from one another and from Chaucer the artist. And in the case of the autobiographical narrators (the Wife of Bath, the Pardoner, and the Canon's Yeoman), an illusion is sustained that there is some reality (though it is represented as being unknowable) to which they refer. Thus, I am taking a position that opposes David A. Lawton's in *Chaucer's Narrators,* 103–104, where he writes: "It is the most rudimentary and token kind of stylistic decorum that provides an echo of the ostensible narrator's voice at the very beginning and end of most, not even all, tales. Apart from these echoes, it is misleading to speak of narratorial *persona* at all in the tales themselves. . . . The *Canterbury Tales,* which seem to offer most for the study of narratorial *persona,* in fact offer least." I also believe that readers are encouraged to speculate about the rhetorical purposes (and thus in some sense the motivations) of each narrator, so I am arguing as well against Jordan, *Chaucer and the Shape of Creation,* 126.

41. Charles Muscatine, *Chaucer and the French Tradition* (Berkeley: University of California Press, 1957), 177. For a more recent narratological analysis of the effect of this kind of discourse, see the discussion of overt narration by Seymour Chatman, *Story and Discourse: Narrative Structure in Fiction and Film* (Ithaca: Cornell University Press, 1978), 222–25.

42. Muscatine was the first to notice the narrative's informing symmetries, *Chaucer and the French Tradition*, 178–81, but others have developed the idea by showing Theseus's role as an artificer. See, for example, Jordan, *Chaucer and the Shape of Creation*, 169–79; and V. A. Kolve, *Chaucer and the Imagery of Narrative: The First Five Canterbury Tales* (Stanford: Stanford University Press, 1984), 135–36.

43. On the meaning of "legende" in this line, see Thomas W. Ross's gloss and summary of criticism in *The Miller's Tale*, A Variorum Edition of the Works of Geoffrey Chaucer (Norman: University of Oklahoma Press, 1983), vol. 2, pt. 3, p. 123. On the narrative strategies of the hagiographers, see especially Hippolyte Delehaye, *The Legends of the Saints: An Introduction to Hagiography*, trans. V. M. Crawford (1907; rpt. South Bend, Ind.: University of Notre Dame Press, 1961), 65–69; Alexandra Hennessey Olson, " 'De Historiis Sanctorum': A Generic Study of Hagiography," *Genre* 13 (1980): 415–25; and Thomas J. Heffernan, *Sacred Biography: Saints and Their Biographers in the Middle Ages* (Oxford: Oxford University Press, 1988), 38–71.

44. With this remark, Harry has accidentally hit upon the humanist defense of fables—but he is employing it here merely to avert the possible revelation of personally damaging information. This is surely the only medieval instance of this precept being employed to circumvent the disclosure of truth! On the "wit" and "urbanity" of the remarks exchanged by Harry and the Cook, see Kolve, *Chaucer and the Imagery of Narrative*, 267.

45. Robert W. Hanning, in "Roasting a Friar, Mis-taking a Wife, and Other Acts of Textual Harassment in Chaucer's *Canterbury Tales*," *Studies in the Age of Chaucer* 7 (1985): 10–16, shows how the idea of distorting texts for personal purposes is actually thematized in *The Summoner's Tale*. It is also raised in *The Friar's Tale*, for the summoner there thinks it is acceptable to ignore a speaker's intent in order to consign his soul to the devil.

46. Other lines in *The Man of Law's Tale* that show its narrator's unreflective confidence in the veracity and historicity of his account and in the truth of his assumptions about Christ's will are 470–74, 507, 701–714, 824–25, 905, and 939–45.

47. See Ellis, *Patterns of Religious Narrative*, 147–63, who shows convincingly that the Man of Law is more interested in decorum than in addressing the knotty problems raised by the existence of conflicting versions of his story.

48. For the tale's sources in Livy and *The Romance of the Rose*, see Helen Storm Corsa, ed., *The Physician's Tale*, A Variorum Edition of the Works of Geoffrey Chaucer (Norman: University of Oklahoma Press, 1987), vol. 2, pt. 17, pp. 4–7. See also Joerg O. Fichte, "Incident-History-Exemplum-Novella: The Transformation of History in Chaucer's *Physician's Tale*," *Florilegium* 5 (1983): 189–207, for an account of the radical generic changes wrought on this tale as it moved through various retellings.

49. See Anne Middleton, "The *Physician's Tale* and Love's Martyrs: 'Ensamples Mo Than Ten' as a Method in the *Canterbury Tales*," *Chaucer Review*

8 (1973): 16–17, for the hagiographical elements of the tale and its strange effects as an exemplum. See also Thomas B. Hanson, "Chaucer's Physician as Storyteller and Moralizer," *Chaucer Review* 7 (1972): 132–39; Ellis, *Patterns of Religious Narrative*, 205; and Emerson Brown, Jr., "What is Chaucer Doing with the Physician and His Tale?" *Philological Quarterly* 60 (1981): 129–49, for demonstrations of how the narrator destroys the moral integrity of the story.

50. For a different reading of *The Physician's Tale* that depends on the rivalry between physicians and lawyers, see Beryl Rowland, "The Physician's 'Historial Thyng Notable' and the Man of Law," *English Literary History* 40 (1973): 165–78.

51. For Virginia's story as comparable to the classical saints' lives in Chaucer's *Legend*, see Middleton, "The Physician's Tale," 27–30.

52. These three Chaucerian narratives almost certainly contribute to the late medieval genre of pseudo-autobiography, a narrative type allowing full exploration of issues such as self-fictionalization, the uncertain value of truth-claims, and the artistic shaping visible in texts representing the recording of an author's life. See G. B. Gybbon-Monypenny, "Guillaume de Machaut's Erotic 'Autobiography': Precedents for the Form of the *Voir-Dit*," in *Studies in Medieval Literature and Languages in Memory of Frederick Whitehead*, ed. W. Rothwell, et al. (Manchester: University of Manchester Press, 1973), 133–52. In addition to Dante's *Vita Nuova*, Machaut's *Voir-Dit* and Froissart's *Espinette amoureuse* are sophisticated examples of this type, and Chaucer surely appreciated their brilliant game-playing with respect to narrative "truth." For commentary on Machaut's narrative, see Beer, *Narrative Conventions*, 73–84; Calin, *A Poet at the Fountain*, 167–202; and Brownlee, *Poetic Identity in Guillaume de Machaut*, esp. 99–100, 125–27, 140–41. See also Boccaccio's interest in the way confession and hagiography can be blended to produce "false autobiography" in *Decameron* 1.1.

53. Burlin, *Chaucerian Fiction*, 222.

54. David Parker, in "Can We Trust the Wife of Bath?" *Chaucer Review* 4 (1970): 94–97, points out this—and other—dubious constructions in the Wife's Prologue. See also Charles A. Owen, Jr., *Pilgrimage and Storytelling in the "Canterbury Tales": The Dialectic of "Ernest" and "Game"* (Norman: University of Oklahoma Press, 1977), 153–54.

55. See Bernard S. Levy, "The Wife of Bath's *Queynte Fantasye*," *Chaucer Review* 4 (1970): 106–22, which argues that the Wife's tale mirrors her own illusions and beliefs, but "backfires" on her. Levy, on page 115n, also lists earlier "wish-fulfillment" critics.

56. On the Wife's skillful use of rhetoric in general, see Lanham, "Game, Play, and High Seriousness," 13–14; and Marjorie M. Malvern, " 'Who Peyntede the Leon, Tel Me Who?': Rhetorical and Didactic Roles Played by an Aesopic Fable in the *Wife of Bath's Prologue*," *Studies in Philology* 80 (1983): 238–52.

57. See David, *The Strumpet Muse*, 136–37, for the sermonlike aspects of the Wife's Prologue and her basically playful intent.

58. *House of Fame*, 474; *Troilus and Criseyde*, 2.78.

59. See Muscatine, *Chaucer and the French Tradition*, 234, for a description of this technique.

60. The Wife's use of male rhetoric to describe herself has been interestingly analyzed by critics. See Burlin, *Chaucerian Fiction*, 225; Lee Patterson, " 'For

the Wyves Love of Bathe': Feminine Rhetoric and Poetic Resolution in the *Roman de la Rose* and the *Canterbury Tales*," *Speculum* 58 (1983): 682–83; and Barbara Gottfried, "Conflict and Relationship, Sovereignty and Survival: Parables of Power in the Wife of Bath's Prologue," *Chaucer Review* 19 (1985): 202–13.

61. Hanning, "Roasting a Friar," 19–20.

62. For a similar view of the Wife's marked interest in the variousness of answers to a single question, see H. Marshall Leicester, Jr., "Of a Fire in the Dark: Public and Private Feminism in the *Wife of Bath's Tale*," *Women's Studies* 11 (1984): 163.

63. See Shoaf, *Dante, Chaucer*, 212 (though Shoaf believes we are to take the Pardoner's confession as "true"). See also Taylor, "*Peynted Confessiouns*," 127; and Robert O. Payne, "Chaucer's Realization," esp. 274–76. For many of the insights that follow I am indebted to the work of John Hofmeister, "Chaucer's Pardoner" (M.A. thesis, The Ohio State University, 1981).

64. See Olson, "Chaucer, Dante, and the Structure of Fragment VIII," 230–32, for the ways in which *The Second Nun's Tale* and *The Canon's Yeoman's Tale* are less fictive than most of the other tales; he also shows how Fragment VIII imitates the structure of the *Purgatorio* 10–27, addressing (but answering differently) some of the questions about literature's role in salvation that Dante raises there.

65. Paul G. Ruggiers, in *The Art of the Canterbury Tales* (Madison: University of Wisconsin Press, 1965), 136, also notes the Yeoman's basic ignorance of the "ultimate secret of the craft."

66. For my analysis of the Canon's Yeoman's narration (and to some extent that of the Wife of Bath and the Pardoner as well), I have benefited from Dorrit Cohn's work with first-person narration in *Transparent Minds: Narrative Modes for Presenting Consciousness in Fiction* (Princeton: Princeton University Press, 1978), 141–72.

67. See Britton J. Harwood, "Language and the Real: Chaucer's Manciple," *Chaucer Review* 6 (1972): 268–79, for an argument about this tale's interest in the relationship between words and things.

Selected Bibliography

Aers, David R. "Chaucer's *Book of the Duchess*: An Art to Consume Art." *Durham University Journal* 69 (1977): 201–205.

———. *Chaucer, Langland and the Creative Imagination*. London: Routledge and Kegan Paul, 1980.

———. "The *Parliament of Fowls*: Authority, the Knower and the Known." *Chaucer Review* 16 (1981): 1–17.

Alain de Lille. *The Complaint of Nature*. Translated by Douglas M. Moffat. Hamden, Conn.: Archon Books, 1972.

Alexander Neckam. *De Naturis Rerum*. Edited by Thomas Wright. *Rerum Britannicarum Medii Aevi Scriptores* 34. London: Longmans, 1863.

Allen, Robert J. "A Recurring Motif in Chaucer's *House of Fame*." *Journal of English and Germanic Philology* 55 (1956): 393–405.

Almansi, Guido. *The Writer as Liar: Narrative Technique in the "Decameron."* London: Routledge and Kegan Paul, 1975.

Atchity, Kenneth John. "Dante's *Purgatorio*: The Poem Reveals Itself." In *Italian Literature, Roots, and Branches: Essays in Honor of Thomas Goddard Bergin*, edited by Giose Rimanelli and Kenneth John Atchity. New Haven: Yale University Press, 1976.

Augustine, St. *The City of God*. Translated by Marcus Dods. New York: Modern Library, 1950.

———. *The Enchiridion*. Translated by J. F. Shaw. Chicago: Henry Regnery, 1961.

Baker, Donald C. "Imagery and Structure in Chaucer's *Book of the Duchess*." *Studia Neophilologica* 30 (1958): 17–26.

Barel Van Os, Arnold. *Religious Visions: The Development of the Eschatological Elements in Mediaeval English Religious Literature*. Amsterdam: H. J. Paris, 1932.

Barney, Stephen A. *Chaucer's "Troilus": Essays in Criticism*. Hamden, Conn.: Archon Books, 1980.

Barolini, Teodolinda. *Dante's Poets: Textuality and Truth in the Comedy*. Princeton: Princeton University Press, 1984.

Bartholomaeus Anglicus. [*De Proprietatibus Rerum*] *On the Properties of Things*. Edited by M. C. Seymour. Translated by John Trevisa. Oxford: Clarendon Press, 1975.

Beer, Jeanette M. A. *Narrative Conventions of Truth in the Middle Ages.* Geneva: Librairie Droz, 1981.

Bennett, J. A. W. *The Parlement of Foules: An Interpretation.* Oxford: Clarendon Press, 1957.

———. *Chaucer's Book of Fame: An Exposition of the "House of Fame."* Oxford: Clarendon Press, 1968.

Benson, C. David. *Chaucer's Drama of Style: Poetic Variety and Contrast in the "Canterbury Tales."* Chapel Hill: University of North Carolina Press, 1986.

Bestul, Thomas H. "Chaucer's *Troilus and Criseyde*: The Passionate Epic and its Narrator." *Chaucer Review* 14 (1980): 366–78.

Bloch, R. Howard. *Etymologies and Genealogies: A Literary Anthropology of the French Middle Ages.* Chicago: University of Chicago Press, 1983.

———. "New Philology and Old French, *Speculum* 65 (1990): 4.

Bloomfield, Morton W. "Distance and Predestination in *Troilus and Criseyde.*" *PMLA* 72 (1957): 14–26. Reprint. *Chaucer Criticism II.* Edited by Richard J. Schoeck and Jerome Taylor, 196–210. South Bend: University of Notre Dame Press, 1961.

———. "Chaucerian Realism." *The Cambridge Chaucer Companion.* Edited by Piero Boitani and Jill Mann. Cambridge: Cambridge University Press, 1986.

Boardman, Philip C. "Courtly Language and the Strategy of Consolation in *The Book of the Duchess.*" *English Literary History* 44 (1977): 567–79.

Boccaccio, Giovanni. *The Decameron.* 2 vols. Translated by John Payne. Revised by Charles S. Singleton. Berkeley: University of California Press, 1982.

———. *[Genealogia deorum gentilium] Boccaccio on Poetry.* Translated by Charles G. Osgood, 1930. Reprint. Indianapolis: Bobbs-Merrill, 1956.

Boitani, Piero. *English Medieval Narrative in the Thirteenth and Fourteenth Centuries.* Translated by Joan Krakover Hall. Cambridge: Cambridge University Press, 1982.

———. "What Dante Meant to Chaucer." In *Chaucer and the Italian Trecento.* Edited by Piero Boitani, 115–139. Cambridge: Cambridge University Press, 1983.

———. *Chaucer and the Imaginary World of Fame.* Chaucer Studies 10. Cambridge: D. S. Brewer, 1984.

Boyde, Patrick. *Dante Philomythes and Philosopher: Man in the Cosmos.* Cambridge: Cambridge University Press, 1981.

Braswell, Mary Flowers. "Architectural Portraiture in Chaucer's *House of Fame.*" *Journal of Medieval and Renaissance Studies* 11 (1981): 101–112.

Breisach, Ernst, ed. *Classical Rhetoric and Medieval Historiography.* Studies in Medieval Culture 19. Kalamazoo: The Medieval Institute, 1985.

Bronson, Bertrand H. "*The Book of the Duchess* Reopened." *PMLA* 67 (1952): 863–81.

Brown, Emerson, Jr. "What is Chaucer Doing with the Physician and His Tale?" *Philological Quarterly* 60 (1981): 129–49.

Brownlee, Kevin. *Poetic Identity in Guillaume de Machaut.* Madison: University of Wisconsin Press, 1984.

Burlin, Robert B. *Chaucerian Fiction.* Princeton: Princeton University Press, 1977.

Calin, William. *A Poet at the Fountain: Essays on the Narrative Verse of Guillaume de Machaut.* Lexington: University of Kentucky Press, 1974.

————. "The Poet at the Fountain: Machaut as Narrative Poet." In *Machaut's World: Science and Art in the Fourteenth Century*. Edited by Madeleine Pelner Cosner and Bruce Chandler, 177–87. New York Academy of Sciences, 314 (1978).

Carson, M. Angela. "Easing of the 'Hert' in the *Book of the Duchess*." *Chaucer Review* 1 (1966): 157–60.

Carton, Evan. "Complicity and Responsibility in Pandarus' Bed and Chaucer's Art." *PMLA* 94 (1979): 47–61.

Charity, A. C. *Events and Their Afterlife: The Dialectics of Christian Typology in the Bible and Dante*. Cambridge: Cambridge University Press, 1966.

Chatman, Seymour. *Story and Discourse: Narrative Structure in Fiction and Film*. Ithaca: Cornell University Press, 1978.

Chaucer, Geoffrey. *The Riverside Chaucer*, 3d ed. Edited by Larry D. Benson. Boston: Houghton Mifflin, 1987.

————. *The Miller's Tale*. A Variorum Edition of the Works of Geoffrey Chaucer. Vol. 3, pt. 3. Edited by Thomas W. Ross. Norman: University of Oklahoma Press, 1983.

————. *The Physician's Tale*. A Variorum Edition of the Works of Geoffrey Chaucer. Vol. 2, pt. 17. Edited by Helen Storm Corsa. Norman: University of Oklahoma Press, 1987.

Chiampi, James Thomas. *Shadowy Prefaces: Conversion and Writing in the "Divine Comedy."* L'interprete 24. Ravenna: Longo Editore, 1981.

Clark, John W. " 'This Litel Tretys' Again." *Chaucer Review* 6 (1971): 152–56.

Claudian. *Panegyricus de sexto consulatu Honorii Augusti*. Translated by Maurice Platnauer. In *Claudian*. Loeb Classical Library. New York: Putnam's, 1922.

Clemen, Wolfgang. *Chaucer's Early Poetry*. Translated by C. A. M. Sym. New York: Barnes and Noble, 1963.

Cohn, Dorrit. *Transparent Minds: Narrative Modes for Presenting Consciousness in Fiction*. Princeton: Princeton University Press, 1978.

Collins, Adela Yarbro. "The Early Christian Apocalypses." In *Apocalypse: The Morphology of a Genre. Semeia* 14 (1979).

Collins, John J. "Towards the Morphology of a Genre. In *Apocalypse: The Morphology of a Genre. Semeia* 14 (1979).

Covella, Sister Frances Dolores. "Audience as Determinant of Meaning in the *Troilus*." *Chaucer Review* 2 (1968): 235–45.

Cowgill, Bruce Kent. " 'By *corpus dominus*': Harry Bailly as False Spiritual Guide." *Journal of Medieval and Renaissance Studies* 15 (1985): 157–81.

Cunningham, J. V. "The Literary Form of the Prologue to the *Canterbury Tales*." *Modern Philology* 49 (1952): 172–81.

D'Andria, Michele. *Beatrice Simbolo della poesia con Dante dalla terra a Dio*. Collana di Cultura 29. Rome: Edizioni Dell'ateneo and Bizzarri, 1979.

David, Alfred. "Literary Satire in the *House of Fame*." *PMLA* 75 (1960): 333–39.

————. *The Strumpet Muse: Art and Morals in Chaucer's Poetry*. Bloomington: Indiana University Press, 1976.

Dean, James. "Chaucer's *Troilus*, Boccaccio's *Filostrato*, and the Poetics of Closure." *Philological Quarterly* 64 (1985): 175–84.

de Bonfils Templer, Margherita. "Amore e le visioni nella *Vita Nuova*." *Dante Studies* 92 (1974): 19–34.

Delany, Sheila. "Chaucer's *House of Fame* and the *Ovide Moralisé.*" *Comparative Literature* 20 (1968): 254–64.

―――. *Chaucer's "House of Fame": The Poetics of Skeptical Fideism.* Chicago: University of Chicago Press, 1972.

―――. " 'Ars simia Naturae' and Chaucer's *House of Fame.*" *English Language Notes* 11 (1973): 1–5.

Delehaye, Hippolyte. *The Legends of the Saints: An Introduction to Hagiography.* Translated by V. M. Crawford. 1907. Reprint. South Bend, Ind.: University of Notre Dame Press, 1961.

DeSanctis, Francesco. *Storia della letteratura italiana.* Edited by Benedetto Croce. Bari: Laterza, 1912.

Dionysius the Pseudo-Areopagite. *The Mystical Theology and the Celestial Hierarchies.* Translated by the Editors of The Shrine of Wisdom. Godalming: The Shrine of Wisdom, 1965.

Donaldson, E. Talbot. "The Ending of *Troilus.*" In *Early English and Norse Studies Presented to Hugh Smith.* Edited by Arthur Brown and Peter Foote, 26–45. London: Methuen, 1963. Reprint. *Speaking of Chaucer,* 84–101. New York: Norton, 1970.

―――. "Chaucer the Pilgrim." *PMLA* 69 (1954): 928–36. Reprint. *Speaking of Chaucer,* 1–12. New York: Norton, 1970.

―――. "Criseide and Her Narrator." In *Speaking of Chaucer,* 65–83. New York: Norton, 1970.

―――. "Chaucer's Three 'P's': Pandarus, Pardoner, and Poet." *Michigan Quarterly Review* 14 (1975): 282–301.

Dubs, Kathleen, and Stoddard Malarkey. "The Frame of Chaucer's *Parlement.*" *Chaucer Review* 13 (1978): 16–24.

Duncan, Edgar Hill. "Narrator's Points of View in the Portrait-Sketches, Prologue to the *Canterbury Tales.*" In *Essays in Honor of Walter Clyde Curry,* 77–101. Nashville: Vanderbilt University Press, 1955.

Dunning, T. P. "God and Man in *Troilus and Criseyde.*" In *English and Medieval Studies Presented to J. R. R. Tolkien.* Edited by Norman Davis and C. H. Wren, 164–82. London: Allen and Unwin, 1963.

Durling, Robert M. "Boccaccio on Interpretation: Guido's Escape (*Decameron* VI.9)." In *Dante, Petrarch, Boccaccio: Studies in the Italian Trecento in Honor of Charles Singleton.* Edited by Aldo Bernardo and Anthony Pelligrini, 273–304. Medieval and Renaissance Texts and Studies 22. Binghamton, N.Y.: MARTS, 1983.

Ebel, Julia G. "Chaucer's *The Book of the Duchess*: A Study of Medieval Iconography and Literary Structure." *College English* 29 (1967): 197–206.

Economou, George D. *The Goddess Natura in Medieval Literature.* Cambridge, Mass.: Harvard University Press, 1972.

Edwards, A. S. G. "The Influence and Audience of the *Polychronicon.*" *Proceedings of the Leeds Philosophical and Literary Society* 17 (1980): 100–119.

Elbow, Peter. *Oppositions in Chaucer.* Middletown: Wesleyan University Press, 1975.

Ellis, Roger. *Patterns of Religious Narrative in the "Canterbury Tales."* Totowa, N.J.: Barnes and Noble, 1986.

Estrich, Robert M. "Chaucer's Prologue to the *Legend of Good Women* and Machaut's *Le Jugement dou Roy de Navarre*." *Studies in Philology* 26 (1939): 20–39.

Farnham, Anthony E. "Chaucerian Irony and the Ending of the *Troilus*." *Chaucer Review* 1 (1967): 207–16.

Ferster, Judith. *Chaucer on Interpretation*. Cambridge: Cambridge University Press, 1985.

Fichte, Joerg O. "Incident-History-Exemplum-Novella: The Transformation of History in Chaucer's *Physician's Tale*." *Florilegium* 5 (1983): 189–207.

Fido, Franco. "Boccaccio's *Ars Narrandi* in the Sixth Day of the *Decameron*." In *Italian Literature, Roots and Branches: Essays in Honor of Thomas Goddard Bergin*. Edited by Giose Rimanelli and Kenneth John Atchity, 225–42. New Haven: Yale University Press, 1976.

Fish, Varda. "The Origin and Original Object of *Troilus and Criseyde*." *Chaucer Review* 18 (1984): 304–15.

Fleischman, Suzanne. "On the Representation of History and Fiction in the Middle Ages." *History and Theory* 22 (1983): 278–310.

Fox, John. *A Literary History of France: The Middle Ages*. New York: Barnes and Noble, 1974.

Freccero, John. *Dante: The Poetics of Conversion*. Edited by Rachel Jacoff. Cambridge, Mass.: Harvard University Press, 1986.

Freeman, Michelle A. "Froissart's *Le Joli Buisson de Jonece*: A Farewell to Poetry?" In *Machaut's World: Science and Art in the Fourteenth Century*. Edited by Madeleine Pelner Cosman and Bruce Chandler, 235–47. Annals of the New York Academy of Sciences 314 (1978).

Freiwald, Leah R. " 'Swych Love of Frendes': Pandarus and Troilus." *Chaucer Review* 6 (1971): 120–29.

French, W. H. "The Man in Black's Lyric." *Journal of English and Germanic Philology* 56 (1957): 231–41.

Fries, Maureen. " 'Slydnge of Corage': Chaucer's Criseyde as Feminist and Victim." In *The Authority of Experience: Essays in Feminist Criticism*. Edited by Arlyn Diamond and Lee R. Edwards, 45–59. Amherst: University of Massachusetts Press, 1977.

Fyler, John M. *Chaucer and Ovid*. New Haven: Yale University Press, 1979.

———. "The Fabrications of Pandarus." *Modern Language Quarterly* 41 (1980): 115–30.

Ganim, John M. *Style and Consciousness in Middle English Narrative*. Princeton: Princeton University Press, 1983.

Gardner, John. *The Poetry of Chaucer*. Carbondale: Southern Illinois University Press, 1977.

Garfinkel, Harold. "Studies of the Routine Grounds of Everyday Activities." In *Studies in Ethnomethodology*, 35–75. Cambridge: Polity Press, 1984.

Gaylord, Alan T. "Chaucer's Tender Trap: The *Troilus* and the 'Yonge, Fresshe Folkes.' " *English Miscellany* 15 (1964): 24–45.

———. "*Sentence* and *Solaas* in Fragment VII of the *Canterbury Tales*: Harry Bailly as Horseback Editor." *PMLA* 82 (1967): 226–35.

———. "Friendship in Chaucer's *Troilus*." *Chaucer Review* 3 (1969): 239–64.

———. "The Lesson of the *Troilus*: Chastisement and Correction." In *Essays on Troilus and Criseyde*. Edited by Mary Salu, 23–42. Chaucer Studies 3. Cambridge: D. S. Brewer, 1979.

———. "Chaucer's Dainty 'Dogerel': The 'Elvyssh' Prosody of Sir Thopas." Studies in the Age of Chaucer 1 (1979): 83–104.

Gellrich, Jesse M. The Idea of the Book in the Middle Ages: Language Theory, Mythology, and Fiction. Ithaca: Cornell University Press, 1985.

Getto, Giovanni. Vita di forme e forme di vita. Torino: G. B. Petrini, 1958.

Gordon, Ida. The Double Sorrow of Troilus: A Study of Ambiguities in "Troilus and Criseyde." Oxford: Clarendon Press, 1970.

Gottfried, Barbara. "Conflict and Relationship, Sovereignty and Survival: Parables of Power in the Wife of Bath's Prologue." Chaucer Review 19 (1985): 202–24.

Green, Richard Firth. Poets and Princepleasers: Literature and the English Court in the Late Middle Ages. Toronto: University of Toronto Press, 1980.

Grennan, Joseph E. "Hert-huntyng in the Book of the Duchess." Modern Language Quarterly 25 (1964): 131–39.

———. "Chaucer and Chalcidius: The Platonic Origins of the Hous of Fame." Viator 15 (1984): 237–62.

Gybbon-Monypenny, G. B. "Guillaume de Machaut's Erotic 'Autobiography': Precedents for the Form of the Voir-Dit." In Studies in Medieval Literature and Languages in Memory of Frederick Whitehead. Edited by W. Rothwell, et al., 133–52. Manchester: University of Manchester Press, 1973.

Hanning, Robert W. The Vision of History in Early Britain. New York: Columbia University Press, 1966.

———. "The Theme of Art and Life in Chaucer's Poetry." In Geoffrey Chaucer. Edited by George D. Economou, 15–36. New York: McGraw-Hill, 1975.

———. "Roasting a Friar, Mis-taking a Wife, and Other Acts of Textual Harassment in Chaucer's Canterbury Tales." Studies in the Age of Chaucer 7 (1985): 3–21.

Hanson, Thomas B. "Chaucer's Physician as Storyteller and Moralizer." Chaucer Review 7 (1972): 132–39.

Harwood, Britton J. "Language and the Real: Chaucer's Manciple." Chaucer Review 6 (1972): 268–79.

Hatcher, Elizabeth R. "Chaucer and the Psychology of Fear: Troilus in Book V." English Literary History 40 (1973): 307–24.

Heffernan, Thomas J. Sacred Biography: Saints and Their Biographers in the Middle Ages. Oxford: Oxford University Press, 1988.

Helterman, Jeffrey. "The Masks of Love in Troilus and Criseyde." Comparative Literature 26 (1974): 14–31.

Henderson, George. Gothic. Baltimore: Penguin Books, 1972.

Himmelfarb, Martha. Tours of Hell: An Apocalyptic Form in Jewish and Christian Literature. Philadelphia: University of Pennsylvania Press, 1983.

Hoffman, Richard L. Ovid and the Canterbury Tales. Philadelphia: University of Pennsylvania Press, 1966.

Hofmeister, John. "Chaucer's Pardoner." Master's Thesis. The Ohio State University, 1981.

Hollander, Robert. Boccaccio's Two Venuses. New York: Columbia University Press, 1977.

Howard, Donald R. The Idea of the Canterbury Tales. Berkeley and Los Angeles: University of California Press, 1976.

———. "Experience, Language, and Consciousness: Troilus and Criseyde, II,

596–931." In *Medieval Literature and Folklore Studies in Honor of Francis Lee Utley.* Edited by Jerome Mandel and B. A. Rosenberg, 173–92. New Brunswick: Rutgers University Press, 1970. Reprint. *Chaucer's Troilus: Essays in Criticism.* Edited by Stephen A. Barney, 159–80. Hamden, Conn.: Archon Books, 1980.

Huot, Sylvia. "Poetic Ambiguity and Reader Response in Boccaccio's *Amorosa Visione.*" *Modern Philology* 83 (1985): 109–22.

Huppé, Bernard F. "The Unlikely Narrator: The Narrative Strategy of the *Troilus.*" In *Signs and Symbols in Chaucer's Poetry.*Edited by John P. Hermann and John J. Burke, Jr., 179–94. University: University of Alabama Press, 1981.

————, and D. W. Robertson, Jr. *Fruyt and Chaf: Studies in Chaucer's Allegories.* Princeton: Princeton University Press, 1963.

Iser, Wolfgang. *The Implied Reader: Patterns of Communication in Prose Fiction from Bunyan to Beckett.* Baltimore: Johns Hopkins University Press, 1974.

Isidore of Seville. *Etymologiae sive Originum.* 2 vols. Edited by W. M. Lindsay. Oxford: Oxford University Press, 1911.

Jauss, Hans Robert. *Toward an Aesthetic of Reception.* Translated by T. Bahti. Brighton: Harvester Press, 1982.

Jeffrey, David Lyle. "Sacred and Secular Scripture: Authority and Interpretation in *The House of Fame.*" In *Chaucer and Scriptural Tradition.* Edited by David Lyle Jeffrey, 207–28. Ottawa: University of Ottawa Press, 1984.

Jones, Charles W. *Saints' Lives and Chronicles in Early England.* Ithaca: Cornell University Press, 1947.

Jordan, Robert M. "The Narrator in Chaucer's *Troilus.*" *English Literary History* 25 (1958): 237–57.

————. *Chaucer and the Shape of Creation: The Aesthetic Possibilities of Inorganic Structure.* Cambridge, Mass.: Harvard University Press, 1967.

————. *Chaucer's Poetics and the Modern Reader.* Berkeley and Los Angeles: University of California Press, 1987.

Josipovici, G. D. "Fiction and Game in *The Canterbury Tales.*" *Critical Quarterly* 7 (1965): 185–97.

Joyner, William. "Parallel Journeys in Chaucer's *House of Fame.*" *Papers on Language and Literature* 12 (1976): 3–19.

Justman, Stewart. "Medieval Monism and Abuse of Authority in Chaucer." *Chaucer Review* 11 (1976): 95–111.

Kellogg, A. L. "Chaucer's Self-Portrait and Dante's." *Medium Aevum* 29 (1960): 119–20.

Kirk, Elizabeth D. " 'Paradis Stood Formed in Hire Yën': Courtly Love and Chaucer's Re-Vision of Dante." In *Acts of Interpretation: The Text in its Contexts, 700–1600; Essays in Medieval and Renaissance Literature in Honor of E. Talbot Donaldson.* Edited by Mary J. Carruthers and Elizabeth Kirk, 257–77. Norman, Okla.: Pilgrim Books, 1982.

Kirkpatrick, Robin. "The Wake of the *Commedia*: Chaucer's *Canterbury Tales* and Boccaccio's *Decameron.*" In *Chaucer and the Italian Trecento.* Edited by Piero Boitani, 201–230. Cambridge: Cambridge University Press, 1983.

Kiser, Lisa J. *Telling Classical Tales: Chaucer and the Legend of Good Women.* Ithaca: Cornell University Press, 1983.

Kittredge, George Lyman. *Chaucer and His Poetry*. Cambridge, Mass.: Harvard University Press, 1915.

Knopp, Sherron E. "Narrator and Audience in Chaucer's *Troilus and Criseyde*." *Studies in Philology* 78 (1981): 323–40.

Kolve, V. A. *Chaucer and the Imagery of Narrative: The First Five Canterbury Tales*. Stanford: Stanford University Press, 1984.

Koonce, B. G. *Chaucer and the Tradition of Fame: Symbolism in the "House of Fame."* Princeton: Princeton University Press, 1966.

LaCapra, Dominick. *History and Criticism*. Ithaca: Cornell University Press, 1985.

Lanham, Richard A. "Game, Play, and High Seriousness in Chaucer's Poetry." *English Studies* 48 (1967): 1–24.

Lawlor, John. "The Pattern of Consolation in *The Book of the Duchess*." *Speculum* 31 (1956): 626–48. Reprint. *Chaucer Criticism II*. Edited by Richard J. Schoeck and Jerome Taylor, 232–60. South Bend: University of Notre Dame Press, 1961.

Lawton, David A. *Chaucer's Narrators*. Chaucer Studies 13. Cambridge: D. S. Brewer, 1985.

Layman, B. J. "Boccaccio's Paradigm of the Artist and His Art." *Italian Quarterly* 13 (1970): 19–36.

Le Goff, Jacques. *The Birth of Purgatory*. Translated by Arthur Goldhammer. Chicago: University of Chicago Press, 1984.

Leicester, H. Marshall, Jr. "The Harmony of Chaucer's *Parlement*: A Dissonant Voice." *Chaucer Review* 9 (1974): 15–34.

———. "The Art of Impersonation: A General Prologue to the *Canterbury Tales*." *PMLA* 95 (1980): 213–24.

———. "Of a Fire in the Dark: Public and Private Feminism in the *Wife of Bath's Tale*." *Women's Studies* 11 (1984): 157–78.

Leitch, L. M. "*Sentence* and *Solaas*: The Function of the Hosts in the *Canterbury Tales*." *Chaucer Review* 17 (1982): 5–20.

Levine, Joseph M. *Humanism and History: Origins of Modern English Historiography*. Ithaca: Cornell University Press, 1987.

Levy, Bernard S. "The Wife of Bath's *Queynte Fantasye*." *Chaucer Review* 4 (1970): 106–22.

Levy, M. L. "'As myn auctour seyth.'" *Medium Aevum* 12 (1943): 25–39.

Lewis, C. S. *The Allegory of Love: A Study in Medieval Tradition*. Oxford: Oxford University Press, 1936.

Lockhart, Adrienne. "Semantic, Moral, and Aesthetic Degeneration in *Troilus and Criseyde*." *Chaucer Review* 8 (1973): 100–118.

McCall, John P. "The Harmony of Chaucer's *Parliament*." *Chaucer Review* 5 (1970): 22–31.

McDonald, Charles O. "An Interpretation of Chaucer's *Parlement of Foules*." *Speculum* 30 (1955): 444–57.

McGrady, Donald. "Chaucer and the *Decameron* Reconsidered." *Chaucer Review* 12 (1977): 1–26.

Macrobius. *Macrobius' Commentary on the Dream of Scipio*. Translated by William Harris Stahl. New York: Columbia University Press, 1952.

Mailloux, Steven. "Learning to Read: Interpretation and Reader-Response Criticism." *Studies in the Literary Imagination* 12 (1979): 93–108.

Mâle, Emile. *The Gothic Image: Religious Art in France of the Thirteenth Century.* Translated by Dora Nussey. New York: Harper and Row, 1958.

Malvern, Marjorie M. " 'Who Peynted the Leon, Tel Me Who?': Rhetorical and Didactic Roles Played by an Aesopic Fable in the *Wife of Bath's Prologue.*" *Studies in Philology* 80 (1983): 238–52.

Mandel, Jerome. "Other Voices in *The Canterbury Tales.*" *Criticism* 19 (1977): 338–49.

Mann, Jill. *Chaucer and Medieval Estates Satire: The Literature of Social Classes and the General Prologue to the Canterbury Tales.* Cambridge: Cambridge University Press, 1973.

Manning, Stephen. "Rhetoric, Game, Morality, and Geoffrey Chaucer." *Studies in the Age of Chaucer* 1 (1979): 105–18.

Marcus, Millicent Joy. *An Allegory of Form: Literary Self-Consciousness in the "Decameron."* Stanford French and Italian Studies 18. Saratoga, Cal.: Anma Libri, 1979.

Markland, Murray F. "*Troilus and Criseyde*: The Inviolability of the Ending." *Modern Language Quarterly* 31 (1970): 147–59.

Marti, Mario. *Storia dello Stil Nuovo.* 2 vols. Lecce: Milella, 1973.

Mazzaro, Jerome. *The Figure of Dante: An Essay on the "Vita Nuova."* Princeton: Princeton University Press, 1981.

Mazzeo, Joseph Anthony. *Structure and Thought in the Paradiso.* Ithaca: Cornell University Press, 1958.

Mazzotta, Giuseppe. "The *Decameron*: The Marginality of Literature." *University of Toronto Quarterly* 42 (1972): 64–81.

———. *Dante, Poet of the Desert: History and Allegory in the "Divine Comedy."* Princeton: Princeton University Press, 1979.

———. *The World at Play in Boccaccio's "Decameron."* Princeton: Princeton University Press, 1986.

Mehl, Dieter. "The Audience of Chaucer's *Troilus and Criseyde.*" In *Chaucer and Middle English Studies in Honour of Rossell Hope Robbins.* Edited by Beryl Rowland, 173–89. London: Allen and Unwin, 1974.

———. *Geoffrey Chaucer: An Introduction to His Narrative Poetry.* Cambridge: Cambridge University Press, 1986.

Middleton, Anne. "The *Physician's Tale* and Love's Martyrs: 'Ensamples Mo Than Ten' as a Method in the *Canterbury Tales.*" *Chaucer Review* 8 (1973): 9–32.

Migne, J. P., ed. *Patrologiae cursus completus: Series Latina.* 221 vols. Paris: J. P. Migne, 1844–65.

Miller, Jacqueline T. "The Writing on the Wall: Authority and Authorship in Chaucer's *House of Fame.*" *Chaucer Review* 17 (1982): 95–115.

Minnis, A. J. *Chaucer and Pagan Antiquity.* Chaucer Studies 8. Cambridge: D. S. Brewer, 1982.

———. *Medieval Theory of Authorship: Scholastic Literary Attitudes in the Later Middle Ages.* London: Scolar Press, 1984.

Montgomery, Robert L. *The Reader's Eye: Studies in Didactic Literary Theory from Dante to Tasso.* Berkeley and Los Angeles: University of California Press, 1979.

Morgan, Gerald. "The Ending of 'Troilus and Criseyde.' " *Modern Language Review* 77 (1982): 257–71.

Mudrick, Marvin. "Chaucer's Nightingales." *Hudson Review* 10 (1957), 88–95. Reprint. *Chaucer's Troilus: Essays in Criticism.* Edited by Stephen A. Barney, Hamden, Conn.: Archon Books, 1980.

Muscatine, Charles. *Chaucer and the French Tradition.* Berkeley and Los Angeles: University of California Press, 1957.

Nelson, William. *Fact or Fiction: The Dilemma of the Renaissance Storyteller.* Cambridge, Mass.: Harvard University Press, 1973.

Neuss, Paula. "Images of Writing and the Book in Chaucer's Poetry." *Review of English Studies* 32 (1981): 385–97.

Newman, Francis X. "*House of Fame,* 7–12." *English Language Notes* 6 (1968): 5–12.

Nolan, Barbara. *The Gothic Visionary Perspective.* Princeton: Princeton University Press, 1977.

———. "The Art of Expropriation: Chaucer's Narrator in *The Book of the Duchess.*" In *New Perspectives in Chaucer Criticism.* Edited by Donald M. Rose, 203–22. Norman, Okla.: Pilgrim Books, 1981.

———. "'A Poet Ther Was': Chaucer's Voices in the General Prologue to *The Canterbury Tales.*" *PMLA* 101 (1986): 154–69.

Norton-Smith, John A. *Geoffrey Chaucer.* Medieval Authors. London: Routledge and Kegan Paul, 1974.

Olson, Alexandra Hennessey. "'De Historiis Sanctorum': A Generic Study of Hagiography." *Genre* 13 (1980): 415–25.

Olson, Glending. "A Reading of the *Thopas-Melibee* Link." *Chaucer Review* 10 (1975): 147–53.

———. "Chaucer, Dante, and the Structure of Fragment VIII (G) of the *Canterbury Tales.*" *Chaucer Review* 16 (1982): 222–36.

———. *Literature as Recreation in the Later Middle Ages.* Ithaca: Cornell University Press, 1982.

Osberg, Richard. "Between the Motion and the Act: Intentions and Ends in Chaucer's *Troilus.*" *English Literary History* 48 (1981): 257–70.

Owen, Charles A., Jr. "The Role of the Narrator in the 'Parlement of Foules.'" *College English* 14 (1953): 264–69.

———. *Pilgrimage and Storytelling in the "Canterbury Tales": The Dialectic of "Ernest" and "Game."* Norman: University of Oklahoma Press, 1977.

Parker, David. "Can We Trust the Wife of Bath?" *Chaucer Review* 4 (1970): 90–98.

Partner, Nancy F. *Serious Entertainments: The Writing of History in Twelfth-Century England.* Chicago: University of Chicago Press, 1977.

Patterson, Lee. "'For the Wyves Love of Bathe': Feminine Rhetoric and Poetic Resolution in the *Roman de la Rose* and the *Canterbury Tales.*" *Speculum* 58 (1983): 656–95.

———. *Negotiating the Past: The Historical Understanding of Medieval Literature.* Madison: University of Wisconsin Press, 1987.

Payne, Robert O. *The Key of Remembrance: A Study of Chaucer's Poetics.* New Haven: Yale University Press, 1963.

———. "Chaucer's Realization of Himself as Rhetor." In *Medieval Eloquence: Studies in the Theory and Practice of Medieval Rhetoric.* Edited by James J. Murphy, 270–87. Berkeley and Los Angeles: University of California Press, 1978.

Peck, Russell. "The Ideas of 'Entente' and Translation in Chaucer's *Second Nun's Tale*." *Annuale Mediaevale* 8 (1967): 17–37.

Pelen, Marc M. "Machaut's Court of Love Narratives and Chaucer's *Book of the Duchess*." *Chaucer Review* 11 (1976): 128–55.

Phebus, Gaston. *Livre de chasse*. Edited by Gunnar Tilander. Stockholm: Almqvist and Wiksell, 1971.

Plett, Heinrich F. "Aesthetic Constituents in the Courtly Culture of Renaissance England." *New Literary History* 14 (1983): 597–621.

Polzella, Marion L. " 'The Craft So Long to Lerne': Poet and Lover in Chaucer's 'Envoy to Scogan' and *Parliament of Fowls*." *Chaucer Review* 10 (1976): 279–86.

Pratt, Robert A. "Chaucer's Claudian." *Speculum* 22 (1947): 419–29.

Praz, Mario. "Chaucer and the Great Italian Writers of the Trecento." In *The Flaming Heart: Essays on Crashaw, Machiavelli, and Other Studies in the Relations Between Italian and English Literature from Chaucer to T. S. Eliot*, 29–89. New York: Doubleday, 1958.

Rabinowitz, Peter J. "Truth in Fiction: A Reexamination of Audiences." *Critical Inquiry* 4 (1977): 121–41.

———. "Assertion and Assumption: Fictional Patterns and the External World." *PMLA* 96 (1981): 408–19.

Richardson, Cynthia C. "The Function of the Host in the *Canterbury Tales*." *Texas Studies in Literature and Language* 12 (1970–71): 325–44.

Robertson, D. W., Jr. *A Preface to Chaucer: Studies in Medieval Perspectives*. Princeton: Princeton University Press, 1962.

Rowe, Donald W. *O Love, O Charite!: Contraries Harmonized in Chaucer's "Troilus."* Carbondale: Southern Illinois University Press, 1976.

Rowland, Beryl. "The Physician's 'Historial Thyng Notable' and the Man of Law." *English Literary History* 40 (1973): 165–78.

Ruggiers, Paul G. "The Unity of Chaucer's *House of Fame*." *Studies in Philology* 50 (1953): 16–29.

———. "Words into Images in Chaucer's *Hous of Fame*: A Third Suggestion." *Modern Language Notes* 69 (1954): 34–37.

———. *The Art of the Canterbury Tales*. Madison: University of Wisconsin Press, 1965.

Scheps, Walter. " 'Up Roos oure Hoost, and Was Oure Aller Cok': Harry Bailly's Tale-Telling Competition." *Chaucer Review* 10 (1975): 113–28.

Schless, Howard. "Transformations: Chaucer's Use of Italian." In *Geoffrey Chaucer*. Writers and their Background. Edited by Derek Brewer, 184–223. Athens: Ohio University Press, 1975.

———. *Chaucer and Dante: A Revaluation*. Norman, Okla: Pilgrim Books, 1984.

Schor, Naomi. "Fiction as Interpretation/Interpretation as Fiction." In *The Reader in the Text: Essays on Audience and Interpretation*. Edited by Susan R. Suleiman and Inge Crosman, 165–82. Princeton: Princeton University Press, 1980.

Schricker, Gale C. "On the Relation of Fact and Fiction in Chaucer's Poetic Endings." *Philological Quarterly* 60 (1981): 13–27.

Scott, J. A. "Dante's 'Sweet New Style' and the *Vita Nuova*." *Italica* 42 (1965): 98–107.

Shapiro, Marianne. "Figurality in the *Vita Nuova*: Dante's New Rhetoric." *Dante Studies* 97 (1979): 107–27.

Shoaf, R. A. *Dante, Chaucer, and the Currency of the Word: Money, Images, and Reference in Late Medieval Poetry.* Norman, Okla.: Pilgrim Books, 1983.

Singleton, Charles S. *An Essay on the "Vita Nuova."* Cambridge, Mass.: Harvard University Press, 1949.

———. "Dante: Within Courtly Love and Beyond." In *The Meaning of Courtly Love.* Edited by F. X. Newman, 43–54. Albany: SUNY Press, 1968.

———. *Dante's* Commedia: *Elements of Structure.* 1954. Reprint. Baltimore: Johns Hopkins University Press, 1977.

———. *Journey to Beatrice.* 1958. Reprint. Baltimore: Johns Hopkins University Press, 1977.

Smarr, Janet Levarie. *Boccaccio and Fiammetta: The Narrator as Lover.* Urbana: University of Illinois Press, 1986.

Spearing, A. C. *Medieval Dream-Poetry.* Cambridge: Cambridge University Press, 1976.

Spiegal, Gabrielle M. "History, Historicism, and the Social Logic of the Text in the Middle Ages." *Speculum* 65 (1990): 59–86.

Steadman, John M. *Disembodied Laughter: Troilus and the Apotheosis Tradition: A Reexamination of Narrative and Thematic Contexts.* Berkeley: University of California Press, 1972.

Stevens, Martin. "Narrative Focus in *The Book of the Duchess*: A Critical Revaluation." *Annuale Mediaevale* 7 (1966): 16–32.

———. "The Winds of Fortune in the *Troilus.*" *Chaucer Review* 13 (1979): 285–307.

Strohm, Paul. "Chaucer's Audience(s): Fictional, Implied, Intended, Actual." *Chaucer Review* 18 (1983): 137–45.

———. *Social Chaucer.* Cambridge, Mass.: Harvard University Press, 1989.

Struever, Nancy S. *The Language of History in the Renaissance: Rhetorical and Historical Consciousness in Florentine Humanism.* Princeton: Princeton University Press, 1970.

Sypherd, Wilbur Owen. *Studies in Chaucer's "House of Fame."* 1907. Reprint. New York: Haskell House, 1965.

Taylor, John. *English Historical Writing in the Fourteenth Century.* Oxford: Clarendon Press, 1987.

Taylor, Karla. "A Text and Its Afterlife: Dante and Chaucer." *Comparative Literature* 35 (1983): 1–20.

Taylor, Paul Beckman. "*Peynted Confessiouns*: Boccaccio and Chaucer." *Comparative Literature* 34 (1982): 116–29.

———. "Chaucer's *Cosyn to the Dede.*" *Speculum* 57 (1982): 315–27.

Thiébaux, Marcelle. *The Stag of Love: The Chase in Medieval Literature.* Ithaca: Cornell University Press, 1974.

Trimpi, Wesley. "The Quality of Fiction: The Rhetorical Transmission of Literary Theory." *Traditio* 30 (1974): 1–118.

Uphaus, Robert W. "Chaucer's *Parlement of Foules*: Aesthetic Order and Individual Experience." *Texas Studies in Literature and Language* 10 (1968): 349–58.

Van, Thomas A. "Chaucer's Pandarus as an Earthly Maker." *Southern Humanities Review* 12 (1978): 89–97.

Von Simson, Otto. *The Gothic Cathedral: Origins of Gothic Architecture and the Medieval Concept of Order.* Bollingen Library. New York: Harper and Row, 1962.
Wallace, David. *Chaucer and the Early Writings of Boccaccio.* Chaucer Studies 12. Cambridge: D. S. Brewer, 1985.
Waswo, Richard. "The Narrator of *Troilus and Criseyde.*" *English Literary History* 50 (1983): 1–25.
Wetherbee, Winthrop. *Chaucer and the Poets: An Essay on "Troilus and Criseyde."* Ithaca: Cornell University Press, 1984.
Wheeler, Bonnie. "Dante, Chaucer, and the Ending of *Troilus and Criseyde.*" *Philological Quarterly* 61 (1982): 105–23.
Wheelock, James T. S. "A Function of the *Amore* Figure in the *Vita Nuova.*" *Romanic Review* 68 (1977): 276–86.
Whigham, Frank. "Interpretation at Court: Courtesy and the Performer-Audience Dialectic." *New Literary History* 14 (1983): 623–39.
White, Hayden. *Tropics of Discourse: Essays in Cultural Criticism.* Baltimore: Johns Hopkins University Press, 1978.
Wilhelm, James J. "The Narrator and His Narrative in Chaucer's *Parlement.*" *Chaucer Review* 1 (1967): 201–206.
Wimsatt, James I. "The Apotheosis of Blanche in *The Book of the Duchess.*" *Journal of English and Germanic Philology* 46 (1967): 26–44.
———. *Chaucer and the French Love Poets: The Literary Background of the "Book of the Duchess."* University of North Carolina Studies in Comparative Literature 43. Chapel Hill: University of North Carolina Press, 1968.
———. *The Marguerite Poetry of Guillaume de Machaut.* Chapel Hill: University of North Carolina Press, 1970.
Windeatt, B. A. *Chaucer's Dream Poetry: Sources and Analogues.* Chaucer Studies 7. Cambridge: D. S. Brewer, 1982.
Wood, Chauncey. *The Elements of Chaucer's "Troilus."* Durham: Duke University Press, 1984.
Woolf, Rosemary. "Chaucer as a Satirist in the General Prologue to the *Canterbury Tales.*" *Critical Quarterly* 1 (1959): 150–57.
Zimbardo, Rose A. "Creator and Created: The Generic Perspective of Chaucer's *Troilus and Criseyde.*" *Chaucer Review* 11 (1977): 283–98.

Index

Adam of St. Victor, 159 n.25
Aers, David R., 9, 43, 46, 152 n.12, 154
  n.4, 160 nn.3, 5, 164 n.13, 165 n.20
Alain de Lille: *Complaint of Nature,* 50,
  54, 162 nn.18–19
Alexander of Hales, 160 n.31
Alexander Neckam, 162 n.21
Allen, Robert J., 157 n.10
Almansi, Guido, 115, 174 nn.13–14
Aquinas, Thomas, 157 n.13
Aristotle, 3
Artist-figures, 16, 18–19, 20, 23, 34, 50–
  51, 54, 63, 91, 111, 115, 117, 122,
  123, 127, 133–34, 162 n.20
Atchity, Kenneth John, 169 n.8
Audience: actual, 8, 9, 10, 54, 64, 80, 87,
  88, 90–91, 93, 97, 103, 104, 110,
  111–12, 113, 117, 123–25, 143, 144,
  148; fictional, 4, 5, 19–20, 58, 60–61,
  63, 64–66, 67, 71, 75, 81, 84–87,
  104, 111–12, 118, 123–25, 127, 135–
  36, 139, 143, 145–46, 148; Harry
  Bailly as, 123–25, 128–29; implied, 4,
  5, 54, 58, 60–61, 64–65, 86, 87, 104,
  124, 135
Augustine, St., 157 n.13, 158 n.15, 159
  nn.22, 25, 160 n.30
Authority, 5, 13, 25, 63, 82, 88–89, 113–
  14; Chaucer's critique of, 5, 6, 7, 8,
  12, 26–27, 29, 40–41, 95–96, 109,
  110, 113, 114, 120, 125–26, 129,
  132, 135, 136, 138–39, 147, 149; narrative assertions of, 2, 4, 6, 7, 8, 13–

14, 82–83, 107, 125–27, 128, 130,
  132, 134, 137, 139, 140, 144–47. *See
  also* Truth-claims
Autobiography, 119, 135–40, 142–47,
  178 n.52

Bailly, Harry, 115, 117, 122, 123–25,
  127, 128–29, 144–45, 176 n.34, 177
  n.44
Baker, Donald C., 155 n.12
Barel Van Os, Arnold, 158 n.16
Barolini, Teodolinda, 107, 152 n.9, 167
  n.37, 169 nn.8, 12, 14, 172 n.37
Bartholomaeus Anglicus, 162 n.21
Battersby, James, 46, 71–72, 110
Bede, 159 n.25
Beer, Jeanette M. A., 173 n.6, 178 n.52
Bennett, J. A. W., 54, 157 n.14, 159 n.28,
  161 n.11, 162 nn.19, 22, 23
Benson, C. David, 152 n.11, 175 n.20
Bernard Silvestris, 162 n.19
Bestul, Thomas H., 164 n.16, 166 n.31,
  168 n.43
Bible, 16, 33, 34, 35–36, 40, 102, 105–
  106, 117, 118, 133, 139, 157 n.7, 159
  n.23, 171 n.31
Bloch, R. Howard, 161 n.8
Bloomfield, Morton W., 162 n.1, 163 n.3,
  164 n.16, 167 n.35, 173 n.9
Boardman, Philip C., 154 n.4
Boccacio, Giovanni, 3–4, 5, 7, 8, 48, 54,
  63, 89, 90, 92, 111–15, 152 n.6, 170
  n.23; *Decameron,* 111–15, 116, 122,

UNIVERSITY PRESS OF NEW ENGLAND publishes books under its own imprint and is the publisher for Brandeis University Press, Brown University Press, Clark University Press, University of Connecticut, Dartmouth College, Middlebury College Press, University of New Hampshire, University of Rhode Island, Tufts University, University of Vermont, and Wesleyan University Press.

Library of Congress Cataloging-in-Publication Data

Kiser, Lisa J., 1949–
Truth and textuality in Chaucer's poetry / Lisa J. Kiser.
   p.   cm.
Includes bibliographical references and index.
ISBN 0–87451–550–5
   1. Chaucer, Geoffrey, d. 1400—Philosophy. 2. Knowledge, Theory of, in literature. 3. Skepticism in literature. 4. Truth in literature. I. Title.
PR1933.K6K57 1991
821'.1—dc20   90–50905